FENG SHUI
A PRACTICAL GUIDE
FOR ARCHITECTS
AND DESIGNERS

VINCENT M. SMITH with BARBARA LYONS STEWART, AIA

KAPLAN AEC EDUCATION

This publication is designed to provide accurate and authoritative information in regard to the subject matter covered. It is sold with the understanding that the publisher is not engaged in rendering legal, accounting, or other professional service. If legal advice or other expert assistance is required, the services of a competent professional should be sought.

President, Dearborn Publishing: Roy Lipner
Vice President and Publisher: Maureen McMahon
Acquisitions Editor: Victoria Smith
Senior Managing Editor: Jack Kiburz
Production Editor: Karen Goodfriend
Creative Director: Lucy Jenkins
Cover Design: Gail Chandler
Typesetting: Janet Schroeder

Published by AEC Education
30 S. Wacker Drive, Suite 2500
Chicago, Illinois 60606-7481
(312) 836-4400
http://www.kaplanAECarchitecture.com

Printed in the United States of America

06 07 08 10   9 8 7 6 5 4 3

Library of Congress Cataloging-in-Publication Data

Smith, Vincent, 1940–
  Feng Shui: a practical guide for architects and designers / Vincent Smith with Barbara Lyons Stewart.
     p. cm.
  ISBN-13: 978-1-4195-3570-3
  ISBN-10: 1-4195-3570-6
  1. Feng Shui. 2. Architecture—Miscellanea. I. Stewart, Barbara Lyons. II. Title.
BF1779.F4S6 2006
  133.3'337—dc22

                                   2006000246

PRAISE FOR *FENG SHUI*

"Planners, architects, and designers can use the universal principles of Feng Shui to take advantage of people's natural tendencies and preferences and create spaces that people feel good in and want to use. This book is about good environmental psychology, and should be of great interest to anyone involved in designing built environments."

REBECCA E. BARRY, PHD.
ARIZONA STATE UNIVERSITY

"As well as an excellent professional guide for architects and designers, this book is also an informative, comprehensive, and provocative manual for anyone interested in creating a serene, stress-free environment conducive to achieving personal goals and spiritual growth. Vincent Smith has expressed in a clear and concise format what we, our friends, family, and clients have been fortunate to learn through his invaluable guidance."

BONNIE TROMPETER LOWE: A.C., A.D.S.,
FORD MODEL, REAL ESTATE INVESTOR, (CLIENT)

NORMAN HAYES LOWE: REAL ESTATE SALES,
THE CORCORAN GROUP, BRIDGEHAMPTON, (CLIENT)

"We would never buy a property without using Vincent Smith as a Feng Shui consultant, and would never hire an architect who has not read this book. Feng Shui: A Practical Guide has made us aware of the universal nature of these principles. This book is a must for every architect and designer."

RENATA BOECK, PRESIDENT,
RENNICK PROPERTIES INC

"Vincent Smith brings the complex, ethereal subtleties of Feng Shui to life in Feng Shui: A Practical Guide for Architects and Designers. From bedroom to operating room, it is clear that everyone can benefit from the teachings presented here—in all aspects of their lives."

DUNCAN B. HUGHES, M.D.

"If you are ready to take yourself to a higher level both personally and professionally, this book is for you, and Vincent Smith is your guide. You will delight in the richness and depth Feng Shui will bring to your life. You will never view yourself, your surroundings, or your work in the same way again."

MARY AND MANUEL RAMOS, READING SPECIALIST,
SR. CLIENT DEVELOPMENT EXECUTIVE

Contents

I want to thank Victoria Smith, our editor, for her gentle and helpful guidance and understanding throughout this exciting process. Barbara Lyons Stewart has been an invaluable part of this book. As an architect and designer and part of our Panergetics team, Barbara has made certain that we are talking your language and has added many architectural suggestions for Feng Shui issues. She has also provided all of the diagrams demonstrating these concepts. I am also indebted to my other Panergetics partners, David Fraser and Lisa Krumins, for their insights and support in this work.

Because Feng Shui is an oral tradition, it is important for me to pay respects to my teachers. I have been extremely fortunate to be a student and disciple of Grandmaster Lin Yun Rinpoche, one of the foremost Feng Shui masters in the West and the leader of the Black Hat School of Feng Shui. Studying and traveling with Professor Lin in China was a profound experience for me. Professor Lin helped me realize that Feng Shui is principally a philosophy of life and only then a design concept flowing from that philosophy.

I was also fortunate to have studied with three of Professor Lin's most experienced protégés, Edgar Sung, Barry Gordon, and Steven Post of the BTB Feng Shui Professional Training Program. These three gentle persons and their wonderful right arm, Cindy, gave me the training and encouragement to become a consultant. It is also important to acknowledge the information and ideas that I have obtained from the authors in the Bibliography. Even though some of the concepts and ideas in this text may appear to differ in places from those writings, the underlying source and intent is the same.

Acknowledgments would be incomplete without my giving thanks and love to my family who have listened to me, probed with me, cared for me, tolerated me, Feng Shuied with me, and loved me. Thank you

Jessica, Alice, Duncan, Lisbeth, Lachlan, and my nieces and nephews. Especial thanks go to my parents who set me on this path. Thank you to all of my students and clients from whom I have continued to learn.

So here we are. We have our work cut out for us. I hope you enjoy this journey as much as I have.

AN ARCHITECT'S PERSPECTIVE

By Barbara Lyons Stewart, AIA

SO WHY SHOULD ARCHITECTS AND DESIGNERS LEARN ABOUT FENG SHUI?

On my first day of graduate school, the studio director announced, "If there's anyone here who wants to design a building that looks like a Swiss chalet, Greek temple, or Italian villa, you should leave right now. You're here to open your minds and create architecture for the future . . . ." This made sense to me at the time but now seems like a questionable approach to the problem of designing space for real people whose basic needs remain constant regardless of time period. I later learned that most of my professors lived in Victorian houses and planned vacations in Tuscany. But no one ever said, "There is something that feels *comfortable* about living in a Victorian house and vacationing in an Italian hill town, so let's figure out why we like those places and interpret those ideas for our own climate and culture." Instead, our professors encouraged a bunch of inexperienced 20- to 24-year-olds to think "outside the box" and "push design in new directions."

As architects and designers, we are trained to worship the gods of originality and novelty, while Feng Shui focuses simply on improving people's lives. By understanding its traditions, we can help those who live and work in the spaces we design, because Feng Shui is *all* about making people comfortable—in whatever design style we choose. It teaches that we need to surround ourselves with the energy, balance, and harmony found in nature to lead healthy and productive lives.

Its basic premise is that we encounter daily (consciously and subconsciously) hundreds of details that can make us tense and uncomfortable. Applying Feng Shui principles to reduce the number of stressful details will make us calmer and happier. These general concepts have been used for thousands of years. Why not study them and see what we can learn?

Switch from thinking about "the Building" to thinking about "the People" and add value to your client's projects.

Incorporating Feng Shui into our design process isn't just adding another layer of knowledge (like learning about furniture placement helps with the design of interior spaces). It actually changes our design process. Most of us were taught that if we design good buildings, then our clients and the future occupants will benefit. So our focus is on designing good buildings, although what defines a "well-designed building" seems to vary with the decade.

Feng Shui pursues the same goal by turning the process inside out. It begins by understanding our human need for "nature" and focusing on creating the best environment for the mental and physical health of the person who will live and work in the space. In Feng Shui, the people are much more important than the building. And there's nothing trendy about designing buildings that are good for people.

Let's look at two examples of the different approaches.

1. An architectural designer might begin schematic design considering complex volumes and an off-center entrance. Feng Shui tradition teaches that humans feel most comfortable in complete shapes and that the major entrance should be centered on the most important elevation because balance is important. This isn't only an Eastern tradition—think about Greek temples, European castles and cathedrals, and most of the important buildings we've studied in architectural history.
2. Designers often develop lobby paving patterns as a graphic exercise to reinforce the overall design concept or the lobby geometry. Feng Shui would recommend a paving pattern that subconsciously and smoothly directs the energy flow of people to their destination: an information desk or the elevators.

Are you already applying Feng Shui intuitively?

Experienced designers often unconsciously follow Feng Shui principles.

- They don't draw a corporate office space plan with an office door at the end of a long straight corridor. Designers think "accent wall," while Feng Shui teaches "too much energy/chi rushing toward the occupant."
- They don't design bedrooms where the only possible bed location puts the headboard against a bathroom plumbing wall. Designers think "potential acoustic problems," while Feng Shui teaches, "The imbalance of water energy can affect your health." (And it will if you can't sleep!)
- They don't generally create rooms with very dark ceilings and very light floors. Designers think "light and airy." Feng Shui teaches, "The balance of nature: light sky, medium forest and fields, and dark earth."
- They wouldn't design a master bathroom with a small north facing window, blue fabric wall covering, brown tiles and carpet, and oil-rubbed bronze fixtures. Designers think "dark and drab"; Feng Shui teaches "too yin."

Feng Shui crossed the ocean in the 1970s along with acupuncture and tai chi, Eastern traditions similarly based upon the flow of Energy. The Mayo Clinic revealed in 2005 that in a study of patients with fibromyalgia, an incurable pain illness, six acupuncture treatments over three weeks significantly improved their symptoms of pain and fatigue. Even if you're a skeptic and only reading this book because your clients have asked you about Feng Shui, think of it the way some people do religion: you don't really know if there's a heaven or hell, but just in case . . . .

And speaking of religion—Feng Shui isn't one. It's a belief system that has never focused on a deity. I wouldn't feel right placing a statue of Buddha in my garden to balance a missing area (an angel or Saint Francis, maybe). So when you read Chapter 9 about the transcendental side of Feng Shui (think "power of positive thinking" and "the importance of visualizing successful outcomes"), be encouraged to find words and hand movements that feel right for you if the traditional cultural symbolism seems too strange. Ancient rituals hold strength and power, but reading this book is probably your first step into Feng Shui, so begin with symbolism that resonates within you.

How do you use this book during the Design Process?

You could follow the steps listed below, but remember to select which Feng Shui principles will be the most helpful while designing your specific new building or renovation project. You won't need all of the principles for every project.

Programming.

- Ask your clients about the Primary Purpose of each space (see Chapter 2). Should the hotel rooms be serene bedrooms or stimulating work/sleep spaces?
- Discuss the energy level they'd like to achieve in each space. Do the litigation attorneys need calming down or revving up? File this information away for future use with this book's sections on *Yin and Yang* and Colors in Chapters 2 and 3.

Site Review and Analysis.
Read the Site Selection Guidelines in Chapter 4 for both residential and business projects. Review the Site Planning Checklist in Chapter 5. (Why do some commercial properties experience constant turnover, whereas those across the street are successful?)

Programming, Adjacency Diagrams, and Space Planning.

- Read about Shapes in Chapter 3. Refer to the *Bagua* diagrams in Chapter 2 to place buildings, departments, and rooms in their most auspicious locations. Yes, this takes a leap of faith, but this is the aspect of Feng Shui most clients expect us to study, and who are we to question clients' desires *and* ancient wisdom?
- Read about the Flow of Energy in Chapter 2 to locate doors and windows and plan corridors like the meandering paths found in nature.

Schematic Design.

- Review the Schematic Design Checklist in Chapter 5 and the applicable project type section in Chapters 6, 7, and 8 for energy and relationship information.

- Review the Commanding Position in Chapter 2 to make sure furniture can be placed to reduce vulnerability before finalizing plans. If you doubt this concept, ask yourself: Why does a Mafia don (in movies, at least) sit in the rear corner of a restaurant with his back against the wall and a view of both exits? And why do dogs sleep facing the door? That's the Commanding Position.

Design Development.

- When you begin thinking about exterior and interior materials, refer to the charts in the Yin and Yang section of Chapter 2 to select materials to produce the appropriate energy level.
- Use the Five Elements Chart in Chapter 2 to select colors and materials for a building exterior. Determine the predominant element in the neighborhood and then select a color for your building that will "overcome" an ugly neighborhood and "support" your own building.

Construction document preparation, and furniture and finishes selection and specification.

- Read Chapter 3 for guidelines in selecting colors, shapes, materials, lighting, sound, signage, art and decorative objects, plants and landscaping, and water features.
- Refer to the Five Elements Chart in Chapter 2 for the tools to either balance a space or enhance a particular element.
- Read the applicable project type section in Chapters 6, 7, and 8 for specific design recommendations.

Why is this a good book for architects and designers?

As an architect in San Francisco, I am increasingly asked by clients what I know about Feng Shui. A few years ago, I began attending seminars and reading books. Many were based on the Compass School of Feng Shui that uses cardinal compass directions to influence our environment—as the Aztecs and Mayas would have done. I found it hard to understand why blue paint on a north wall (arctic ice) would be best or how locating a bed auspiciously depended upon the birth date of only one of the bed's occupants. The Compass School is the most popular Feng Shui school in Asia today, but I couldn't reconcile it with my Westen architectural education.

Then I attended a seminar taught by Vincent Smith at the University of California at Berkeley from the viewpoint of the Black Sect School of Feng Shui. I began to see ho e Feng Shui concepts of a natural Energy and Balance logically to our man-made environment—and I first felt the pull from the illogical, transcendental side of Feng Shui. It has never been a fixed doctrine but incorporates beliefs from India, Tibet, China, and other cultures. It has endured because it's based on universal beliefs. Feng Shui practitioners through the ages have added their own interpretation and wisdom—and Vincent is an excellent Feng Shui interpreter for those of us who don't merely want to decorate our projects with bamboo flutes, crystals, and purple candles.

This book could just as easily be titled *A Universal Philosophy of Environmental Psychology*. As architects and designers, we've always known that our spaces affect people's lives. Studying Feng Shui gives us another set of tools—one with 5,000 years of history—to help make those lives a little happier and more comfortable: a good goal.

I hope you enjoy reading this book and learning how to apply some of these principles to your own projects. And if you decide to embrace its ideas and continue studying Feng Shui, then you'll never look at buildings quite the same way again . . . .

FENG SHUI:

A Universal Philosophy of Environmental Psychology and the Squint Test

Welcome to the world of Feng Shui! Feng Shui is the study of all forms of energy, including the energies of spaces, and how those energies affect people. The mention of Feng Shui no longer draws a blank stare from many Americans but instead is making news with great regularity. Rupert Murdoch, Donald Trump, Citibank, Coca Cola, Hewlett Packard, and other big players are using these ancient principles to develop sites and properties to create positive and productive living and working spaces. No longer considered the realm of New Agers, Feng Shui is now recognized as a tool for improving our everyday lives, both for today and for the long term.

The intent of this book is to demystify and de-Easternize Feng Shui and make these universal principles accessible to our Western culture. Many skeptics think of Feng Shui as a form of Chinese hocus-pocus. Unfortunately, much of our Western press demonstrates a lack of understanding about Feng Shui and makes fun of some of the techniques that have been used by the Chinese, because those particular tools are strange to us. Most Westerners justifiably look askance when they read about hanging Chinese firecrackers and flutes. The important point, however, is that the underlying principles are valid for everyone in any time or place. The specific tools that are used to adjust the energies of a space can be adapted by any individual or business to be appropriate in any geographic or cultural region, whether it be England, New England, the American Midwest, or California. The fact that these principles are more than 5,000 years old certainly indicates their validity. Because these concepts are not about particular styles of design, there is every reason to believe they are just as important today as they were yesterday.

Our goal is to provide you with an in-depth understanding of the underlying concepts and principles of Feng Shui so that you will be able to take your designs to a new level. Feng Shui can help you analyze, and provide solutions for, *any* situation. Understanding and applying the principles of Feng Shui will lead to the creation of spaces that enhance the well-being and productivity of the individual or business and make your client want to return to do business again. Although Feng Shui covers all of the energies that affect us, not just those in our physical spaces, this book will limit itself primarily to the physical environment.

The ancient principles of Feng Shui are a universal form of environmental psychology. All of the energies that surround us, especially those in our physical spaces, reflect how we feel about ourselves and, at the same time, affect our behavior, often on a subconscious level. These principles are not just Chinese, but are universal in nature. They are tools that everyone can use to create spaces that will reduce stress and maximize people's potential and well-being. This book will first discuss the concepts of Feng Shui, then apply them to architectural project types in a manner that is consistent with any style. Because our goal is to make Feng Shui accessible to you, we generally will not use Chinese terms.

Practicing the art of Feng Shui is learning the art of experiencing all the energies in a space. It is critical for professionals to live inside their designs—not just seeing space but experiencing it. How does it feel to walk through the door and immediately face a wall? And then have to decide which way to go? In a dark area with gray walls? The list of questions goes on and on. Visualize the experience your clients will have once they live and work in the space you have created. Is the experience one they want? Does it enhance the purpose of the space?

It is easy to give a client advice on a space that is exactly like the one in the Feng Shui book that you just read. However, how often does that happen? In our Feng Shui practice, we have found that there is no such thing as the "same space." Spaces may be similar in some respects but not the same. Even when two areas appear to be identical in shape, the energy in each, as well as in the area leading into them, will be very different. In addition, it is important to consider the particular occupants and their personalities and needs. As we know, no two individuals are alike. Place a unique individual in a unique space and we have a Feng Shui challenge.

Throughout this book, we refer to the Squint Test. The Squint Test is a technique for ascertaining the impact that visual images have on the subconscious. By closing your eyes to a slit, you no longer see objects as identifiable conscious images but instead perceive only the color contrasts and patterns. This underlying image impacts the subconscious and creates a sense of calmness or chaos, or something in-between.

Most professionals lay out a design with "north" at the top of the sheet. Our diagrams will be oriented with the entrance to the space at the bottom of the page, allowing you to feel as if you are entering and moving into the area. We are also trying to move away from the left brain's tendency to read sequentially toward the right brain's method of feeling. We will discuss this concept further in Chapter 2.

Whenever we give several ways to resolve an issue, we list them in order of preference. Throughout this book, we occasionally will appear to repeat a point that we have discussed in a prior chapter. Be patient. Frequently, what appears to be redundant is often a similar idea in a slightly different context or with a different spin. I have found that discussing the same concept in different situations often makes understanding the underlying significance easier. Throughout this book, the word *I* refers to me, Vincent, and the word *we* refers either to our Panergetics team or to Panergetics and the client, because we try to involve the client in the Feng Shui process to the greatest extent possible.

To help you understand my approach to Feng Shui, let me briefly describe my journey to becoming a Feng Shui consultant and teacher. I grew up in Louisville, Kentucky, in a Quaker family with parents who were involved in the musical and theatrical world as directors and teachers. With this influence, I began acting and singing at an early age. After graduating from Harvard College, I was faced with the decision of whether to act, sing, and eat peanut butter sandwiches or go to Yale Law School and earn a living. Because I did not expect that I would become a star, I chose the law and practiced real estate law in New York City for 25 years, becoming the senior real estate partner at a large law firm. However, once the stage bug has bitten you, it is with you for life. My nights and weekends were often spent in the theater, acting, directing, producing, and designing sets. It was my work designing sets that led me to the New York School of Interior Design and Donna Lang, a nationally known designer and author from whom I learned a great deal and with whom I formed the design firm of Lang, Winslow, and Smith in Chatham, New Jersey. In the mid-1980s, I attended a lecture by Sarah Rossbach on Feng Shui and knew immediately this would be my next career. After studying Feng Shui for six years, I retired early from the law in 1995 and formed the VMS Feng Shui Design Company. In 2002, I founded Panergetics, LLC, a national Feng Shui consultancy for businesses. My love for the theater has been fulfilled by teaching college credit courses in Feng Shui at Williams College in Massachusetts and at Berea College in Kentucky and by lecturing on Feng Shui in universities, such as Berkeley and Arizona State, and at numerous companies around the country.

One word of caution that I want to mention here and will undoubtedly repeat throughout this work: Feng Shui is more than "book learning." It is an intuitive, energetic process that is both very simple and very complex. Do not be too hyperactive about following the precise instructions in an analysis of a space or a technique. Frequently, we have been taught in Western education that we must "color within the lines" to perform "correctly." As you will see, there is a correct way to perform Feng Shui, but you will not find it in any book. You will only find it in yourself and often only by "coloring outside the lines." The goal of this book is to give you the tools with which you can enter a client's space and Feng Shui the environment. On many occasions, you will respond to a situation from deep inside yourself and not from your book learning. Those are very exciting moments. You will feel as if you are the conduit of information from another source. You are.

1

A HISTORY AND OVERVIEW OF FENG SHUI

The winds are mild
The sun is warm
The water is clear
The trees are lush
—The Chinese Burial Book

The Chinese words *Feng Shui* mean *wind* and *water* and come from this ancient Chinese poem. Notice that the poem is about the various aspects of nature. It is also no coincidence that air and water are the two most essential necessities for our survival. The ancient term that was used for the concepts of Feng Shui was *k'an yu*, words meaning *cover* and *support* and loosely translated as "under the canopy of heaven."

Nature will play a large role throughout this book. By nature, however, we are not just talking about plants and water features that can bring energy to a space. When we think of making our environments more in tune with, or feeling more like, nature, we will be talking about incorporating in our man-made spaces the proportions and scale of natural elements and the shapes, materials, textures, color values and relationships, lighting, and other visual and sensual elements that are found in nature.

This chapter will give an overview of the philosophy, history, and development of Feng Shui. Feng Shui consists of a practical and tangible approach to energy as well as a very important transcendental aspect. This book focuses primarily on the practical side, but will briefly discuss the transcendental elements in Chapter 9. We will also explain why

1

these universal principles have come down to us through the Chinese and not through other cultures in which they previously existed.

Feng Shui is frequently described as "the Chinese art of placement and design." It is a discipline that deals with choosing an appropriate building site, with locating the building on the property, with arranging the rooms within the building, and with placing the furniture within the rooms. These elements, however, are only the visible tip of the iceberg; as we all know, the ice beneath the ocean's surface is considerably greater than the portion we see.

Feng Shui is not a decorating style. Its principles apply equally to any décor or furnishing and embrace much more than interior decorating. Feng Shui covers all forms of energy and life experience and has been described as art, science, philosophy, psychology, ecology, superstition, and magic.

In reality, Feng Shui is a way of life, the discipline of tuning the human instrument to be sensitive to the energies around us. Feng Shui is the art of listening to, trusting, and following your intuition. The principles of Feng Shui teach us how to access what we already know. I realize that may sound a bit far out, but bear with me!

THE UNIVERSAL NATURE OF FENG SHUI

Although Feng Shui comes to us as a 5,000-year-old tradition, the principles are universal in nature and are based on being in harmony with the natural flow of the forces of energy. For some reason, these principles became lost in other cultures. In visiting and studying the architecture and design of ancient cultures, such as the Minoan and Mayan civilizations, as well as that of cultures that we tend to call "primitive," I became even more convinced of the universality of Feng Shui. The Greeks, the Egyptians, the Scandinavians, the Navajo Indians, and many other cultures embraced the same concepts. Some specific examples are the Delphi and the Parthenon in Greece, the Taj Mahal in India, Chichén Itzá from the Mexican Mayan culture, and the great pyramids of Egypt. An analysis of the homes and structures of the early Indian tribes in the United States also reveals an observance of the same basic ideas. Even animal homes are constructed along similar principles.

When I began teaching Feng Shui in college courses, I realized that I needed to find some basis for the concept that these principles were universal and not just Chinese. My research led me to several books on the evolution of language. The first human communication was oral and was a series of mental pictures; e.g., "He was as big as a bear and as woolly as a mammoth." This immediately creates a visual image, which is a right brain function relating to our subconscious brain activity. The first written languages were pictographs and hieroglyphics—still very right brain. However, as our Western languages evolved, the pictographs became abstract letters that do not create pictures but only have meaning when they are strung together in a sequence of similar abstractions. As Western languages evolved, our left brain, which governs our sequential and conscious thought processes, became more dominant, overriding many of our right brain functions. When we look at Chinese and other Asian languages, they still consist of pictorial characters. The nature of these Asian languages, therefore, has stimulated the development and retention of the right brain images that are the substance of Feng Shui.

The principles of Feng Shui relate to the way the images of our environment impact our subconscious behavior. Being aware of the nature of this influence is a very right brain activity. Although we realize that the brain is complex and cannot be easily categorized, we describe below some commonly understood brain distinctions to which we will refer throughout this book.

Right Brain	Left Brain
Imagery	Written words
Simultaneity	Linear
Subconscious	Conscious
Intuition	Speech
Metaphor	Logical
Left side	Right side
Left hand	Right hand
Holding	Reaching
Gathering	Hunting

Particularly note the last four concepts of each column and the side of the brain to which they relate. We will refer throughout this book to the concepts of the right brain and left brain and the way in which they affect design decisions.

In our Western, strongly left brain culture, we can develop our right brain abilities by focusing on techniques such as those set forth in *Drawing on the Right Side of the Brain* by Betty Edwards or the principles of Feng Shui. Because Feng Shui is about the impact that energies have on us, developing our right brain's subconscious is critical. As Anna Wise describes in *The High Performance Mind*, one of the easiest ways to shift into the subconscious is to change one's brain wave patterns through meditation. Meditation is therefore an important part of a Feng Shui consultant's daily activity that we will discuss in greater detail in Chapter 9.

SCHOOLS OF FENG SHUI

If you have read more than one book on Feng Shui, you are undoubtedly confused. Although there are many different approaches to the concepts of Chinese Feng Shui, they are all based in the same principles of energy. We have set forth below a very superficial description of a few of the better known disciplines.

The Form School

According to existing historical information, the early schools of Feng Shui arose between 4,000 and 5,000 years ago in the small villages in the north of China. These people lived in a region where the mountains were to the north, the flat plains and waters of the Yellow River Basin and the seas were to the south and east, and the less friendly climates were to the west. To protect themselves from the harsh northern weather and benefit from the warm southern sun, the physical placement of their homes in relation to the natural land formations was a primary concern. As a result, the earliest schools of Feng Shui focused on the contours and shapes of the land and related them to the four cardinal directions of the compass. Having a culture in which animals played an important symbolic role, the Chinese associated each of the four directions with an animal. The north was the black tortoise, the east was the green dragon, the south was the red phoenix, and the west was the white tiger. The village or house that was surrounded by natural geographical shapes resembling these four animals was considered to be located in the most auspicious setting. This early approach to Feng Shui is called the Form School.

The Compass School

As the culture spread and the rivers changed their courses, Feng Shui evolved with the civilization. As the community grew, it was necessary to accommodate more and more people in a way that made each person feel they were facing a good direction. The Compass School that developed is considered by many to be the traditional approach and today is the most prevalent method of Feng Shui practiced in China.

This approach uses the *lo p'an*, a compass that has anywhere from 8 to 36 concentric circles, depending upon the sophistication of the Feng Shui practitioner. Individuals determine their auspicious direction based on their birthday. They then use the *pa kua*, an octagon with a trigram from the *I Ching* on each of the eight sides, and the *lo shu* magic square, both of which we will describe in detail in Chapter 2. In the Compass School, the *Kan*, or Path in Life, portion of the octagon is always placed to magnetic north to determine how to orient the individual's front door, bed, chair, and other elements of life based on that person's most favorable direction.

There are many variations on the use of the compass and other mathematical approaches in different schools of Feng Shui. These tools give many people comfort in the "factual" nature of the Feng Shui consultant's recommendations. However, if several people inhabit a space, a decision must be made as to whose "most favorable direction" will be used. In addition, there are two north points, the north pole and magnetic north. The magnetic north shifts one degree every five years. As a result, someone using the Compass School will need to shift the arrangement of the front door and the placement of the bed, desk, and other key elements of the space every five years.

I do not raise these points to be negative but to be informative. Although moving the front door is not realistic, moving one's furniture every so often may be beneficial, as long as it does not create another issue. It is very easy for us to become too static and rigid if everything always remains the same.

The Black Sect School

The most recent evolution of Feng Shui has become prominent in the United States and Europe and is known as the Black Sect School, or

Black Hat Sect Tantric Buddhist Feng Shui. The Black Sect School has been led by Grandmaster Thomas Lin Yun Rinpoche. Although this approach to Feng Shui incorporates many of the concepts of the other schools, it does not use the *lo p'an*, or compass, and focuses less on the magnetic compass points and the importance of the best directions for an individual. The emphasis of the Black Sect is on the natural flow of chi, or energy, in a particular space, the balancing of energies, and the use of both tangible and intangible solutions to correct the problems in our environments. The Black Sect also uses the *Bagua*, or *pa kua* as the Compass School calls it, but always applies it by placing the *Kan*, or Path in Life, section of the *Bagua* on the same line as the entrance to the space rather than orienting it to magnetic north. Some Compass School practitioners consider the Black Sect School to be a simplified and Westernized version of Feng Shui. Our feeling is that the Black Sect may indeed be closer to the original concepts of Feng Shui before the many layers of evolution added increasing complexity. The bottom line, however, is that all of the approaches stem from the same basic principles and are intended to make our environments more conducive to a happy, productive life.

The Black Sect may have a more spiritual approach to Feng Shui than other schools because it gives one a direction to use in our constantly changing world where every space and individual is unique. By *spiritual* we do not mean *religious* but "of the spirit" or "related to the subconscious and unconscious levels of the human psyche." The psychologist Carl Jung was fascinated by the concepts of the *I Ching* and Feng Shui and referenced them in his work. Our feeling is that a Feng Shui master or consultant needs to be a very centered person and come from a psychologically sound base.

Black Sect Tantric Buddhism (BTBH) originated from the indigenous Tibetan Bon religion. When Buddhism was introduced from India into Tibet, it quickly became the dominant religion and evolved into five traditions: Sakya, Nyingma, Kagu, Gelug, and Black Sect. The Black Sect was the result of the blending of the Bon religion and Buddhism and is considered the second stage of BTBH.

The third stage of BTBH occurred when Tibetan Buddhism spread into China. Although the Sakya, Nyingma, Kagu, and Gelug traditions retained their purity when they moved into China, the Black Sect became a further blend of religions, adopting much of the Chinese culture, including the philosophies of Taoism, *yin and yang*, the *I Ching*, Feng Shui, holistic healing, and divination. At this stage, BTBH had become a blend of the Tibetan, Indian, and Chinese cultures.

The fourth stage of BTBH seeks to bring this ancient tradition into the present era and to blend the philosophies of these ancient cultures with our modern, Western world. Over the last three decades, Professor Lin Yun, the current leader of BTBH, has spread the concepts of BTBH throughout the United States and Europe by incorporating modern, Western knowledge, sciences, and disciplines into the traditions of Feng Shui. The Black Sect approach is a blend of the mundane and tangible with the transcendental and intangible. The concepts set forth in this book are primarily those of the Black Sect.

The Intuitive Feng Shui School

You may occasionally hear about Intuitive Feng Shui. Although some Feng Shui consultants speak disparagingly about such a concept, we feel that all animals, including human beings, have an intuitive instinct to follow these universal principles. As our societies have evolved and become more complex, we have often moved away from those principles and created environments for other reasons—to our detriment. All of us experience spaces that "just feel good" because some part of our psyche is telling us that the space is a "natural" one.

THE FENG SHUI CONSULTANT'S APPROACH

Feng Shui is an integration of practical and tangible issues and solutions with the transcendental and intangible aspects of the universe. Our current society is often in tune with a television channel instead of being in tune with nature, ourselves, and our environment. The Feng Shui consultant works with the architect and designer in the capacity of an environmental psychologist on the practical and tangible issues of a space to create a psychologically healthy environment for the client. The consultant may then move into the more transcendental areas if the client is so inclined. We will discuss this area further in Chapter 9.

We can use Feng Shui to enhance a person's life by doing the following:

- Creating a new space that optimizes the environment for the individual's life
- Improving an existing space where the environment may be adding to a person's problems
- Giving a client the tools to change a personal belief and pattern of behavior

In the event that a particular aspect of a person's life is blocked or not successful, a Feng Shui analysis of the person's home and office environment often will reveal the source of that block and lead to the key psychological element that is the source of the problem. We are most affected by what is closest to us. At the same time, we are often attracted to an environment that reinforces our blocks and continues us along the path we want to leave.

For example, a person may have no problem starting projects but have great difficulty in completing them. In most instances, this block will be reflected in the environment that the individual has chosen or created, making it even more difficult for that person to move ahead. An analysis of the physical space often leads to a discussion of the underlying factors causing this pattern of behavior. When a client acknowledges the problem and understands the connection with a space, it is then possible for the individual consciously to alter the environment and move in a new direction.

THE DETERMINANTS IN LIFE

The Chinese believe the following five determinants in life are all interrelated and create the person we are at any one moment in time. See Figure 1.1.

Karma. Whether or not you believe in past lives, even science is emphatic about the tremendous degree to which our DNA determines who we are as individuals. Our DNA is a physical manifestation of some of the traits we bring to this life from the past.

Fate. The Compass School emphasizes the importance of astrology and the moment of birth. Although we will obtain this information about a person, family, or business, it is only part of the picture. The "person" who exists "today" is a complex composite of the five Interrelated Determinants and should be analyzed at the current moment, not by relying on a birth date. By sensing who that individual is and what the issues are, even if they have not been articulated, we will know how best to help the client.

Luck. This is an arbitrary word to describe our daily experiences. Every situation, from the weather conditions to contact with another person, affects the way we feel and behave and continues to mold who we are.

Education. Our education is broader than our formal schooling. Everything we read, hear, or experience adds to our wealth of information and becomes part of us.

Feng Shui. The word *environment* encompasses a great deal. The environment that affects us goes from the distant sun, moon, and tides to

FIGURE 1.1 *Determinants in Life*

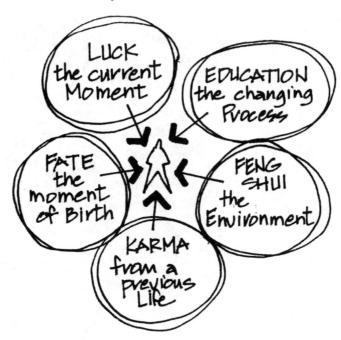

our country, our community, our office, our neighborhood, our street, our house, our bedroom, and our bed. The energy of all of these forces has an impact on us. The closer the energies get to our body and the more time we spend in a space, the stronger the effect.

ANALYZING THE ENVIRONMENT

In the following figure and tables, the last item is always "Other." These are not "checklists" to be gone through item by item but are examples of the type of features that may be relevant. The most important factor in an analysis is often in the "Other" category.

One of the most important items in Figure 1.2 is often the history of the prior owners or occupants of the property. We will discuss these factors in more detail in Chapter 4.

In analyzing a property, a building, or a space, the Feng Shui consultant will consider the following elements:

FIGURE 1.2 *Feng Shui Analysis*

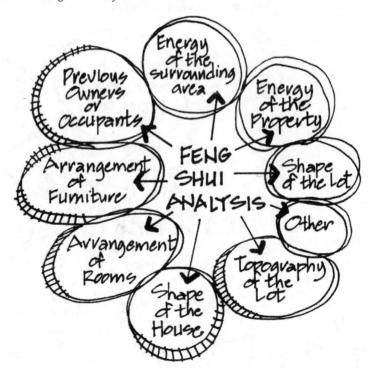

Set forth below are some of the elements of the neighborhood surrounding a property that may be relevant in analyzing the energies that are affecting the clients as they approach their spaces, as well as when they are inside. Being aware of the state of a person's personal energy as a result of the process of arriving at a home or office is critical in making decisions on how to reverse, balance, or otherwise compensate in the design of the client's own space. For example, if the buildup of energy as one approaches an office is dismal and very low, it may be important to make a dramatic shift in the energy of the person's individual space to emphasize that you have now entered an exciting environment that is clearly distinguishable from the unpleasantness outside. Another example is the "poison arrow." When a sharp object, such as the corner of a building across the street, is aimed directly at a space, the energy off that corner is considered to be an unnatural and too strong force that can affect the occupants of the space.

TABLE 1.1 *Neighborhood Features Affecting People and Their Spaces*

Bodies of Water	Structures	Entrances
Vegetation	Cemeteries	Lighting
Roads	Neighbors	Sounds
Bridges	Transformers	Odors
Houses of Worship	Telephone Poles	Colors
Buildings	Trees	Other

TABLE 1.2 *Interior Features Affecting People and Their Spaces*

Entrance Area	Lighting
Shapes of Rooms	Position of Beds
Pattern of Flow	Position of Desks
Hallways and Stairs	Position of Stove
Ceiling Lines, Beams, and Columns	Position of Bathroom Fixtures
Placement of Doors	Colors
Placement of Windows	Clutter
Placement of Fireplaces	Occupants' Problems
Electrical Appliances	Other

Once we are inside a residence or business, we will continue the analysis of the energies in the spaces and consider the internal elements set forth in Table 1.2, among others.

In a business or other type of environment, this list would also include every aspect of that particular space.

In the Black Sect school of Feng Shui, we often use some of the following tangible additives as adjustments for the problems we encounter. These are only intended to give you an idea of the nature of the tools, not to indicate that these are the only items that may be used. On the contrary, it is very important that an adjustment be appropriate for the space and the particular individuals who occupy the space. You will notice that all of these objects are forms of energy that will be used to shift the energies in a space, from stimulating to stabilizing.

TABLE 1.3 *Items That Can Shift the Energies in a Space*

Brightness	Mirrors	Lights	Crystal	Polished Metal	
Sound	Bells	Wind Chimes	Waterfalls	Radio/TV	
Life	Trees	Flowers	Plants	Fish	Pets
Dynamics	Waterfalls	Fountains	Wind Chimes	Flags	Uplighting
Weight	Statues	Heavy Rocks	Fences	Large Planters	
Fragrance	Flowers	Incense	Essence of Oils	Cooking Aromas	
Touch	Fabrics	Surfaces	Rugs	Textured Materials	
Color	Hue	Intensity	Value	Shade	Tint
Other					

2

BASIC FENG SHUI PRINCIPLES

This chapter will discuss in detail basic Feng Shui concepts and tools and their applicability to the design of our physical environment. Whenever a space is not working well and does not maximize the potential of its occupants, it invariably is out of sync with one of these principles.

Almost every problem that arises in a space will relate to the following:

- The Flow of Energy
- The Balance of Energies

To enhance the potential of the space and its occupants, we use the following Feng Shui tools:

- The Commanding Position
- The *Bagua*
- The Five Elements

The most important question to ask about any environment, whether it be a town or a room, is,

"What is the Primary Purpose of this space?"

A. THE FLOW OF ENERGY: CHI

The way in which the chi, or energy, flows through a space impacts our level of stress and our behavior. In nature, there is no such thing as a straight line, a right angle, or a square edge. Yes, perhaps you can come up with something, but don't waste your energy! The point is that nature is filled with round forms, from the sun and moon to the trees and humans to the atom. And when energy moves, whether as light waves or people, it moves in a curved motion. We do not walk in a perfectly straight line unless we are forced to prove our sobriety!

If you watch people walk down a broad empty street, you will see that they meander in a natural way like a stream until something catches their attention and pulls them in a specific direction. There are interesting photographic studies of a college campus with many right-angled walkways. In the winter, when the campus is covered with snow, it becomes obvious that the students and faculty do not follow the walkways or go in straight lines from one building to another. Instead, they create curved paths in the snow that truly meander across the campus. Highways provide another example. People will inevitably drive more quickly on a long straight road than on one that curves. By designing long, straight corridors and walkways, we force people to move in an unnatural motion against their natural inclination.

Most people are right-footed and lead off with their right foot, which initially pulls them to the right. To compensate, we shift our energy back to the left and move in a counterclockwise direction. Studies indicate that when people are lost in the woods or another indefinite environment, they move in large, counterclockwise circles. In Feng Shui, we often use this natural inclination to begin moving to the right when we first enter a space and place certain pieces of furniture, such as a reception desk, to the right inside an entrance to make visitors feel as if they are naturally moving in the correct direction as they come into a space.

Basically, think of yourself as a form of energy, and be very aware of the way in which you move into and through a space. If the energy is blocked or pinched or prevented from flowing smoothly and freely, our stress is increased and our ability to perform to our maximum capability is reduced. Repeated 90-degree turns in a path or hallway are neither natural nor comfortable. In addition to the awkwardness of the angle, the uncertainty of what is immediately around the corner is unsettling. Most of the time, these impediments are small and seem insignificant. The problem arises, however, when one small block is followed by another and another, until we are consciously or subconsciously in a stressed condition before we even reach our destination. By opening up the flow of energy, we increase the opportunity for people in the space to live up to their potential.

All forms of matter and energy vibrate at their own specific cycle per unit of time. That apparently solid and inert desk at which you are sitting is in fact a group of molecules in motion. Visible light is only a small part of the electromagnetic spectrum. Invisible but measurable frequencies and wavelengths constitute a large portion of the spectrum, but there is also a very large unknown part. All of these forms of moving energy constantly affect us on a conscious, subconscious, and unconscious level. Energy, or *ley*, lines run throughout the earth. Geological fault lines are one of the most extreme producers of high mineral deposits. We are all aware of certain places that do not appear to be conducive to life; where wild life and natural plants do not thrive; where people are not happy, become aggressive, or become ill; and where something is clearly "out of sorts," as my grandfather used to say. It may be that the site is over a negative energy line.

For years, I lived on a street that was one block long. In the 13 houses on the block, six women developed breast tumors. Three died. Try to avoid building along an extreme energy line or in an area with energies that are incompatible with our normal human lives. However, in an existing situation or where there is no choice, neutralizing a negative stream, whether water or another energy, can be accomplished by releasing the negative energy from the earth with transcendental Feng Shui techniques.

The First Impression

The first thing we see sets our subconscious to work. This is a principle that you should always keep in mind when designing a space. The first impression we have of someone creates a powerful image. It may or may not be accurate, but it is certainly strong and will take some work to overcome. Similarly, the first thing we see in a space and our first impression of it immediately impact our subconscious, and often our conscious mind as well, and lead us psychologically in a specific direction. Our goal is to make those first impressions totally consistent with the purpose of the space.

For example, in a home environment where you enter the front door and immediately see a bedroom, you are at least subconsciously reminded of how little sleep you have had and feel tired. This encourages a state of exhaustion whenever you come home. When you first see a kitchen, your subconscious makes you want to eat. This can lead to eating issues. We recently worked on an office space in which most of the employees entered through a door that was directly opposite a restroom door. An extremely high percentage of the people who came in this entrance immediately used the restroom. This was their first impression of their workplace, as opposed to an exciting, upbeat lobby area.

Blocking the Flow of Energy

Our spaces can create blocks in many different ways. One of the most common is found in residences when we enter the front door and are immediately confronted with a wall that is less than six to seven feet from the door. This proximity, which is roughly equivalent to the height of a person, is too close and may make people feel blocked in their progress into the space. The "blocking wall" also creates an immediate question: "Which way should I go?" Not only have we stopped the person's energy, we have created further tension by requiring them to make a decision as to what to do next. Even though the process may not happen on a conscious level, we have added one touch of stress to another. The odds are that this blockage is just the first in a series of many stressful irritants.

Avoid designing a blocking wall. The typical Feng Shui solution for a preexisting wall that cannot be removed is to hang a mirror that opens up the space and gives the wall a feeling of greater depth. We have found in our practice, however, that this adjustment is usually not the best. The mirror reflects the viewer back out into the space from which they have just come rather than pulling them into the room they have just entered, obviously with the intention of coming into the space, not of leaving it immediately. The mirror is apt to reflect the outdoors, where most of us might prefer to be, or it may associate the viewer with an unattractive scene, such as a dingy, impersonal hallway in an apartment building.

In many situations, the most effective solution is to hang a picture that has depth to it and reads in a direction that will subconsciously lead the person in the best direction. If the picture is one of an interior scene, it will continue to pull the viewer into the room, whereas a nature scene may send the viewer's subconscious intent back outdoors. In Chapter 3, Section G: Art and Decorative Objects, we will discuss in detail the way art can be used to lead the viewer subconsciously.

Doors

Pair of Doors. Doors are a metaphor for an invitation to enter a space. The width and height of a doorway and the number of doors at the entrance of a building are subtle indicators of the intention of the occupants. Double doors and doors that are larger than normal indicate that all are welcome and are appropriately used on public buildings and businesses. On a residence, this message is often confusing. Even though double doors convey an image of the home being open to the public, we realize this is probably not the case. To further complicate the matter, one of the two doors is often permanently locked, even though there are handles on each of the two doors. The locked door is invariably the first one a person tries to open! This turns what originally appeared to be a very welcoming image into one of rejection. In any situation where there are double doors, especially in a business environment, both doors should be capable of being opened.

Dutch Doors. A Dutch door, in which the upper portion of the door can be opened and the bottom part kept closed, does not communicate the same greeting of warmth that a full door conveys. The message here is, "I will be happy to talk with you, but I reserve the decision as to whether or not you are welcome." In a home where the residents want more energy to enter, especially in a situation where there is a home office, a Dutch door should be replaced or always treated as a single unit.

Door Swings. When we approach a building or a room, we intend to enter *into* the space. Our natural inclination is to continue our forward movement and push the door in. If the door opens out, we are required to interrupt our forward flow and take a step backward before continuing forward. To enhance the natural flow of energy, doors should always open in. We are fully aware that building and fire codes impose restrictions on the way in which doors may swing. Try to plan a door swing that pulls people in rather than stopping their forward movement. Revolving doors, automatic sliding doors, and doors that swing in both directions accomplish the desired goal of eliminating that first impediment to the flow of energy.

Most professionals are aware that a door should open inward to expose the largest, or most important, part of the room. This allows the people entering the room to feel in control, because they immediately see the key elements of the space. Similarly, anyone inside the room will also feel more comfortable, because someone who enters cannot surprise them. Although this may seem like common knowledge, we were recently in a hospital in which the office doors did not open against the wall, but swung into the room, hitting anyone in the back who was standing at the desk talking to the occupant of the office and blocking the view of the doorway from the desk.

Door Handing. Many professionals are not aware of the effect of the right-handed door versus the left-handed door concept. Our goal is to make it as easy as possible for a person to enter every room. As we pointed out in the discussion of the left brain and right brain in Chapter 1, the left hand tends to be used for carrying and the right hand for reaching. As a result, most people carry purses, briefcases, and other objects in their left hand and reach out to shake hands with their right hand. This is true even for many left-handed people. As we approach a door and reach for the knob with our right hand, a right-handed door will swing open to the right and allow us to proceed smoothly into the room. If the door is a left-handed door that opens to the left and we have grabbed the knob with our right hand, we suddenly find that our right arm is in front of us, blocking us from easily entering the space. Because our goal is to eliminate all possible impediments to the smooth and uninterrupted flow of energy, whenever possible create a right-handed door that opens inward to expose the most important part of the room. See Figure 2.1.

FIGURE 2.1 *Door Handing*

for a Righthanded Person
enteving a room...

A "lefthanded"   A "righthanded"
Door blocks   Door provides
access.   clear access.

A number of door issues are frequently discussed in Feng Shui. Although they may seem extreme to you at first blush, bear with us.

Conflicting Doors. "Conflicting" or "fighting" doors exist when two doors hit one another if they are opened at the same time. See Figure 2.2. The conflicting doors may indicate, or increase the likelihood of, the possibility of a conflict in a particular aspect of the occupant's life. The area of life that may be affected depends upon where the doors are located in the house from the perspective of the *Bagua*, which we will discuss in detail in Section D of this chapter. The *Bagua* is a template that relates the various aspects of our life to particular areas in our spaces. For instance, if the doors of a home or office are in the Helpful People portion of the *Bagua*, the occupant may be in conflict with the boss or with people who would normally be of assistance, such as an attorney or publisher. Energy forbid! If one of the doors is a closet door, it may be that the conflict is coming from a source that is not immediately apparent.

FIGURE 2.2 *Conflicting Doors*

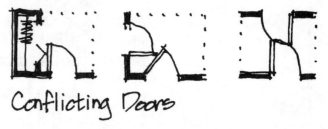

Even if you cannot subscribe to these more esoteric concepts, it is certainly easy to understand that conflicting doors should be avoided. A person opening one door may hit the person who is using the other door. Even as one starts to open one of these doors, he or she will experience a subconscious moment of hesitation about whether someone is in the way: another slight moment of being blocked from a smooth flow of energy.

Piercing Heart Doors. The term *piercing heart doors* describes three or more doors centered in front of you as you proceed forward, a situation shown in Figure 2.3 that can result in health problems. As the energy goes through the succession of doors, the chi accelerate, in much the same way as when energy flows down a long hallway, but it is pinched as it goes through each door. The repeated opening up and closing down can create stress that leads to health issues.

Centered Doors. In the case of doors that are directly opposite one another, be very aware of the functions of the rooms behind the doors, because a person's energy will naturally be pulled into the opposite room rather than turning at a sharp right angle down the hall. We recently worked on a dormitory and recommended relocating the communal bathroom door that was directly opposite a student's room door. Envision the feeling of leaving your room every day and being pulled into the group bathroom, as well as having the energy from the bathroom, and probably that of the many people exiting the bathroom, coming into your private space. In a residence, having bedroom doors directly opposite one another is an invitation for Johnny to end up in his sister's room more than she would like. Once a person's energy has made the turn into a hallway and is proceeding in a specific direction, the individual is less inclined to make a sharp right-angled turn into another room.

FIGURE 2.3 *Door Relationships*

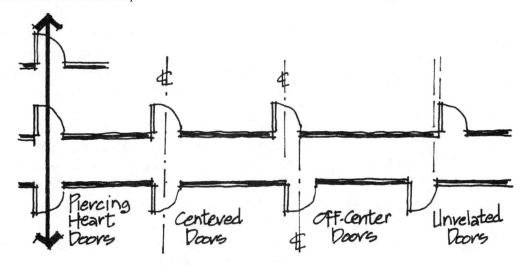

Off-Center Doors. If doors that are opposite one another are off center or misaligned, the energy flowing through the first door is partially interrupted, or blocked, by the next doorway. In addition to the problem discussed in the prior paragraph, there is the issue of the even flow of energy being interrupted. It is as if one half of a person is being pulled into the opposite room and the other half is being blocked by the opposite wall. It is thought that this imbalance in the uninterrupted flow of energy can lead to an increase in health problems and that the occupants may incur headaches and illnesses relating to the central nervous system. Regardless of how you react to this conclusion, the natural flow of energy will clearly feel better if the doors are not misaligned. The traditional adjustment for correcting this imbalance of energy is to mirror the portion of the walls that are directly opposite the open doorway.

Unrelated Doors. When doors are unrelated to one another and open facing the opposite wall, it is important to lead people subconsciously in a specific direction so that they do not have to "think" about which way to go. The easiest technique to accomplish this is with artwork that "reads" in the desired direction. We will discuss this tool in greater detail in Chapter 3, Section G: Art and Decorative Objects.

Exit Doors. A door that exits the back of a home or a bedroom is considered to portend a problem with respect to certain areas of the residents' lives. Referring to the sections of the *Bagua*, which we explain in Section D of this chapter, a door in the Prosperity area of a home or bedroom that leads out of the home or bedroom can indicate financial issues, with money flowing out of the family. This energy can often be reflected in tax problems. Similarly, a door that goes out of the home or bedroom in the Primary Relationship area of the Bagua can indicate that the relationship that is intended to occur in the home or bedroom may occur outside the home.

The metaphor is that the energy that should be staying in a person's life has an opportunity to escape. In an office context, money may be leaving the business too easily, or some of the partners may be engaged in outside activities that are detrimental to the business.

Dead Doors. A "dead door" is one that is not used. A door is a metaphor for entering one's private space or going out into the world. If a door that appears to be an entrance is not used as one but is the equivalent of a wall, the metaphor becomes one of being both physically and psychologically blocked and not allowed to progress in a natural way. By covering as much of the door as possible with a mirror on the interior, the image then becomes one of being in the space, as opposed to being blocked. Be very aware, however, of what is being reflected in the mirror and make certain that the image is appropriate for the intended purpose of that particular part of the space.

Windows

When we enter a space, our intention is to be inside that space. If a window is directly opposite the door when we come into a residence, an office, a room, or any other area, our energy is pulled straight through the space and out the window. Most people will be immediately drawn to the natural light, trees, colors, and other elements of the outdoors. See Figure 2.4. This can divert us from our intended purpose, even if for just a moment. Sometimes the impact is much greater, however. Placing the windows off to the side from a direct line opposite the door will avoid this problem.

If the windows already exist, place a plant or other attractive object in front of the window to stop the energy from exiting the space. Pulling the drapes or lowering the blinds can also prevent energy from leaving.

FIGURE 2.4 *Opposite Doorways*

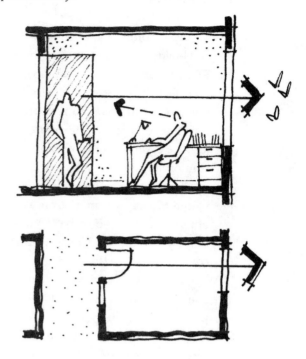

In an individual office situation, we recommend that the occupant lower the blinds when leaving at the end of the day so that upon arriving the next morning the person's energy stays in the office rather than flying outdoors.

One striking example of this occurred in a home that had been on the market for almost a year. Directly opposite the front door was a long wall of windows and French doors that looked out on a beautiful garden with steps at the far end that curved away like a funnel. When prospective buyers entered the house, their energy was immediately pulled out the wall of glass, into the yard, up the steps, and into the distance. Psychologically, they had left the house before they ever looked at it. The house was not selling. Fortunately, the window wall had draperies that could be pulled. We recommended that these draperies be closed before a buyer arrived. After potential buyers had inspected the entire house, the broker could say, "Oh, did you see the wonderful view from this beautiful room?" Once the brokers followed this very simple principle of keeping the energy of the client inside the space until the right moment, the house sold quickly.

Furniture Created "Doorways"

Any professional who has worked on a building is well aware of code and building requirements for the minimum width of door and corridors. These requirements are for both comfort and safety. We often forget, however, that the placement of furniture can also create a "door" or "corridor" from one space to another. See Figure 2.5. When two pieces of furniture, or a piece of furniture and a wall or column or other fixed object, are close to one another, the passage between them can become uncomfortably narrow. A doorway that is 30 inches or more in width is a comfortable space through which to move. Similarly, furniture that is placed 30 inches or more from another object will allow for an easy flow of movement. However, be careful about that 30 inches; it may not really be a passageway of 30 inches. If an object has a sharp corner, we are subconsciously aware that hitting it would hurt, so we steer clear of that corner. Subtract 4 inches from that side. If the other side of the passage is another sharp corner or wall, subtract another 4 inches. If the wall has a picture on it at this point, we do not want to hit the picture, so subtract 6 inches instead of only 4 inches. The 30-inch "doorway" has become 30 minus 4 minus 6, or only 20 inches in width, uncomfortable to move through, causing some degree of tension, if only on a subconscious level.

FIGURE 2.5 *Furniture Created Doorways*

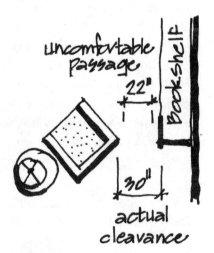

FIGURE 2.6 *Beams*

Beams

Overhead beams may create a pressure that can lead from discomfort to headaches to more serious illnesses. See Figure 2.6. The concept is that, as the energy flows around the room and hits the beam, it is forced down. A person who is sitting or sleeping under a beam physically feels the difference in height between the ceiling and the beam. We have watched people become drowsy and even ashen as they sat in a meeting underneath a soffit. In one case, a woman who was visibly feeling discomfort was greatly relieved when I suggested that she move her chair several feet. She later asked, "What was that all about?" I assure you, she will never sit under a beam again. Our personal list of client experiences goes on and on.

The height of the ceiling and the size of the beam are both relevant. A 7-foot ceiling with an 8-inch beam will be a greater problem than a 12-foot ceiling with a 12-inch beam. A barn house with even higher ceilings and beams that have air space above them will usually not be a problem at all.

If the beams are existing, avoid placing a sitting area, desk, or bed directly under a beam. If the bed is wider than the space between two beams, try to place the bed so that no one will be lying underneath a beam. In a small space where this is unavoidable, a relatively simple, fun, and inexpensive technique is to "drop the ceiling." A billowing fabric creates a soft "ceiling" with colors that enhance the Primary Purpose of the room. We will discuss Primary Purpose in Section F of this chapter.

Columns

Columns block the flow of energy in much the same way as beams. If they are round, the energy will flow smoothly. If they are square or project into a room with a sharp corner, they can create the same feeling of discomfort or illness. Sitting or sleeping near the sharp corner may be uncomfortable. The farther away one is from the corner, the less the impact. See Figure 2.7.

Structural columns in the corners of rooms, especially offices, are usually the biggest problem. If possible, avoid having the column project

FIGURE 2.7 *Columns*

into the room at all by revising the plan or furring out the wall. The next course of action is to place any important piece of furniture, such as a bed, desk, or frequently used chair, as far as possible from the column. The last resort is to hang a plant, decorative fabric, or some other item that is appropriate for the space so that it softens and absorbs the harshness of the energy from the sharp corner.

Slanted Ceilings

Slanted ceilings cause energy to accelerate and compress as it circulates around the room and is forced down by the slope of the ceiling. See Figure 2.8. This causes both a physical and a psychological pressure. Other than leveling the ceiling and eliminating the problem, the solutions are primarily transcendental, because they are in the mind and do not truly alleviate the pressure of the ceiling. Either mirror the entire short wall or the top 18 or 27 inches of that wall. This mirror will reflect the tall wall and give the perception of the shorter wall being as tall as the opposite wall. Other solutions are to cast light on the short wall or place plants that reach upward to give the sense of an upward energy raising the short wall. The artwork on the short and tall walls should be hung at the same height to give the illusion of the walls being the same. Hanging pictures high on the tall wall will only accentuate the difference and height of the taller wall and throw the room even more out of balance.

FIGURE 2.8 *Slanted Ceilings*

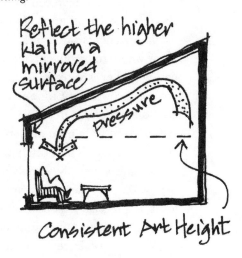

Slanted and Angled Walls

Slanted and angled walls give a sense of things being off balance and create a "missing" portion in a space. We will discuss the effect of "missing areas" in Chapter 3, Section B: Shapes. If at all possible, avoid including angled walls in a space. One solution to an existing situation is to mirror the angled wall to reflect the straight part of the room. When using a mirror, however, the professional must always be aware of what will be reflected in the mirror and make certain that the viewed images are not creating an even greater problem.

Clutter

When we tell a group that clutter is one of the primary focal points in a Feng Shui analysis of a space, virtually everyone in the audience shakes their head knowingly, "Yes, that applies to me!" Have you ever noticed how clutter follows us everywhere, whether in our closet, basement, attic, dresser, desk, purse, wallet, or car? All of us undoubtedly have many areas of our life that are filled with items that have outlived their usefulness and could be thrown away without being missed. Why don't we?

We undoubtedly have many rationales, but one of the primary reasons is a deep-seated fear of letting go of the past and moving forward. As was once said, "The only thing we have to fear is the unknown." However, all of us have found that the unknown is much less frightening once we become involved in it than it was when we were just thinking about how difficult it was going to be.

Many clients say to me, "But it is too overwhelming. I don't even know where to begin." I have found that a very easy way to begin eliminating clutter is with small steps. I recommend that a client first set a goal of throwing out nine items each day, no matter how insignificant each one may be. After a day or two, the client has gotten started and is well beyond only nine objects. If you are trying to clear out a closet, choose nine items that you have not used in the past two years. The two-year rule is generally a good one. If you have not used or touched an item within the past two years, you probably won't miss it and it's time for it to go. Clear exceptions to this rule are antiques, certain financial records, or objects of sentimental value, but be careful and make those exceptions rare. Exceptions do not include old shoes or a sweater with

FIGURE 2.9 *Block of Clutter*

Energy Blocking Clutter

holes in it that your ex-spouse gave you. Clearing out clutter is a perfect opportunity to let go of that part of your past that may be blocking you and keeping you from moving on. See Figure 2.9.

Clutter saps us of our energy in several ways. Let us take a desk for example. If we are surrounded by piles of paper that relate to work other than the project we are focusing on at the moment, our concentration is fragmented by the piles, notes, and other objects that impinge on our vision. In addition, we are subconsciously being reminded on a constant basis that we have all of those uncompleted tasks. Consequently, we are unable to devote all of our energy and attention to the task that we are trying to perform. All of us keep more paper than we need. Of course, some paper is important and necessary for us to retain. The answer is to file it out of sight and with a system. Not only will it no longer interfere with your concentration, but papers filed in an orderly way will be easier to locate.

When you have finished work, leave the desk clear. You will find it much less overwhelming when you return the next day to be greeted by a clean desk as opposed to stacks of paper. I have had clients who have told me, "I can't work in a neat office, and I know exactly where everything is." Although almost anything is possible, that stretches my credulity a bit. I encourage them to try eliminating some of the clutter as a test. You can lead a horse to water, but . . . However, in this case, the water tastes good!

Filling your bookshelves with unused materials ties you to the past psychologically and does not give you the shelf space or the psychic space to add new books and new ideas. I have solved the old book problem for myself by giving books to friends with instructions not to return them but to pass them on to someone else. A school or library will often take books or magazines, and libraries and other charities will frequently resell books to raise money. I find it much easier to remove books and magazines from my space when I know they will have a new home where they will be more frequently used.

Photographs, by definition, are a part of our past. This is a tricky area for the professional. I am frequently presented with a wall or table top that contains dozens of family pictures. Photographs can suddenly move from the interesting and attractive category to that of clutter. It is, of course, inappropriate for me to tell a client how many, or which, photographs should be removed. The consultant can, however, assess the situation and give suggestions.

Frequently, pictures have been added to a display instead of replacing an earlier shot. If there are a large number of pictures on the wall of each person in the family, recommend that three pictures of each person from three different stages in life be chosen for display. The fewer the pictures, the easier it is to see and appreciate the ones that are being shown. The photographs that are taken down do not need to be thrown away but can be saved in an attractive album. I suggest that clients review any tabletop groupings of pictures at least once every six months, because they tend to accumulate faster than pictures that are hung, which should be considered every year or so.

Most of us have a collection of some sort. In many cases, the collection overwhelms the environment, and the space appears to have become about the objects being collected rather than the people who are living in the space. It is healthy every so often to reflect on why you have the collection. Are these items ties to a past that is no longer relevant? Is it time to begin passing these objects on to family and friends and keep your favorite as a reminder of a wonderful time that you had collecting? This may not be that time. If not, circulate your collection. Have only a portion of the collection on display at any one time and rotate the pieces that are out, much as museums do. Changing a part of the environment will shift the energy in the space and also stimulate those who are in the space.

Remember that the fewer the number of objects on a shelf or in any space, the easier it is to see them. I have often recommended that a shelf that is filled to the edges with objects be pared down dramatically. Take everything off the shelf. Wipe it clean so that you are starting fresh in every way. Now pick the one object that you would want to have if you could only have one. Next, your second most precious possession. Now, the third. By this time, you have really started to look at the pieces and to realize why they were there and how many of them have lost their significance. As I discuss in Section B, an odd number of objects is apt to create a more dynamic image. Even when the space can hold more, the client frequently decides to leave some space for new items and give away, discard, or store the other pieces. These unneeded objects are often perfect for the yard sale or thrift store.

B. THE BALANCE OF ENERGIES: YIN AND YANG

The balance of complementary aspects of our environment, whether colors, shapes, materials, or other design components, greatly affects the way we feel and behave. When the complement is absent, our body often forces itself to "create it," causing unnecessary stress. The most obvious example of this is in the world of color, where we physiologically create and see spots of a complementary color if it is missing from a space. Try staring for several seconds at a green wall and see how long it takes for your eye to create red spots.

We are all familiar with the symbol for yin and yang.

FIGURE 2.10 *Yin and Yang Symbol*

Yin and yang are often thought of as being opposites. A more accurate interpretation is that yin complements or completes yang, and yang complements or completes yin. They are always together. Without one, the other does not exist. The feminine does not exist without the masculine and vice versa. The receptive primal power of yin is the perfect complement, not the opposite, of the creative power of yang. The receptive does not combat or conflict with the creative but makes it complete.

In addition, as we see from the symbol, within the yin is the yang and within the yang is yin. Within anything is the possibility, potential, or seed of its complement. Within day is the potential of night. The yin and yang are also continually moving and changing, mutually integrating and at the same time maintaining their continuous balance and harmony. One should also keep in mind that yin and yang are relative concepts. See Figure 2.10. Yellow is yin when compared to the more yang energy of red but is yang when compared to the more yin energy of purple.

Set forth in Table 2.1 are a few examples of the complementary nature of yin and yang that may be helpful.

TABLE 2.1 *Yin and Yang Aspects*

Yin	Yang
Energy that is receptive, yielding, and passive	Energy that is assertive, creative, and initiating
Feminine	Masculine
Unconscious	Conscious
Right brain	Left brain
Intuition	Logic
Night	Day

TABLE 2.1 *Yin and Yang Aspects*

Yin	Yang
Dark	Light
Earth	Sky
Cold	Hot
Stillness	Motion
Inward	Outward
Contracting	Expanding
Smaller	Larger
Denser	Thinner
Even numbers	Odd numbers
Houses	People
Interior	Exterior
Open areas	Built-up areas
Cool colors	Warm colors
Intrusions	Protrusions
Round	Sharp
Curved	Straight
Liquids	Solids
Empty	Full
Soft	Hard
Areas of inactivity: garages, empty dwellings, residences left vacant for long periods of time, schools, offices, toilets, and closets	Areas of activity: dwellings with frequent activity

You will note above that the feminine and cool colors are yin and that the masculine and warm colors are yang. This reflects the fact that women are apt to be more drawn to the cooler colors and men to the warmer colors. We can frequently determine the sex of designers of a space by looking at the color choices. It is important for designers to put aside their own personal predilections and consider what colors will enhance the space in light of the people who are actually living or working

FIGURE 2.11 *Yin and Yang Materials*

Be aware of the Energy associated
with the materials you specify.

Remember that yin-yang relationships are
entirely relative depending upon Color,
Pattern, and Texture.

Blue matte finished ceramic tiles can appear more
yin than high gloss red painted gypsum board walls.

Polished Cherry flooring can
appear more yang than green
integrally colored concrete . . .

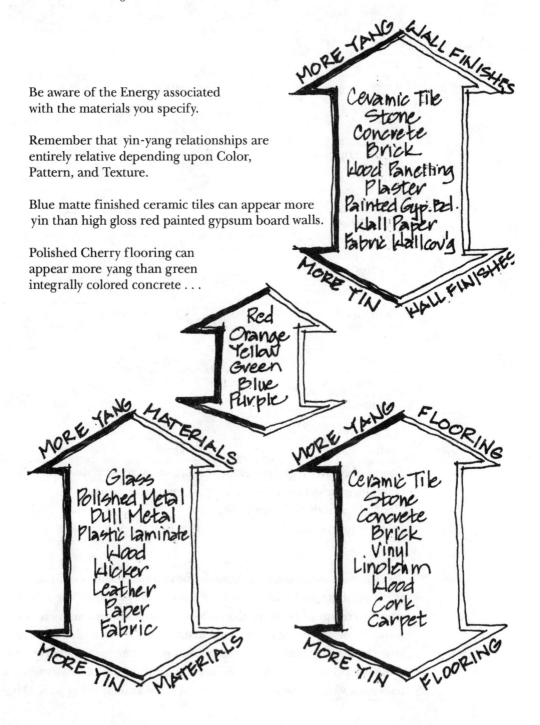

there. See Figure 2.11. In a residence, the color energies are frequently out of balance because one person has made all, or most, of the design and color choices and not taken into consideration the needs of the other individual.

Cases of Extreme *Yin and Yang*

Extreme imbalances of yin and yang can adversely affect one's feelings and behavior. Two of the most important uses of balance in the design world are the balance of colors, which I discuss in detail in Chapter 3, and the balance between Unity and Complexity. When a space is so plain that it appears as a single visual image, such as a truly monochromatic space, the psyche will crave some variety and will begin to create those images in an artificial way on its own. This could include seeing patterns in the chair fabric or the carpet that do not really exist. Needless to say, when people physiologically create something that is not there, their stress level is increased and their health can be affected. On the other hand, if the space is filled with an extreme variety of colors, patterns, and shapes, possibly with several sounds added to the cacophony of visual and aural sensations, one can instantly feel the need to flee from this extreme complexity.

Balanced Entry Doors

The right side of a house, as you are facing it, is the male side, and the left side is the female side. If the front door of an apartment building is in the center of the building, there is apt to be a roughly equal number of men and women in the building. If the main entrance is to the right side as one faces the building, the left side of the building will be dominant, and there may be more women in the building than men. Similarly, if the doorway is to the left side of the structure, the male side of the building will be more dominant, and men may outnumber women in the building.

In a private home, the location of the door may reflect the sex of the person who is the more dominant in the household. One may well ask, "Which comes first, the chicken or the egg? Did the dominant female choose a house in which the female side of the house was stronger, or did she become more dominant as a result of living in the space?" We have almost always found in our practice that when a couple's relationship is out of balance, the imbalance is reflected in the image of the front of their home.

As you read the last two paragraphs, you may have raised an eyebrow as to the accuracy of that concept or thought it was merely some strange Chinese idea. If you think about it in other contexts, however, you may begin to make Western connections. Remember the last wedding you attended. As you looked at the couple who were being married, what were their positions and that of their guests?

C. THE COMMANDING POSITION

The placement of furniture can enhance our being in control of our spaces and our life. Have you ever seen a CEO who sat with his or her back to the door? The CEO wants to make it clear to everyone entering the office who is in control of the space and, by extension, the company. Everyone I know who has ever gotten divorced has had a major Feng Shui problem in the bedroom, and it is inevitably the placement of the bed. We will explain later! Because we want to empower everyone to realize their maximum potential, we should design spaces so that clients can arrange the furniture in their home and office to accomplish that goal.

The Commanding Position is the place in the room with the greatest control over the space. The concept is the same whether we are talking about a bed, a desk, or any other seat or position in a room. A person should have a view of the door and of as much of the room as possible within sightlines that encompass 90 degrees based on the straight-ahead view (i.e., 45 degrees to either side of the nose). Repeatedly turning one's head to see the door or others in the room is uncomfortable and can cause physical stress that leads to psychological stress or vice versa. In our practice, the primary concern is the position of the bed or desk in relationship to the entrance to the space, not the compass direction. Do not worry about whether you are facing north, east, or any other direction. You want the person to be in control of the door and the room.

Figures 2.12 and 2.13 show possible bed and desk placements numbered around the room. Let's talk about the problems or virtues of each placement.

FIGURE 2.12 *Commanding Position–Beds*

FIGURE 2.13 *Commanding Position–Desks*

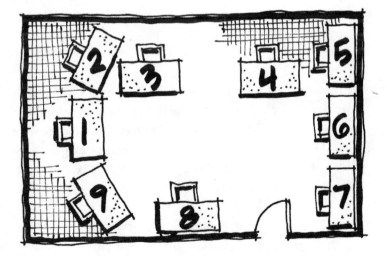

Bed and Desk Positions 1, 2, and 3. These three positions are the strongest, because the door and most of the room is within a 90-degree angle of view. In a rectangular room like that shown, positions 1 and 2 have slightly more control and, everything else being equal, would be the best choices. It is preferable to have the support of a wall at one's back at a desk or above your head in a bed. If windows are placed in the middle of a wall, position 2 is often the best position. Because most people are unaccustomed to this position, it may initially seem strange. However, people often grow to like the angled placement in the corner. When a bed is placed in the corner, we advise placing a tree, lamp, or table with a lamp on it in the corner to fill the dead space behind the bed. The other issue that arises with a bed at this angle is the placement of bedside tables that are large enough for table lamps and do not interfere with getting in and out of bed. We have designed triangular bedside tables to eliminate this problem.

Bed and Desk Position 4. This position might appear to have the most control over the door, but it is not a good placement. The traditional Chinese explanation is that this is the "coffin" position, because a coffin is carried straight out the door. In fact, this is not a good position because it is confrontational. Any person or other energy that enters the room and approaches the desk or bed comes directly toward the occupant in a straight line. As discussed earlier, a straight line is not a natural movement and becomes uncomfortable fairly quickly. In addition, position 4 does not have most of the room within the angle of view and is, therefore, not in control of what is happening in the rest of the space.

Desk Positions 5, 6, and 7. These three positions have a common problem in that they are all behind the door and face into the wall. This position offers no comfortable view of the door. In addition, facing a wall is more blocking than sitting with open space in front of you. As a result, these placements may restrict a person's ability to think openly and creatively. If this location is the only possibility, the traditional solution is to place a mirror on the wall or on the desk. Although this tactic may open up the space in front of the person at the desk, it will probably not give them a view of the door and may add to a sense of chaos in the person's line of sight with the reflected view in the mirror.

Desk Positions 5 and 7. These desks have the additional problem of having one side against a wall. The concept here is that half of the person's mental abilities may not function as well as possible because of the physical block. If the blocking wall is on the person's left side, right brain activity may be hindered; and if the wall blocks the individual's right side, the person's left brain activity may not function to its maximum ability. (We discussed these right brain/left brain concepts in Chapter 1.)

Bed Position 5. Because bed position 5 is behind the door and against a wall, it has several problems. Being hidden from the entrance to the room by the door swing may raise a feeling of insecurity, because visitors will physically be in the room before the occupant can see them. In addition, the blocking wall can inhibit both the mental and physical development of the individual, as described in the preceding paragraph. Several of our clients were rather surprised when a doctor's visit after our Feng Shui consultation confirmed that the side of their children that was against the wall when they were sleeping was in fact not as physically developed as the side of the body that was exposed to the open part of the room. The best placement is out in the room with open space and equal energy on both sides of the bed. The traditional Feng Shui recommendation is to mirror the wall beside the bed to create the illusion of openness if there is no other place for the bed.

Bed Position 6. This bed position is vulnerable because it is both close to the door and behind it. Although this position has control over much of the room, it does not have command over the entrance to the space.

Bed Position 7. This is the bed placement that I have encountered where people have later divorced. Does that mean that a couple with their bed in this position will necessarily have marital discord? Of course not. The point is that in this placement, neither person has a natural view of the door. They are, therefore, subconsciously anxious and not able to sleep as deeply as they would if they were in a Commanding Position. Not sleeping creates tension. Who better to take this out on than one's partner? This unnecessary stress may be the straw that breaks up the relationship. The professional should avoid designing a plan that runs this risk for the occupants. If there is absolutely no other place in the room for the bed, a mirror can help alleviate the problem. Because the goal is to have a view of the door and a feeling of control over any person or energy entering the room, the mirror should be placed in a position that gives the occupants a clear view of the door without having to turn their heads. In a bedroom, the tendency is to center the mirror opposite the foot of the bed. This position rarely gives a view of the door because of the angle of viewing and is frequently impossible because of windows opposite the bed. In most instances, the best solution for a bed in Position 7 is to use a standing mirror that can easily be positioned at exactly the right angle to give the occupants a view of, and a feeling of control over, the doorway.

Desk Positions 8 and 9. Desk position 8 is similar to desk position 6 in that it is not in control of the space and is blocking the person's thought processes by facing the wall. Although desk position 9 has a view of the room, it is more hidden from view as one enters the space than positions 1, 2, and 3. Being hidden conveys a subconscious desire not to be noticed, which in most cases would not be a good idea in an office environment.

A desk that faces out a window is a common situation. This placement is clearly not in a Commanding Position. Why is the person at the desk? To work. The distractions outside the window will pull the person's attention away from the tasks at hand. A person can always take a conscious break from work to look at the scenery.

When we give a lecture to a business client, we also discuss the Commanding Position in a conference room and explain that once you are aware of the psychological nature of the various positions in the room, you can place people around the table to empower the client, potential client, or yourself, depending upon your goal for the particular meeting. Of course, window walls or glass conference room walls will also be a part of the psychological interplay in the room. Similarly, in a living room situation, you might want to make a guest feel empowered rather than taking the Commanding Position for yourself.

One of my favorite examples of successfully using the Commanding Position occurred when we were working in a college fraternity room. Because of the small room, we decided to build a loft over two thirds of the high-ceilinged space. In most student lofts, the bed is placed on the upper level. In this case, however, the student was set on achieving extremely high academic goals and graduating with highest honors. To further this goal, we placed the desk on the upper level. To ensure a sense of security when he was in the bed with his desk above him, we built the loft with such sturdy supports that it would have held the second story of a house. With his chair on the higher level and facing the door, the student was sitting above anyone who entered the room. Talk about being king of his domain! Achieving all of his extremely high goals for the year, he said, "I have never felt so much in control of everything in my life as I did when I was sitting at my desk."

D. THE *BAGUA*

The *Bagua*, one of the principal tools of a Feng Shui analysis, is a template that can be used to lay out a space in a way that will maximize the potential of each aspect of our individual life, our family, and our business. Analyzing and utilizing the *Bagua* in your designs may require a leap of faith in the beginning, but as you incorporate the ancient principles in your designs, you will begin to see the positive effects that have been proven over thousands of years of use.

The *Bagua* is an octagon, shown in Figure 2.14, with each of the eight sections and the center representing particular aspects of life and of the flow of events. Although the historical derivation and development of the *Bagua* is fascinating, suffice it to say here that the empirical study of man and his environment has led to the association of specific *guas*, or sections of the *Bagua*, with specific areas of our life. Despite the fact that the teacher in me shudders at oversimplifying a highly multilayered concept, we will not explore in detail the extreme complexity of the *guas*. Suffice it to say that each has many different attributes, and only two of the most basic, color and element, have been set forth in Figure 2.14.

Several of the *guas* are frequently described in terms other than those used in Figure 2.14. These are generally as follows:

- *Path in Life.* Although this *gua* is often referred to as *Career*, many people do not have what is commonly considered a career, but everyone has a Path in Life, a Journey that defines us. In addition, the words Path in Life also refer to the entrance into a private space, which, of course, is also the way out of the space into the public world.
- *Self-Knowledge.* Self-Cultivation, Spirituality, Illumination, Self-Development, and Personal Growth are all part of what is included in the Self-Knowledge *gua*.
- *New Beginnings and Family.* This is the *gua* identified with both Biological and Nontraditional Family Units. We have found in our

practice that when a person or company is having trouble getting started on projects, or New Beginnings, this area often reflects the basic underlying issues. This area is sometimes called Health. Because all of the *guas* have various body parts attributed to them, to focus on this as the only Health area could be misleading.

- *Prosperity. Wealth* is probably considered the most common word for this *gua*. Because the impact of this *gua* cannot be limited to money but represents our Talents and Abundance in all parts of life, we feel that Prosperity is a more accurate definition.
- *Reputation.* Some Feng Shui books will describe this area as *Fame.* Because very few of us are, or aspire to be, famous, Reputation is a more appropriate word. Everyone has a reputation.

FIGURE 2.14 *The Bagua*

- *Primary Relationship.* Often referred to as *Marriage*, Primary Relationship refers to the most significant relationship in one's life, including a spouse, life partner, or other mate.
- *Completion and Children.* Although *Creativity* is sometimes placed in this *gua*, it is probably more appropriate in the center area of the *Bagua*, because all of the areas of our life come together in our creative process. We have found that when a client is able to start many projects, but has trouble finishing any of them, this Completion area often reveals the problem issues.
- *Helpful People.* Travel is also associated with this *gua*. However, one's relationships with people who are not family members, like clients, neighbors, and office personnel, tend to be a bigger issue for most people.
- *The Essence.* All of the aspects of one's life come together to make up the essence of a person's being in this central *gua*, also called *Health, the Tao, Tai Chi,* and the *Center.*

One's inclination at first is to look at the assignment of these characteristics to a particular area of a space and say, "Sure!" in an extremely skeptical voice. I was one of those people 20 years ago. As I began to teach college courses in Feng Shui, however, I needed to go deeper and truly understand what was behind the *guas'* attributes. And they did make sense—to my left brain as well as the right!

In an intensive class, I will spend at least one day on each of the *guas* and explore in depth its many characteristics and why they are associated with that particular *gua*. Remember: These concepts derive from 5,000 years of tradition. Although no extensive scientific data of the type that our current left brain culture often requires exists, a great deal of real-life experience supports these ideas. And they really do make sense. Let me give you an example.

The Path in Life area is the middle third of the front line of the space, as well as the area in which the door is located if the door is not centered. This area often reveals the underlying cause of a person's issues in this area of life. For example, if the door is in the Self-Knowledge area, a person's issues with respect to Career or Path in Life problems may well stem from not knowing what he or she really wants to do in life or the direction to take (i.e., self-knowledge). On the other hand, if the door is in the Helpful People area, career problems may arise from difficulties in relating to, or working with, coworkers.

As we will discuss in Chapter 3, Section B: Shapes, a space will feel more balanced if the entry door is in the center of the main entrance elevation. The entrance is truly one's path into the more private world of that space. Correspondingly, the doorway is also the pathway from the inner private arena out into the world itself. Design features, such as colors and pictures, that are in this area of a space will have a subconscious effect on how we feel about where we are going, whether it is our path into our personal life or our entrance into the outside world. If you head off to work in the morning and the last thing you see in your house is a picture beside the front door of you and your family on vacation, your mindset may not be conducive to spending ten hours in the office.

Applying the *Bagua* to Building Design and Analysis

To analyze a property, house, room, or any other physical area, even a desk, the Black Sect *Bagua* is applied to a space by placing the Path in Life position of the *Bagua* on the same line as the main entrance to the space, the "door wall." This is the case even if the entrance is not in the middle of that line. If there are several entrances to the space, always place the Path in Life on the door wall of the principal entrance to the space, even if it is not the one that is used the most. For example, the front door of a house determines the Path in Life area, even if it is never opened and everyone uses the side door. In a room, the door wall will be the wall on which the main door to the space is located. If there are two doors of equal size and importance into the room, the primary door will be the one that is the most direct route into the space from the front door of the building. In the case of a multistory, single-family home, continue to orient the *Bagua* on the second floor in the same direction as you did on the first floor, because throughout the house you will always feel the importance of the principal entrance. Although there are differing approaches to this concept, this orientation will usually be the most appropriate. The location of the door wall can be a very relevant factor in a Feng Shui analysis.

Because the *Bagua* is an octagon, trying to apply it to a square, rectangle, or other shape can be confusing. We find that the simplest technique is to think in terms of the tic-tac-toe board and divide the shape into nine equally sized shapes. In Figure 2.15, we have labeled each *gua* with the characteristic that we have most often experienced. We have used a rectangle to indicate how each section does not need to be a square. Please remember that this diagram is simplified.

If a property or building has an extremely complex shape that is difficult to analyze with the *Bagua*, you may skip that step and apply the *Bagua* to the house or to the rooms in the house. Do not skip over it lightly. Look at the shape intuitively to determine what you are really seeing. The traditional Chinese approach to an irregularly shaped space would be to identify an object or animal that is similar to the shape. If this image is a positive one, that would be considered good. If the metaphor of the revealed shape has negative connotations, such as an axe, steps would be taken to alter or change the subconscious impact of that shape.

As you apply the *Bagua* to a property, a building, and then to a specific room, you may find that you have to turn the plans around to place the Path in Life *gua* on the entrance wall to that particular space. Remember that the compass direction is not a factor in placing the *Bagua* on a space. See Figure 2.16.

FIGURE 2.15 *Bagua Grid*

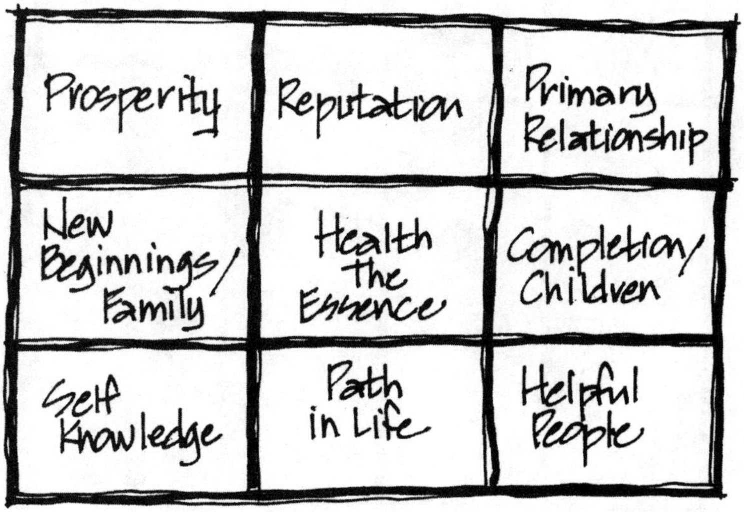

Prosperity	Reputation	Primary Relationship
New Beginnings/ Family	Health the Essence	Completion/ Children
Self Knowledge	Path in Life	Helpful People

FIGURE 2.16 *Applying the Bagua*

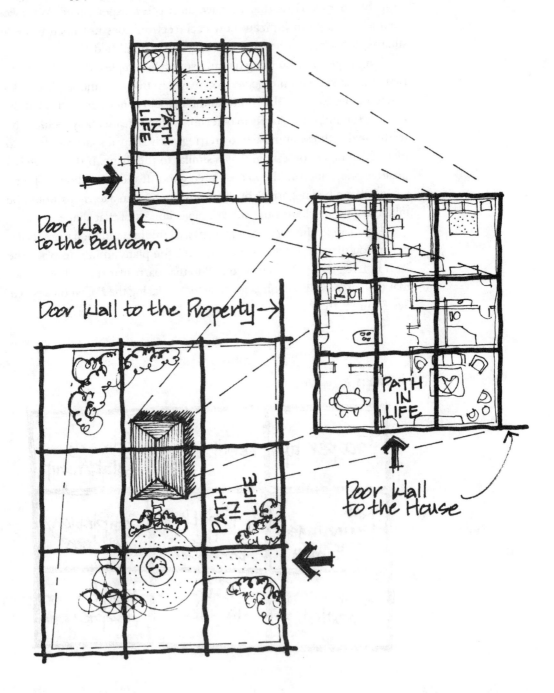

Applying the *Bagua* to Interior Design Details

In addition to using the *Bagua* to help create and analyze architectural floor plans and room layouts, it is also a tool for selecting and locating interior design elements. Selecting objects, materials, and colors, and placing them in a space based on their corresponding relationship with the *Bagua* and their ability to increase energy can be an effective way to enhance an environment. This technique also gives an individual an opportunity to improve a part of his or her life and have fun doing so. If individuals wish to focus on adding energy to a particular aspect of life, such as his or her Primary Relationship, that individual can choose an object that is made of a material and color that will act as a metaphor in that area of life and place it in the appropriate section of the *Bagua*, or the individual can select an appropriate object from Chapter 1, Table 1.3. Throughout this book you will find many examples of how to apply the *Bagua* to enhance an area in life through plan layout, color, material, lighting, sound, art, and landscaping.

E. THE FIVE ELEMENTS

The concept of the Five Elements of Water, Wood, Fire, Earth, and Metal shown in Figure 2.17 is a tool that enables a designer to create a more balanced and, therefore, more comfortable, pleasing, and productive environment.

Over 2,000 years ago, the Chinese Naturalist School developed the theory of the Five Elements. The elements of Water, Wood, Fire, Earth, and Metal were considered to be more than just inactive matter. Instead, they were viewed as dynamic and interrelated processes by which individuals and environments could be understood. The Five Elements represent the forces of nature as well as the characteristics of all aspects of the human being, both physically and psychologically. Each of the elements was given the characteristics of its natural state.

Some of the Characteristics of the Five Elements

Although round is the shape that is traditionally associated with Metal, the word *round* today often conveys a feeling of the earth. These

FIGURE 2.17 *The Five Elements*

THE FIVE ELEMENTS

WATER	WOOD	FIRE	EARTH	METAL
Fluid Black	Expansive Green	Intense Red	Firm Yellow	Heavy White
Wavy Reflective	Tall Vertical	Pointed Triangular	Low Horizontal	Spherical Hard
Downward	Upward	Upward	Stable	Inward
Wisdom to Poor Judgement	Easy Going to Stubborn	Swallowing Anger to Explosive	Sacrificing Self to Using Others	Talkative to Shy
Fountain Stream Pond Glass Chrystal Mirror	Wood Wicker Cane Paper Tree Plant	Candle Fireplace Light Lamp Stove Incense	Plaster Pottery Ceramics Brick Statuary Rocks	Steel Brass Silver Bronze Copper Gold

associations are all related to how the object, color, or image impacts the subconscious of the occupants of the space. For instance, even though we listed lamps as Fire, a round, ceramic lamp of earth tones with a cream-colored shade is more apt to convey an image of the Earth being warmed by the sun.

Because each person has at least some of the characteristics of each of the Five Elements in them, the role of the professional is to create a space that will either bring about a better balance or keep an existing balance that will continue to maximize the individual's potential.

The Five Elements are viewed in their relationships with one another in many different ways, two of which are depicted in Figure 2.18. Remember that these concepts are metaphors for the relationships and interactions of different types of human and spatial energies.

FIGURE 2.18 *The Five Elements–Producing and Overcoming Cycles*

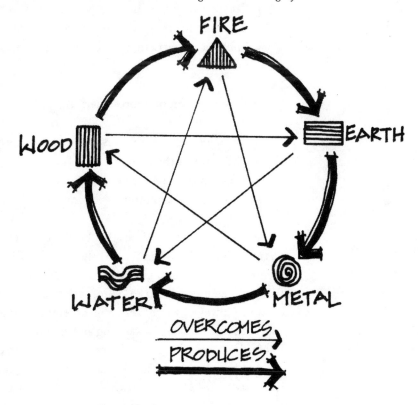

Producing Cycle.   *Water nourishes Wood*
Wood produces Fire
Fire leaves ash and creates Earth
Earth produces Metal
Metal produces condensate - Water

Overcoming Cycle.   *Water extinguishes Fire*
Fire melts Metal
Metal cuts Wood
Wood takes up the Earth
Earth absorbs Water

The Five Elements are used primarily to:

- Create a very specific energy in an environment
- Balance the energy of the people in a space
- Enhance a particular aspect of a person's life or a company's business

An Element can be represented by:

- An object or finish that is made of, or represents, the element
- The color of the element
- The shape of the element
- A picture of something that connotes that element

I will discuss throughout this book how these tools can be used effectively in specific situations in the design of buildings and spaces to create a feeling of being complete and in balance. That does not mean that each element needs to be represented in exactly 20 percent of the design. However, the absence of an element may certainly make the space feel incomplete. In arriving at a balance in a space, one also needs to consider the energies of the people in that space.

For instance, an office that is chrome, steel, and glass with gray and white walls and a blue-gray carpet is primarily a Metal environment with some subtle hints of water. It is apt to be a harsh environment that does not feel very welcoming, especially because many of us are being bombarded outside the office by a world filled with many hard, cold energies. By balancing this coldness with plants, color, and other forms of energy that represent the elements of Wood, Fire, and Earth, the space will undoubtedly be more comfortable and more conducive to its Primary Purpose.

F. THE PRIMARY PURPOSE

The most important question to ask about each environment is, "What is the Primary Purpose of this space?" The answer to this question then becomes the starting point for every decision. When preparing floor plans, selecting colors, or deciding any other aspect of the design process, we must always ask ourselves, "Does this choice enhance the Primary Purpose?"

When asked the Primary Purpose question, clients will often say, "Well, the purposes are . . . ." No, what is the *Primary* Purpose? Get the client to focus on the primary use of the space. Obviously, many areas have multiple uses. If we do not focus on the Primary Purpose, however, the environment is apt to become unfocused.

Here are some examples.

- *Bedroom.* A bedroom in an apartment or a child's bedroom often contains both a bed and a desk. In most cases, the Primary Purpose would be sleep rather than study. It *is* called a bedroom. With "good sleep" as our basic concern, we would first place the bed in the Commanding Position in the room to maximize the ability of the occupant to obtain the best rest possible, as well as to enhance the subconscious self-image of the individual. If several possible placements for the bed are of relatively equal strength, we can decide which of them would allow for the best positioning of the desk. Rarely, however, would we want to compromise the bed's location.

    Color choices for the room might vary greatly, depending upon the Primary Purpose of the bedroom. A desire to create a peaceful space for rest, as opposed to a more energetic environment for work, would undoubtedly lead to a different color selection. This color direction could also be influenced by the particular individual's needs, as we will discuss in Chapter 3, Section A: Colors.

- *Office.* In discussing the position of the desk in an office, clients will often say, "I want to place my desk so that I can look out the window." When asked what the Primary Purpose of the office is for them, they will inevitably begin talking about their work and their desire to be creative, productive, in control, and so on. When we elaborate on the reasons why the Commanding Position for the desk will undoubtedly enhance their professional career and point out they can always take a break from the stress of their work by turning around and looking at the view, they inevitably grin sheepishly and say, "Well, okay, I guess you're right. That does make sense."

During the information-gathering phase of the planning process, this Primary Purpose question should be asked at a number of different levels. The building itself has a purpose, and each individual room or area within the building will have its own purpose. You may want a multiuse condominium complex to convey a specific image as a whole, but then want the retail spaces, the residences, and the activities room to communicate very different feelings. Remember that the Primary Purpose is always related to the energy required or desired in a space. A small conference room in a hospital for meetings with doctors and their patient's families might have the same programming requirements as a conference room in an advertising agency. However, one space is meant for healing and comfort; whereas the other should promote an energetic exchange of creative ideas. Energy and function are equally important in designing a space based upon its Primary Purpose.

3

THE FENG SHUI APPROACH TO ARCHITECTURAL AND DESIGN ELEMENTS

This chapter will discuss Feng Shui concepts with respect to certain architectural and design elements. In many instances, your reaction will, and should, be, "Of course, that is just good design." You will be correct. The problem occurs when these basic principles of environmental psychology are overlooked or given short shrift for the sake of locating the electrical and data outlets. Spaces are designed for people, and our goal is to use these universal principles that have evolved over the past 5,000 years to enhance their life and productivity through the following design elements:

- *Colors.* The psychological effect of the use and balance of color
- *Shapes.* The ramification of various shapes, including "missing" areas
- *Materials.* The balancing of the elements through the use of materials
- *Lighting.* The use of lighting to change the energy in a space
- *Sound.* The many ways that sound can be used to affect the energy of a space

- *Signage.* The design and placement of signage to enhance the flow of energy and image of a business
- *Art and Decorative Objects.* The use of art and other decorative objects to guide the flow of energy and to balance a space
- *Plants and Landscaping.* The ways in which plants and landscaping can affect our behavior and attitudes
- *Water Features.* The placement of water features to enhance the environment

A. COLORS

Colors affect us both physiologically and psychologically and impact our psyche on the conscious, subconscious, and unconscious levels. This commonly accepted principle has been explored in great depth for centuries. Although you are familiar with many of the following color concepts, we feel it is important to mention them in a discussion of the psychological effects of color on people. For example, grays are said to be the color of choice of depressed people, and the low energy of a gray is apt unknowingly to pull down the energy of the occupants of a space.

The human being reacts first and foremost on a biological level to the different wavelengths of the different colors and their values and intensities. Our personal gathering of the color stimuli affects both the brain processes and the nervous system. In addition, it is felt that the human being reacts to colors on the level of Jung's collective unconscious. Our reaction to certain images is innate to our development as a species. On a third level, probably in descending impact, is our reaction to colors on a cultural basis. This bias can include everything from longstanding cultural traditions to the trend of the day.

Our sensation of color derives from a variety of factors. An object either absorbs or repels light rays, depending on the molecular nature of the matter on which the light falls. What we perceive is also affected by the juxtaposition of the perceived object with other hues and by their value or intensity. The qualities of color are often associated with the memory of other sensations; and sight therefore is often connected to our other senses.

Color studies resulting in different conclusions were probably conducted with different controls and groups. For instance, whether the individuals in the group were predominately men or women could clearly affect the outcome of a study.

We occasionally hear someone say, "Colors don't affect me." Nonsense. Although everyone is affected by color, individuals tend to have different needs for specific colors at various times to create a balance within themselves. When professionals are designing a space for an individual or family, they can take into consideration the needs of that client. Notice, I said "needs." Not wishes. When a client says, "I really want the room red," it is important to explain the effect that this color choice will have on the occupant and the activity that is planned for that room. The individual's needs can occasionally be accommodated in a business environment, but here one's approach generally has to focus on the business needs and the way the average person will react.

Sir Isaac Newton was the first to reveal the components of white light by placing a prism in the path of a beam of light. When Newton projected the rays that were refracted by the prism onto a screen, he was able to identify seven colors in the same order as the colors of a rainbow. These colors range from the shortest wavelength to the longest: violet, indigo, blue, green, yellow, orange, and red. They comprise the full visible spectrum, the first four being the cooler colors and the last three the warmer hues. One color blends continuously into the next, and each change in wavelength creates a separate and individual hue. Our language does not have a name for each color created by each change in wavelength.

Warm and Cool Hues

Hue is the term used to define the specific color, such as red, yellow, or blue. The warm yang colors are those in the red, orange, and yellow spectrum; and the cool yin colors are those in the green, blue, and purple range. Our eyes will tire in direct proportion to how colors excite the retina. Red will cause the greatest fatigue and purple the least. Red advances and pushes itself forward more than any of the other colors. Therefore, when a child is given a choice of colors, the infant reaches for the object that appears to be the closest, the red one. We then, perhaps erroneously, come to the conclusion that red is the first color that the child notices.

At the risk of being accused of a gross generalization, we believe that women tend to prefer the cool colors and men lean toward the warm hues. Think of the color choices that existed in the bed linen market prior to Ralph Lauren's introduction of warm-hued prints. They were predominately blues, greens, purples, and whites, undoubtedly because the buyers were primarily women and the market data supported that color direction. Each individual has the need for both the yin and the yang colors but in different proportions, with men more likely to be drawn to the yang colors and women to the yin colors.

The primary colors of pure red, yellow, and blue are not subtle colors. A color is called subtle when it is a mixed color, such as the tertiary and quaternary colors. These colors will appear to vary in different light and at different times of day because they are created from a mixture of pigments. These colors are usually more interesting because as the light changes, first one ingredient of the hue appears to come forward and then another becomes more visible.

Color "Temperature" Concepts

- Warm colors come forward.
- Cool colors recede.
- Cool colors tend to lower energy.
- Warm colors tend to excite energy.

Complementary Colors

It is critical to balance a color with its complement. This neutralizes, or balances, the color. Our brains need the complement and if it is not present, we will start to create it. In an all-green room, our eyes will begin to see red spots, fulfilling the physiological need for the complementary color. In Feng Shui, we recommend using three touches of the complement to create a circular motion for the eye. A single spot of red in a green room will cause us to fixate on the red. Two red objects will have our eyes going back and forth from one to the other as if we were watching a Ping-Pong match—not comfortable for very long. The introduction of three red items will lead us from one object to the next to the next and back to the first in a circular motion, creating the most comfortable condition for our eyes and therefore for our psyche.

Values or Tonal Value

The value, or tonal value, of a color is the lightness or darkness of the color. Adding white to the color creates a lighter value of the same hue. The word *tint* is also used to describe a light value of a color. Adding the complementary color to a hue or adding black or gray to the color will create a darker, or lower, tonal value of the hue. The word *shade* is often used to designate a dark value of a color.

Color Value Concepts
- Light colors recede.
- Dark colors come forward.
- Light colors are youthful and happy.
- Dark colors are mysterious, dignified, and mature.

In nature, we experience a general separation of the light, medium, and dark color values in the light value of the high sky (blue with white clouds), the midrange values in the objects at our eye level (buildings, forests, distant hills), and the dark value of the earth below our feet. See Figure 3.1. Of course, this assumes we are talking about daytime. Because we are more naturally awake during the day and asleep at night, we tend to feel more alert during the day. As a result, we tend to feel more comfortable and balanced when the color values that we use on our floors, walls, and ceilings reflect this natural daytime separation.

Our ceilings are usually the lightest value in our spaces, and our walls and furniture tend to be in the mid-range, but frequently the floors are treated with a lighter color value than the mid-range values. When this happens, people may not feel as grounded and may behave in a scattered or flighty manner. Having the darkest value beneath our feet helps create a more stable psychological environment. Where the floors are a light wood, a darker area rug under the primary seating area can create a more grounded feeling.

FIGURE 3.1 *Color Values*

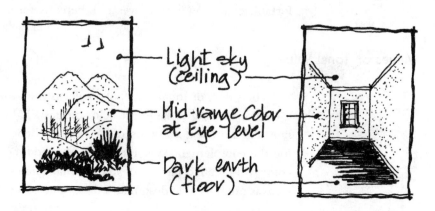

Having said this, once we are aware of the basic principle, we can always choose to "break the rule" if doing so enhances the Primary Purpose of the particular space. If not, stay with the norm. In some instances, we will want to paint a ceiling a dark, nonreflective value to make the unsightly pipes and ventilation conduits disappear. In a restaurant that focuses on dinner as its main source of revenue and needs to paint the ceiling a dark value to eliminate unsightly ceiling constructions, we can think of the values as reflecting the natural aspects of the night. Although the sky is dark, the walls and furniture will still be in the mid-range value, and the earth or floor beneath our feet will still be a dark color value.

Intensity or Chroma

The intensity of a color is increased when we see it with its complement. Complementary colors accentuate the intensity of each other more than do colors with less contrast. Green on red will appear more intense than green on blue, because red is the complement of green. Because there is blue in the green, the contrast is not as great as with the green on its complementary red.

The more intense a hue, the more arousing that color will be on the occupants of the space. Excitement and fatigue are produced by the use of intense, or strong chromatic, values of the primary and secondary hues and by patterns of strongly contrasting tonal values. Conversely, neutralizing tertiary and quaternary colors and patterns with mildly contrasting values will be more peaceful and restful on both our eyes and psyche. This is an important concept to keep in mind as we proceed to create environments that are conducive to lowering stress and maximizing the potential of the occupants.

Color Compositions

Each of the following classical color compositions will have a very different effect on a person.

Complementary. Many color theorists feel that this color scheme is one that scientifically and psychologically produces the best result, because it is the closest to nature and fulfills the chromatic equalization that is a natural demand of the eye. A more agreeable harmony is often attained if both of the complementary colors are slightly tinged with a third color that is the same in both cases. In a red and green scheme, tinge both colors with yellow. If the red is on the blue side, the green should also be on the blue side.

Analogous. Analogous colors are any 3 adjoining hues in a 12-color wheel or any 3 of 6 adjoining colors on a 24-color wheel. To add greater vitality, use a complementary accent. If the accent is intense or strong in chromatic value, though small in area, it will have an impact and will increase the perception of the hues of the dominant color scheme.

Neutral and One Color. A neutral, such as gray, white, or beige, alternates with another color for the dominant areas of a room. Because gray and white are very cool, it is best to use a warmer hue as the other color. Because of its very low energy, gray is usually not a good color to use in most spaces.

Monochromatic. The dominant areas are different tonal values of the same hue. This color scheme will often result in a space that may look dramatic, but is out of balance in color and in the representation of the Five Elements and will usually not be comfortable for most people.

Monotone. A single neutral color in the same tonal and chromatic value is used throughout the design. This scheme is best used as a background for the display of objects. In a retail space, for example, the objects for sale should be the focus of attention.

The Placement of Color

Colors are affected by the hue, intensity, and value of adjoining colors, sometimes in dramatic ways. Strong contrasts in tonal values will cause the lighter areas to appear lighter and the darker areas to appear darker than they would if the tonal values were closer. Colors that are adjacent to one another on the color wheel seem stronger when seen together. A russet, the tertiary color from red and orange, looks more orange when compared to red and more red when next to orange.

Where color is placed in the room will also impact an individual. Because our eyes are about four feet off the ground when we are sitting and six feet from the floor when we are standing, we "live" between four and six feet off the floor. See Figure 3.2. We are most comfortable seeking the color that we need in that range. If your design intent is to use green as the principal color to create a specific impact, then you should place the green on the walls in that primary four- to six-foot eye range. If the only green is on the floor or on a chair seat, the psyche will have to search for it and will be required to work at finding what it needs.

FIGURE 3.2 *Color Zone*

Our goal is to make the process as easy as possible for the client. The floor and the chair can be used to balance the primary design color with the complementary color or to complete the color spectrum.

The larger areas of a room should usually be covered in the most neutral colors of the scheme. As the areas to be covered with color reduce in size, the intensity of the color may be increased proportionately. In other words, a little bit of intense color goes a long way.

In general, a room is divided into dominant areas (walls, floors, ceilings), medium areas (draperies, large pieces of furniture, and fabric), and small areas (small pieces of furniture, chair seats, pillows, and accents of piping, welting, fringes, lamp bases, vases, plants, and flowers. The color scheme in a room is principally formed by the colors in the dominant and medium areas with the colors of the small areas providing the balance.

The Effect of Lighting on Color

Light is absolutely necessary for color. See Figure 3.3. Natural daylight is the most balanced color, consisting of the full spectrum. When the quality of the light changes, because of a variation in the intensity, direction, or color of the light itself, the color of the perceived object will change. For instance, a green leaf will appear black in a dark room.

Practical Painting Issues

Before painting an entire room, we always suggest painting several three-foot square areas on walls in different parts of the room that are exposed to natural light as well as artificial light. View them at varying times of day. Even though I have studied color extensively, I once erroneously assumed that I had made a superb color choice. When I returned home after the painters had completed the work, I found that I was living in a lemon-lime green forest. The painters were back at work after I had chosen, and tried a sample of, another color!

We generally recommend using an eggshell finish for the walls and a semigloss for the woodwork. An eggshell has more sheen than a matte finish and marks, such as fingerprints, are more easily cleaned. If darker tones are being used on a wall, a semigloss might be used to give the walls a greater luminosity, because a semigloss reflects more light. Keep the reflectivity in mind, however, and remember that as paint becomes glossier, it will reveal more of the blemishes in the surface of the wall. If your walls are not in great condition, stick to lighter values of color and use an eggshell finish.

The decision as to whether the woodwork in a room should be a different color than the walls depends to a great degree on the nature of the woodwork. Keep in mind that the more contrasting the colors, the more evident an object becomes. If the doors and woodwork are visually outstanding architectural elements, you may choose to highlight them with different colors. Be aware, however, that the contrasting trim will attract attention and may make the room appear cluttered with vertical and horizontal woodwork lines.

FIGURE 3.3 *The Effect of Lighting on Color*

Wall Color	Effect of Incandescent Lighting	Effect of Cool Fluorescent Lighting
Red walls will appear...	red orange	purplish
Blue walls will appear...	greenish	blue grey
Yellow walls will appear..	more intense	greenish
Green walls will appear...	yellow green	bluish green
White walls will appear...	yellowish	bluish

Feng Shui Color Theories

Several overlaying approaches can be used to select colors for a particular environment. We usually find that one approach will be the most appropriate for a particular project. It is very important not to be tied to one color system over another but to be aware of the many factors at play in the specific situation and to use the color approach that will enhance the Primary Purpose to the greatest degree.

The *Bagua* Color Theory. Remember that each section of the *Bagua* has a color attribute. When we discuss these colors, we are not limiting ourselves to a pure color but are referring to a hue in the general area that conveys the image of the desired intention. For instance, in a particular situation where we are trying to enhance the Reputation or Image of a client, a pure red might convey the wrong image, whereas a red mixed with a little blue, more like a burgundy, could communicate a Reputation (red) that was filled with Self-Knowledge (blue), precisely the image that your client wants the world to have of its business. This approach can be used in the client's environment and on its business cards and other corporate materials to communicate a consistent and powerful image.

FIGURE 3.4 Bagua *Colors*

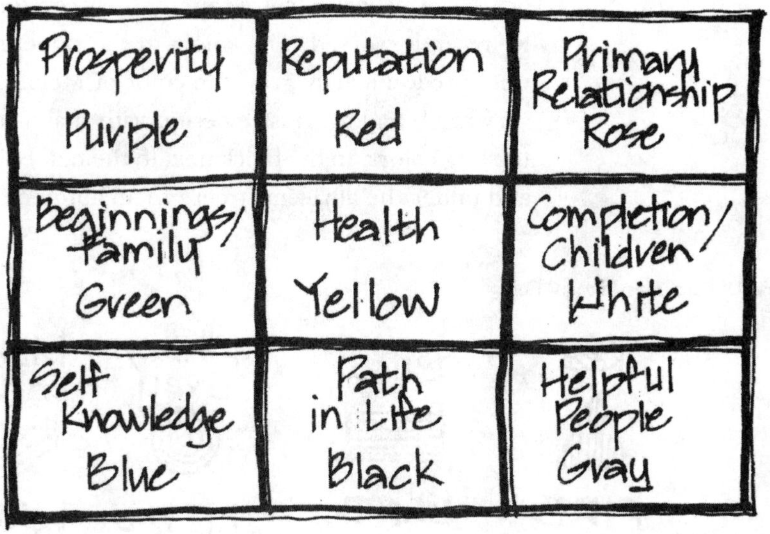

Prosperity Purple	Reputation Red	Primary Relationship Rose
Beginnings/ Family Green	Health Yellow	Completion/ Children/ White
Self Knowledge Blue	Path in Life Black	Helpful People Gray

These *Bagua* colors can be used in a general sense, as in the above example, or as the starting place in the selection of a color for a specific space. See Figure 3.4. If you have used the *Bagua* for the layout of a home and have located the master bedroom in the Primary Relationship area, using the *Bagua* color for this area would lead us in the direction of a warm, passionate color. Do not be rigid about the process. You can suggest this direction to your clients and see how they react. It may be that they want to use green for a very specific reason, such as the need for a more restful night's sleep. You can then explore with them the psychological consequences of their preference, always balancing the choice with the complementary color and considering the overall balance of the Five Elements in that particular person's space and life.

The Five Elements Color Theory.   The colors of the Five Elements shown in Figure 3.5 are used to balance the elements in an environment. When we discuss these colors, we are not limiting ourselves to a pure red, yellow, or green but are referring to a hue in one of those color ranges that conveys the image of the particular element. For instance, if we wanted to increase the Fire element in a space, we would choose a color that reads more like Fire than any other element. Because we deal with the effect that the color has on the subconscious, we can easily accomplish our goal in a subtle way.

An example of the way in which the colors of the Five Elements can be used effectively involved a multistory condominium project on which we recently worked. The colors in the surrounding warehouse district were predominately gray, the color of Metal. A nearby building had a very harsh and aggressive design with sharp angles and extremely contrasting colors. In the block next to the new building was a train station, and under the adjacent street ran an automobile tunnel. In addition, a

FIGURE 3.5 *Five Element Colors*

nearby naval air station completed the picture of an excess of harsh Metal elements represented by trains, planes, and automobiles.

Given this neighborhood environment, our recommendation was to use a red surface on the exterior of the building, with green trim and awnings, and gold design elements on the balconies. This color scheme used the Five Elements to balance the excessive Metal energy in the environment by adding the Fire element. The metaphor is that Fire melts the Metal. See Figure 2.18 in Chapter 2, Section E. A red exterior, the color associated with Fire, will help balance the overwhelming Metallic feeling of the neighborhood. By using a very dark green accent on the railings, window frames, awnings, and the like, the metaphor continues as the green of the Wood element further fuels the Fire. The fact that red and green are also complementary colors is not a mere coincidence and "completes" the composition. The gold accent panels on the balconies also relate to the Five Elements in that the Wood (green) produces the Fire (red), which produces the Earth/Ash (yellow).

By using mixed colors and colors of a lower chromatic value or intensity rather than the pure hues of these colors, the building will also convey the image of elegance and avoid suggesting "Christmas!" Red as the exterior color will also raise the energy level of the property and make it stand out as a strong building among its more somber gray neighbors.

Full Spectrum Colors in Building Interiors and Exteriors. The full color spectrum of red, orange, yellow, green, blue, and purple represents the components of light. Using all the colors of the spectrum in a space will make the environment feel more like nature and therefore more complete and fulfilling. The colors do not need to be used in equal amounts. Once the principal color has been selected for the space and the corresponding other colors have been chosen to fill in the secondary features, the balance of colors comprising the full color spectrum can be added in the accessories.

The Primary Purpose Color Effects on Behavior. The Primary Purpose of a space is probably the most important determinant in the choice of the basic design color for that particular environment. In addition to using the *Bagua* and the Five Elements as directions for the selection of colors, you can also choose colors based upon their psychological effects. Set forth below are some of the characteristics and influences that certain colors may have on an individual.

Color Theory Applications to Private Spaces

Once you and the client have decided on a color direction based on the Primary Purpose of the space and using the *Bagua*, the Five Elements, and colors' psychological effects as guidelines, you could use a technique that we have found to be very effective when the space is the client's home or private office. For instance, if the color green is chosen, then we will select a large number of acceptable green color chips based on our Feng Shui knowledge of the client and the space. We might take 27 color chips ranging from pure green to a more yellow green. We will then randomly pick three cards at a time and ask the client to select their favorite based on nothing but their instinctive choice. If they hesitate more than three seconds, the cards disappear and three more cards appear. We then work our way through all of the cards until the client has narrowed the selection down to one or two. This is almost always the best color for the space.

Although we provide a great deal of guidance in the process, the client chooses the final color. They subconsciously may know which color will accomplish what they need in that space. By eliminating a conscious thought process, the client is more apt to pick the best color for their needs. The short response time encourages a more intuitive selection. We are taking them out of left brain logic and into right brain imagery, because that is what the colors in the space impact. Remember that testing a sample of the color on the wall is still necessary.

A dominant color in the room is essential. Repeat the color of the walls in small areas of the room, such as in fabrics or accessories, to complete the color composition.

To create more balance in a space, it is often advisable to use warmer colors in rooms of a northerly exposure and cooler colors in rooms that have a great deal of sunlight. A room that is dark from lack of natural light tends to neutralize all colors, thus pulling them together and making them appear harmonious. As a consequence, in a dark room slightly more intense colors should be used than in a sunlit room.

The Psychological Effects of Color

Red	Brings a jolt of energy to an area of life that may need a boost
	Relates to speech
	Stimulates the appetite
	Is the color of power and strength
Orange	May cause aggression or agitation
	Is a difficult color for most spaces, except as an accent
	May make children cry more
Yellow	Represents the energy of the sun
	Is the color of joy, happiness, tolerance, acceptance, and honesty
Gold	Provides a sense of being grounded
	Improves communication
	Is associated with prosperity
Green	Enhances new beginnings, growth, and abundance
	Is reminiscent of foliage
	Calms emotions and promotes rest
	Is the color of hope and vitality
	Stimulates career productivity and success
Blue	Is calming, soothing, and tranquil
	Lengthens time
	Is historically a color of royalty
	Symbolizes understanding
Purple	Is associated with wealth and royalty
Brown	Creates a feeling of being grounded and stable
	Is less intimidating than blue
White	Represents purity and death
Black	Is the color of knowledge, seriousness, and justice
Gray	Pulls down our energy
	Should be avoided in almost all cases

Ways to **C**reate **C**olor Interest

- Contrast of hues
- Contrast of tonal values
- Contrast of intensity
- Contrast of color areas
- Contrast of surface treatment—pattern versus plain
- Contrast of materials
- Distribution of color

Selecting a Default Color

White is currently the color that is generally selected when someone cannot decide what color to use. A warm white or pale cream with a slight hint of yellow is probably the best default color. Yellow is in the middle of the visual color frequencies, is the least energetic of the warm colors, and will add some yang energy to a space that is apt to be out of balance in the yin direction. It is also reminiscent of the sun, an energy that most people find healing and pleasant. In addition, yellow is a color that men and women alike are apt to find comfortable. Obviously, in certain very hot climates, the coolness of the white may be more appropriate to balance the overall energies of the environment.

B. SHAPES

The Feng Shui concept that a regular shape (rectangle, square, or round) has the most comfortable impact on an individual is based in mathematics and philosophy and is found in many cultures. From Pythagoras in the sixth century B.C. to the present, philosophers and scientists alike have considered mathematics to be of utmost importance in every aspect of our lives. Numbers have long been used as the basis for determining shapes and the origin of geometry. Leonardo Fibonacci, a 13th-century Italian mathematician, set forth what has become known as the Fibonacci Sequence. The Fibonacci Sequence is an unending sequence of numbers in which the first two numbers are 0 and 1 and each succeeding number is the sum of the two immediately preceding numbers: 0, 1, 1, 2, 3, 5, 8, 13, 21, 34, 55, 89, and so on. The geometric ratio of any two successive numbers of the sequence, such as 8 to 13 or 13 to 21, is frequently found in nature, most notably in the curve of the nautilus shell, the leaf pattern of many plants, and the human body.

Leonardo da Vinci used the mathematical ratio of the Fibonacci Sequence in his work. Leonardo is considered the creator of the concept of the Golden Rectangle, the proportions of which approximate the Fibonacci Sequence as the numbers in the Sequence get higher. Leonardo's Golden Ratio is 1 to 1.618. As shown in Figure 3.6, the ratio of A, the smaller part, to B, the larger part, is the same as the ratio of B, the larger part, to the sum of A and B.

As Leonardo demonstrated, the Golden Rectangle reflects the proportions that are most often found in nature, from a flower to the proportions of the human figure. By using the shape of the Golden Rectangle in our buildings and spaces within a building, we are approximating nature and creating spaces with which we will feel more comfortable. Most of the great monuments throughout the ages and around the world, such as the Parthenon, have been built, consciously or subconsciously, using the Golden Rectangle. See Figure 3.6. We recommend using these properties for designing "complete" and comfortable spaces.

FIGURE 3.6 *The Golden Rectangle*

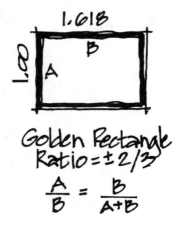

Regular Shapes

During your schematic design phase, begin by planning a building or room in the regular shape of the Golden Rectangle. As a room becomes longer and thinner, it will begin to feel squeezed and less comfortable. As the space moves towards the shape of a square, it will begin to feel static. When we talk about rectangular spaces throughout this book, we will assume that you begin designs with the proportions of the Golden Rectangle in mind. See Figures 3.7A and 3.7B.

When we approach a rectangular building and the entrance is on the long side of the rectangle, the building appears grander. Because we are often unable to see the depth of the building, our mind visualizes a greater depth than may actually exist. When the entrance is on the shorter side of the building, the approach to the building will not appear to be as imposing. In the interior of a building, the opposite is generally the case. Because we cannot anticipate the width of an interior room as we approach it, a room that extends away from us in the longer direction will appear to be grander.

FIGURE 3.7A *Shape Structure*

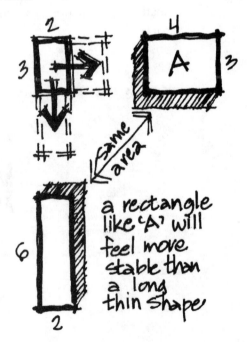

FIGURE 3.7B *Elevation Study*

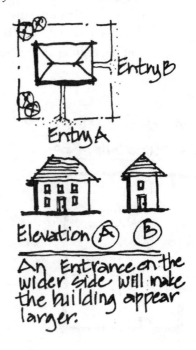

Elevation Ⓐ Ⓑ

An Entrance on the wider side will make the building appear larger.

Irregular Shapes, Missing Areas, and Projections

The shape of a property, house, or room may be symbolic at a deep psychological level. Our goal is to strive for regular geometric shapes that feel complete. If a space is irregular, there are several ways to analyze the shape and its impact on the occupants. In ascertaining the shape of a structure, do not include a porch or deck that is not enclosed and part of the indoor living space, unless it is under a common roof with the rest of the building. See Figure 3.8.

Irregular Shapes. There are several ways to approach an irregular shape. First, see if you can easily envision the shape as a particular "object." The imagined shape may be sending your subconscious a subliminal message. For instance, it is thought that if you are spending a great deal of time in the blade portion of a house shaped like an ax, it will adversely affect your relationships. The message of the shape may have some effect on a person, even if the shape is not clearly visible, because one may be subconsciously aware of the image that the space creates.

Your goal is to avoid creating a disturbing shape or to find ways to alleviate an existing negative situation.

A second approach is to look at what is "missing" or "projecting" from the regular shape. See Figure 3.8.

FIGURE 3.8 *Irregular Shapes*

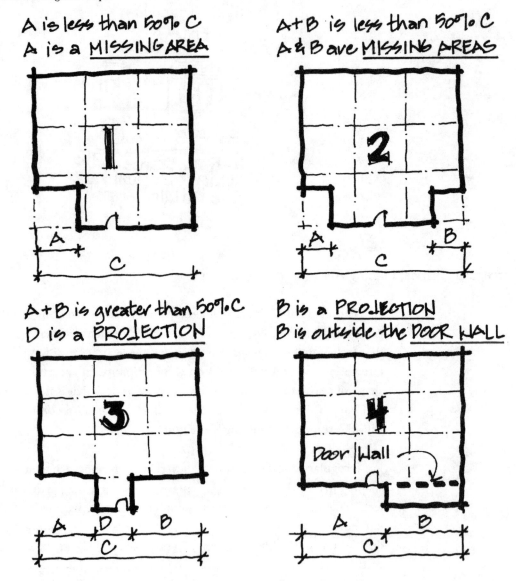

Plan 1: In looking at a shape to determine the nature of the irregularity, the traditional guideline is that if the length of A is less than half of C, then the area within A is "missing" as in Plan 1.

Plan 2: Because the width of A plus B is less than half of C, the areas within A and B are both missing.

Plan 3: Because the width of A plus B is more than half of C, the area within D is a "projection." The one caveat that we would make to this general guideline is, "Do not get hung up on precise measurements, but react to what you are seeing and feeling."

Plan 4: It might well be that if we were standing in front of a building like the one in Plan 4, it would feel as if area A were missing, despite the fact that the yardstick would tell you that area B is projecting. The more complex the shape becomes, the more intuitive the process of determining whether the structure is missing an area that could adversely affect the lives of the occupants.

Missing Areas. Once you have determined that the space has a missing area, apply the *Bagua* to the property, building, or room to ascertain what *gua* is missing or affected. A missing area in a particular *gua* of a home or office may reflect a need or issue in the life or health of one of the inhabitants in the area related to that particular *gua*. Note which element is represented by the affected area. In applying the *Bagua* to Plan 1 of Figure 3.8, for example, missing section A is in the Self-Knowledge area, which may either reflect an existing condition or inhibit the natural development of that area of the lives of the occupants.

Projections. When a projection exists in a property, building, or room, this may well reflect a positive enhancement in that particular area of the occupants' lives. In applying the *Bagua* to the space in Plan 3 of Figure 3.8, the extension is in the *gua* that relates to one's Path in Life. In this case, the shape may reflect an enhancement or success in that aspect of the occupants' lives.

The Door Wall

In Plan 4 of Figure 3.8, you will note that area B is behind anyone who is entering the building, or "outside" the door wall, the plane on which the main entrance is located, indicted by the dashes on the figure.

In this situation, it is commonly felt that the activities intended to occur in space B may end up occurring outside of the home or office. If this were a dining room, the occupants might well eat out more than they eat at home. A home office in this area might indicate that the person travels a great deal in connection with work, and a master bedroom in this location could reflect the fact that one of the residents engages in activities outside the home that are intended to occur within the confines of the family residence. In an office context, the people who occupy desks in area B may be more inclined to travel, engage in activities outside the office, or even leave the company more quickly than the norm. See Chapter 7, Sections B and C, and Figure 7.6 for information about applying the door-wall analysis to Office Spaces.

Filling in Missing Areas

In the event that an existing building is missing a portion, you will want to add energy to this area to make it feel complete. The number of ways this can be accomplished is limited only by your imagination and creativity. For instance, you might add a light pole at the corner of what would be the complete shape with the light directed upward at the structure. If a *gua* is missing from the land itself, add energy to the area adjacent to the boundary. A light pole with a spotlight pointing toward the house or a tall flagpole will give you a feeling of completion and fullness in this area. If the missing area were in the Prosperity area, the element of which is Wood, planting trees or painting a wooden fence green to symbolize the strength of Wood will strengthen the feeling of power in the Prosperity *gua*. See Figure 3.9. Filling in any missing area will involve using a combination of the *Bagua* and the Five Elements as they relate to that portion of the property.

When using a flagpole to compensate for a missing area, it is often recommended that the height of the flagpole be equal to the distance from (a) the corner of the existing structure to (b) the point that would be the corner of the building if it were a complete shape. This creates a sense of lifting up the missing corner by the height of that distance, the height of the flagpole.

FIGURE 3.9 *Filling in the Missing Area*

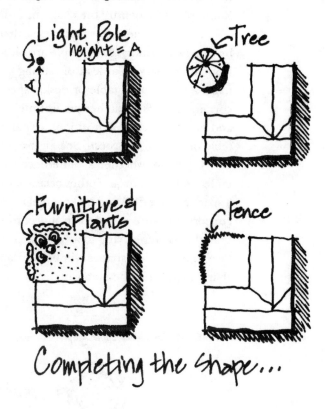

Completing the Shape...

Furniture Shapes

As I discussed in Chapter 2, Section A, energy flows more smoothly and effectively when the corners of counters, cabinets, tables, desks, and other pieces of furniture are rounded. In addition to having round corners, bull-nose edges on counters and other surfaces will also create a more comfortable feeling.

The overall shape of a table or desk will affect the dynamics of what occurs in a meeting. A round table is comfortable and has a feeling of equality with no designated power position other than the Commanding Position dictated by its position in the room. An oval table or desk is a comfortable shape but has a stronger position of authority at the wide part of the long side of the oval. If two people are sitting opposite one another at the widest point, they will not feel as confrontational as they would if the sides of the surface were straight. See Chapter 7, Section C: Office Spaces, Figure 7.12, for Large and Small Conference Room plans to identify the chairs in Commanding Position locations.

A square table is less embracing than the round table and tends to be somewhat static. Two people are either facing one another in a confrontational way or awkwardly sitting at right angles to each other. Finally, a rectangular table or desk, especially one with sharp edges and corners, creates a harsher environment with a series of more powerful and more subordinate positions, depending upon the placement of the table or desk in the room. See Figure 3.10.

Any table, whether a conference room table, coffee table, bedside table, end table, or any other accessory type of table, is apt to open up a space a great deal and make it feel more comfortable if it has rounded corners, because people can move around the furniture more easily than if they were trying to avoid sharp corners and hard edges. In addition, the rounded shapes will help balance all of the straight lines and sharp angles that inevitably occur in every space.

FIGURE 3.10 *Conference Table Shapes*

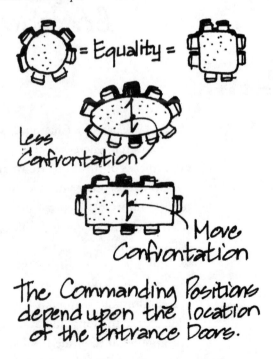

C. MATERIALS

From the floors to the ceilings, our spaces are filled with a variety of substances. Although colors tend to be the dominant visual technique in creating a balanced environment, the materials that we use in a space create a definite energy and can enhance the Primary Purpose. It is often difficult to differentiate the impact of the materials from the effect of the colors because they are working on us simultaneously. Sometimes the colors and materials provide a common sensual experience, but sometimes they produce a tension that is not always intended.

The energy of a room is also affected by the furniture fabrics, window treatments, and wall coverings. All of these hard, cold, soft, fragile, and tactile materials create a visual expectation and sensation in the psyche, even before you have stepped on the shiny hard marble flooring or touched the soft velvet fabric or the cold stainless steel arm of the chair. Our choices of materials and finishes should be conscious decisions that will add to the Primary Purpose of the space.

Whenever possible, use natural and sustainable materials to create a healthy, more natural environment. Although we realize that the selection of materials involves practical maintenance considerations, we are focusing here on the way materials affect us psychologically.

Flooring Materials

We begin with the flooring, because the feeling we have as we step into a space gives us our first subliminal sensation of comfort or tension. Our subconscious mind immediately processes the questions, "Is the surface slick, soft, hard, stable? Will it make me feel as if I am walking over a wet surface, soft sand, hard rock, stable wood? Do I need to be careful? Will it be comfortable?" The reaction to a flooring material is a combination of the image or perception that it creates and the actual sensation one experiences when stepping onto the surface.

A hard marble floor, a wood floor, and a soft carpet create different images and sensations. When we enter a building, we are often coming from a concrete, stone, or other hard outdoor paving surface. We tend to associate hard surfaces with the harshness of the outside world or of large public areas. When we enter a lobby with a hard stone floor, we still feel as if we are in a very public place. This may be appropriate in an office building, but in a hotel lobby we want to make people feel as if they have left the harshness of the outside world behind and reached their home away from home. By using a softer feeling wood or carpet on a hotel lobby floor, we have caused a visual, as well as a physical, shift in the energy of the hotel guest.

Even within an office or residential space, we can shift the experience from one room to another by changing the floor texture. Stepping from a hallway with wood or a tight loop carpet into an office with a more plush cut pile carpet causes an immediate shift of energy from "public and practical" to "comfortable and private." A statement has been made. Moving from wood flooring in a living room onto a carpeted bedroom floor immediately confirms that you are moving into a softer environment. An area rug can also define a separate and special seating area within a room.

The finish of a flooring surface can also affect your level of tension. A highly polished marble or shiny vinyl composition tile (VCT) or wood surface may create the feeling that the surface is wet or slick and therefore dangerous. This may create immediate stress when the desire is to make people feel more relaxed than they were outside of the space.

The flooring material, combined with its color and finish, creates the subconscious image of a natural element that can increase or reduce our tension. None of us feels comfortable walking on a watery surface. If the flooring is a shiny black or dark blue marble or VCT, it may come across subliminally as water. For a split second the mind hesitates as it processes the information before deciding that it cannot be water. The floor creates an unnecessary tiny irritant that adds to the list of small items that increase stress. A concrete or dull hard surface may give the sensation of walking over rocks, not the most comfortable path and another mark on the stress scale. On the other hand, a wood surface immediately appears solid and supportive, and a carpet conveys the more inviting feel of a grassy lawn. The wide variety of patterns, colors, and textures of VCT can be used to communicate a number of intended physical sensations. The important point for the designer is to be aware of the subconscious image that the flooring creates and make certain that it is enhancing the Primary Purpose of that particular space.

Furniture Construction and Materials

Furniture materials, finishes, and fabrics also affect people's feelings and behavior and should enhance the Primary Purpose. A room that is filled with chrome and glass chairs and tables is apt to have a much colder and more aloof feeling than a space filled with wood and fabrics. Because the flooring and walls in a space are often a given, we frequently use pieces of furniture to create a particular feeling or to shift the balance of energy to accommodate the energy of a new occupant. In many cases, a client's life is filled with a great deal of harshness and coldness. As a consequence, the professional will generally want to choose furniture that will look welcoming and balance that hardness, metaphorically redirecting the client's energy in a more gentle direction.

The patterns on furniture and window fabric clearly convey a specific energy. It is very important for you to be aware of the effect that patterns have on the viewer. We frequently use the Squint Test when determining the effect of a pattern. By squinting your eyes so that all you see are the contrasts, you will experience the effect of the pattern on the subconscious. A striped pattern may well vibrate, and a bold check may appear chaotic. A large print may appear overwhelming in scale. Make certain that the effects are consistent with the Primary Purpose of the space. If not, make another selection.

Wall Patterns and Materials

We tend to think of walls primarily in terms of colors. The patterns on wallpapers, however, have a tremendous effect on the psyche. Once again, use the Squint Test. See Figure 3.11. Because most striped wallpapers will visually vibrate, they are apt to add a feeling of excitement to a room. Although this may be exactly what you want for a family room, it is usually not a good choice for a bedroom. We have worked on several children's rooms in which the child's sleep became much more peaceful when we changed the walls from the excitement of bold patterns to calmer plain colors. Changing a child's nighttime sleep will always affect their daytime behavior. Even in the context of a family room, make certain that the energy of the particular family and the other energies in the space will not be thrown out of balance with the additional excitement of striped wallpaper. It may be that the energy of the three

FIGURE 3.11 *Wall Patterns*

teenage boys, the television, the hockey game, the pool table, and their friends does not need the addition of a strong pattern to create an energy level in the room that is tolerable for the parents.

Different materials on the walls can also have an impact. Putting aside the effect of their colors, concrete, ceramic, or stone walls convey a hardness and coldness. If these surfaces are rough, the impression can be one of "be careful" or "stay away" that can add to a tension in the space. Wood paneling can convey warmth and is an effective way of adding the Wood element. If the paneling goes from the floor to the ceiling, however, the image becomes one of tall trees surrounding the area and, depending upon the color, can close in a small room to the point of feeling overwhelming.

Ceiling Materials

The texture of a ceiling can also affect us. Most ceilings are smooth and painted a very light color so they will feel as high and light over our heads as possible. When a ceiling has a rough texture, it is apt to feel heavier and more uncomfortable. The lighting and the height of the textured ceiling obviously make a difference. If the ceiling is not high and the lighting accentuates the roughness of the surface, we will want to keep a greater distance from the ceiling than we would if it were a smooth surface. In effect, the roughness and lighting may "lower" the ceiling from its actual height, which may be comfortable, to an apparent height that may become very uncomfortable.

A similar feeling of oppression overhead can be experienced when a ceiling has beams that are relatively low. As we discussed in Chapter 2, Section A: The Flow of Energy, sitting, standing, or sleeping under a low beam can have a negative impact on a person's physical condition. If the beams are a dark wood in strong contrast to the rest of the ceiling color, they will appear heavier than if they match the ceiling color. This will not alter the physical effect of the beams but may somewhat reduce the feeling of heaviness overhead.

Using the *Bagua* to Select Materials

Selecting materials and fabrics and placing them in a space based on their corresponding relationship with the *Bagua* can be an effective way to enhance an environment. This technique also gives individuals an opportunity to improve a part of their life and have fun doing so. If a person wishes to focus on adding energy to a particular aspect of life, the person can choose an object that is made of a material and color that will act as a metaphor in that area of life and place it in the appropriate section of the *Bagua*. For example, if a couple wants to focus on their relationship, you might suggest that they place a lamp or other object in the Primary Relationship *gua* of their bedroom using a material and color that is consistent with their intention. The element that is symbolic of that area is the Earth and the color is a pale rose. A round porcelain vase lamp base of earth tones with a soft translucent rose-colored shade would clearly be a more appropriate choice of materials and colors for this purpose than a slender metal-base lamp with a deep blue or black shade. The Earth nature of the porcelain vase is clearly more consistent with their goal and the Earth element of the Relationship *gua* than the Metal harshness of the metal base, which metaphorically takes from the Earth. The rose shade is also more appropriate than the Water-colored shade, which symbolically muddies the Earth. The use of the ritual technique described in Chapter 9 would further enhance their desired intention when they place the lamp in their bedroom.

Using the Five Elements to Select Materials

When we look at materials from the perspective of the Five Elements, we find the following correlations.

EARTH In the form of ceramics, tiles, and other similar claylike substances as well as carpets that represent the feeling of the land.

METAL In chrome, steel, iron, and other forms of metal, as well as concrete and other hard surfaces.

WATER In the reflective nature of glass or other shiny dark surfaces.

WOOD In the many varieties of actual wood or wood imitations.

FIRE Does not tend to have a material that we can use in designs, although a fireplace, stove, or candle certainly represents Fire. As a result, we usually balance the need for the Fire element through the use of color and objects.

A space is frequently out of balance in its effect on the occupants when the colors and the materials are primarily of the same elemental nature. For example, an office lobby space that has a great deal of glass, polished blue-gray tiles, white and gray walls, and stainless elevator doors and frames communicates the coldness and harshness of Water and Metal and is missing any touch of the Earth, Wood, or Fire elements. By adding wood trim to the metal door frames and overlaying the tile floor with a dark earth tone carpet, we have balanced the feeling of the space with a combination of colors and materials that begin to bring us back to a more natural environment.

When a person or space is out of balance and doesn't reinforce the Primary Purpose of the space, we can use the attributes of specific materials to convey the feeling of a particular element. If an office space is harsh and cold, covering the guest chairs in gold or burgundy velvet symbolizing the Earth or Fire elements would add an inviting feeling of warmth and affluence. The rich velvet cries out to be touched and visually feels soft and comfortable, even from across the room. In a residence, clients may feel fractured and unstable in their relationship with family members and friends. This might suggest the need for more of the stabilizing Earth element. Without being rigidly bound by the system of the Five Elements, a good place to begin in the design process of selecting flooring would be to look for materials that connote the stability of Earth. In this case, the stability of terracotta tiles is apt to feel more grounding than the watery feel of highly polished marble tiles. If you want to select a softer surface to balance the harshness of a person's attitude toward others, mixing the feel and visual metaphor of colors with materials might lead you to choose a dark green cut pile carpet that subconsciously reminds us of a grass lawn. As is always the case, the color and the material should work together to promote the same psychological goal.

D. LIGHTING

Light is the primary source of energy, and the human being has a tremendous need for light in order to function effectively. How often does someone enter a room and turn on the lights, regardless of the time of day? Because most of our interior spaces are yin and lacking in energy, lighting is an extremely strong and vital form of yang energy that can help bring a space into balance.

Light can be very warming, cheery, and enabling. When we do not have enough light, we strain to see and immediately feel tense. A well-lit environment is a pleasant place to be, as well as a space where we can function more effectively and easily. Adding lamps, especially in an office environment that is lit primarily from the ceiling, can dramatically affect the energy and warmth of a room.

In traditional Feng Shui, the lack of light is considered to have a negative effect on virtually every aspect of life. For instance, if a home is too dark, the occupants may have problems with money. This is especially true if the entry is dark. When you think about the way in which light makes it easier for us to function, it is easy to understand that the lack of light may very well impede our ability to maximize our income. In effect, the lack of light shuts us down on many levels, just as if we were preparing to go to sleep, even when we are trying to function productively during the day. It is accepted generally that good lighting will enhance an environment.

The Color of the Light

As we have discussed in Section A: Colors, the color of the lighting in a room will have an impact on the colors of the walls and fabrics. In addition, the color of the light itself will have an impact on the individual. Incandescent and warm fluorescent lamps give the warmest glow to a space. Although daylight bulbs have a natural feel to them because they are closest in color to natural daylight, remember that the intense natural light and heat energy of the sun will have a much stronger impact on an individual than a daylight bulb in a fluorescent ceiling fixture, which will actually read as cooler than daylight. Because of their daylight color balance these lamps are often used in helping people who have a light-deficiency-based condition. However, many people feel more comfortable with the energy of a warm or incandescent light.

The Types of Light Fixtures

Motion lights are a very effective way to bring instant energy into an environment. When we approach a building and the lights immediately go on, the energy is welcoming. The instant light also makes it easier to proceed, thereby eliminating an element of stress. When we open a front door and a motion light illuminates the entry, it floods the area with instant energy without the effort of searching for the light switch in the dark.

Overhead fluorescent lights with a green/blue/gray cast, often the standard fixture in offices, can sap energy. In an office with this type of lighting, it is critical that we add task lighting to increase the yang energy in the room and balance a cool yin environment.

The use of three-way light fixtures is a very good way to create either a subdued energy or a more highly energized space as appropriate. The most important point about a three-way fixture is that it is designed to use a three-way light lamp and should *only* be used with the appropriate bulb. Otherwise, the fixture does not function as intended. When a lamp is first turned on and nothing happens because the fixture contains a 100-watt bulb, the image that is being conveyed is that the lamp, the space, and its occupants are not working as well as they are capable of functioning. The message that we should consistently be giving ourselves and everyone else is just the opposite: this space and the people in it are operating at maximum potential.

It is generally most effective to use light fixtures with traditional translucent shades in which the light shines both up and down, as well as through the shade. A translucent shade allows for a more even distribution of light and the feeling of a more balanced space.

In a home, restaurant, spa, or other intimate and personal environment, candlelight is a very effective way to increase warmth. Selecting the number of candles can be a fun source of positive imaging. Although we all recognize that two candles on a table signify a couple, a candle on the dining room table for each person in the household can be a way of recognizing symbolically the importance of everyone in the family. Using differently colored candles can also create an overall energetic feeling and add that complementary color or missing piece of the full color spectrum to balance the energy of a space.

In selecting light fixtures, be very much aware of the relative visual weight and impact of the base and the shade. If the base is not balanced or the shade appears heavier than the base, a person may feel that the fixture is about to topple over. This feeling of instability may create an unneeded tension and contribute to an occupant's unsettled frame of mind.

The Placement of Fixtures

In placing lights in a room, the professional should focus on several issues:

- What is the Primary Purpose of the space?
- Where are the primary needs for lighting?
- Where are the dead spots in the room?

We live approximately four to six feet off the ground, four feet when we are sitting and six feet when standing. By this, we mean that our eyes, the primary receptors of light energy, are at this level. When the lighting in a room is in the ceiling, the energy is above us and can make us feel somewhat inferior, because we are below the light in an area with less energy than is in the ceiling. In addition, the intensity of the light dissipates as it moves away from its source in the ceiling.

People will inevitably gravitate to an energy spot in a room and avoid a dead space. If a person ends up in a low-energy spot, you can often watch that individual's energy begin to drop fairly quickly, even to the point where the person has a difficult time staying awake.

The amount of lighting that is needed in a single office space varies, depending upon its use at any particular time. This concept is often ignored. The amount of light that is ideal for task lighting is four to five times that needed for using the computer. Similarly, an office in which people meet should be evenly illuminated throughout and not leave anyone literally in the dark.

We always recommend having at least three light fixtures in a room and distributing them throughout the space to avoid uneven energy. If there is only one spot of light in the room, our eyes will be drawn to, and fixate on, that energy like a moth. Two light sources tend to create a tension because a person's energy is drawn first to one and then to the other, much like watching a tennis match, creating discomfort. Three or more lights that are placed in various areas of a room will cause the eyes to move from one to the next to the third and back to the first in a circular pattern, the most natural and comfortable motion.

We are frequently confronted with lobby and reception areas where recessed accent and downlighting create an uneven pattern of light and dark areas on the floor. It is preferable to use wall washers and ceiling floods that cast a broader spectrum of light that overlap with the light cast by adjacent fixtures. This will create a smooth flow of visual and psychological energy.

FIGURE 3.12A *Task Lighting*

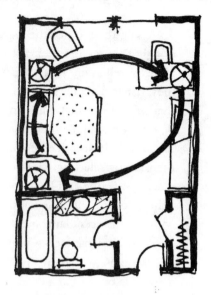

"Three Points of Light"

FIGURE 3.12B *Ceiling Lighting*

Wallwashers for Even Light

Using the *Bagua* and the Five Elements in Lighting Design

Using the tools of the *Bagua* and the Five Elements in the selection of light fixtures and their placement, people can enhance their environment as well as improve an aspect of their life—and have fun doing so. If they wish to add energy to a particular *gua*, they can choose a light fixture that will act as a metaphor and place it in the appropriate section of the *Bagua*. For example, people who literally wants to concentrate on "illuminating Self-Knowledge" could metaphorically cast light on that part of their life by selecting a lamp associated with this positive intention and placing it in the Self-Knowledge section of the bedroom. Using the attributes of this *gua*, the lamp might be a deep blue round earthen vase with a translucent lampshade. The use of the transcendental technique described in Chapter 9 would further enhance their desired intention.

We can also use the Five Elements to adjust the energy of a space. If a room is out of balance in its elements and needs more of the Wood element, an upright, dark wood base with a pale green shade would be a simple way to introduce balance. Similarly, the upward motion of a standing lamp with a reddish wood base and a rose shade will add a feeling of more Fire to a room and increase the sense of strength and energy in the space.

E. SOUND

Sound is energy. From the beginning of time, sound, music, and rhythms have been associated by philosophers and scientists with the creation, or primary vibrations, of the universe itself. A four-month-old fetus can hear sounds that are outside the womb. Sound and rhythm are extremely powerful influences and are with us every moment of our life, whether we are awake or asleep.

Sound brings back memories. Every time I hear the distant sound of a train, I am immediately back on my grandparents' farm in Indiana. Sound is a friendly companion in the tinkling of wind chimes. It is the wind in the trees, the rain on the roof, the roar of the ocean. It is the sound of our own nervous and circulatory systems. It is music.

In the ancient world, music and rhythms were consciously used as mysterious and powerful tools for attuning and influencing the physiological and psychological conditions of the mind and body. We have all experienced the power of music as it excites us, saddens us, or makes us trip the light fantastic. Music brings back memories, keeps us company, and lifts our spirits. We have music at home, at work, at play, and at prayer. Music is a universal language and brings together people of completely different cultures.

Scientists have long known that music can affect the growth of plants. An increasing body of scientific research supports the idea that music and sounds can increase the ability of the human being to withstand stress and other causes of illness and to heal. Scientists believe that sounds can release endorphins and cause other positive hormonal and neurological changes. On the other hand, sounds can also be harsh and unfriendly and cause the very stress we are trying to alleviate.

Many theories over the centuries have correlated the wavelengths of different sounds with the same responses elicited by different colors. Rimsky-Korsakov felt that F-sharp was "decidedly strawberry red." We have enjoyed working with individual clients in having them free-associate colors with the sounds of particular tuning forks. Although we have not done enough testing to establish a validated theory, we have gotten some consistently fascinating responses. In addition, the comfort level of people with certain notes clearly demonstrates that certain sounds evoke certain responses in the same way that colors do.

Rhythms also affect us on many levels. All cultures use rhythms to affect people, even if only in their national anthem, and many groups use rhythm in their spiritual traditions to induce trances and similar states.

We need the energy of sound. How often do people enter their home and immediately turn on the radio, TV, or stereo? They have just come from the outdoors, which usually is filled with a great deal of sound and other forms of energy, and have entered an empty yin space that feels out of balance. Immediately feeling the lack of energy in the space, one of the first things they do is to add sound, which immediately creates more yang energy. If you can introduce sounds and the opportunity to create sounds in a space in a natural way, you can begin to shift a person's physiological and psychological condition. Let's begin at the entrance to a home.

Wind Chimes

Wind chimes are a wonderful tool to introduce sound into an environment. If wind chimes are near the entrance to a residence, we are greeted by the gentle sound of pleasant musical chords. This is both a welcoming sound and a way of adding energy to an entry that may lack energy, such as a recessed doorway that is dark and even perhaps slightly hidden. Have your clients select the sounds that resonate with them. This is their space, and they need to relate to the sounds that greet them on arriving home. Chimes that have been tuned to particular chords, such as the chimes made by the Woodstock Company, are the most effective. Because these chimes also come in a variety of colors and finishes, the colors and elements of the *Bagua* and the Five Elements can be incorporated in selecting wind chimes to place in a particular part of a property.

When a person opens the front door, door chimes can create an instant welcoming sound, filling the empty yin entryway with immediate yang energy. A door chime that rings when the door is opened also acts as a warning and helps alleviate anxiety, thereby increasing one's ability to rest and work peacefully. Door chimes should be attached firmly to the upper corner of the door above the doorknob. This placement allows for the maximum swing of the door to increase the sound of the chimes. If the chimes are merely hung on the doorknob or in some other impermanent manner, the residents may feel they are in a temporary home, an impression that we want to avoid, even if it is true.

In addition to being decorative and playful, wind chimes can also be used on a transcendental level. A wind chime may prevent negative energy from entering a space, disperse chi that is moving too quickly or in a direction that you wish to alter, or keep energy from leaving a space. Ringing your own wind chimes is a private method for bringing attention to yourself. As you ring the chimes, envision the energy that you have stimulated going out into the universe and flowing back to you. If you have a client who is receptive to this transcendental aspect of Feng Shui, a wind chime is a readily acceptable tool to shift the energy of a home and its occupants. We will discuss the specifics of this transcendental technique in Chapter 9.

Water Features

The sound of water can also be an effective way to introduce pleasing yang energy to a space. A fountain in front of a building or inside an entrance can add both a cooling sensation and a welcoming sound to a home or office. Because water has so many subliminal connotations for people, it can very effectively enhance an environment. We will discuss the use of water and how it can relate to the *Bagua* and the Five Elements in Chapter 3, Section I: Water Features.

Music

Although we are all familiar with music in our interior spaces, music can effectively be used outdoors to create a feeling or shift the energy before we even enter a space. One of the most interesting uses of music we have experienced was in a hospital parking lot where people are immediately greeted with the gentle sound of a calming music. By the time they actually enter the hospital, their energy from the stress of travel and the fear of what lies ahead has begun to shift, even if only slightly. When the music continues in the lobby, the transition from the natural outdoor environment to the indoor spaces is less abrupt, and people may subliminally continue to connect the sound with the healing attributes of nature. The same positive shift of energy and change of mood can be created by the use of outdoor music in other places, from a restaurant to a more corporate environment.

Other Sources of Sound

Although we have focused primarily on sound at the entrance area of a building, sound can be introduced effectively into other areas of a building and in ways other than with chimes or water features. In doing so, be aware of the particular areas of the *Bagua* in which you are placing the sound. Because sound itself is not one of the Five Elements, the source of the sound may well connote a specific element in the way that the sound of a fountain is associated with the element of Water and the sound of a chime with Metal. Make certain that the source of the sound is consistent with the area of the *Bagua* in which it is placed.

One of the most common sources of sound is a radio or stereo system. These units are usually placed in rooms where the client wants a great deal of yang energy, such as a family or living room. On the other hand, the sound of calming music can also enhance a peaceful space, such as a massage, meditation, or bedroom area. Because your clients will select their own music, it may be helpful for you to point out to them that the energy from a radio or stereo will be a large part of the energy in the space and may affect their mood and behavior.

Many sources of sound can be fun, energetic, and decorative in a client's space. Rain sticks that a person can pick up and shake or interior wind chimes or bells one can touch gently with a finger and create a pleasant sound when passing by are only a couple of ways to introduce sound, a tool that we often forget when we are looking for ways to add energy to a space.

F. SIGNAGE

Although signage is always intended to convey information, its most important, and often forgotten, purpose is to communicate a psychological statement about the person, company, town, or other entity that is represented by the sign. The large sign, the corporate logo, and the business card are all part of the energy and image of an institution, and the energies of these "signs" should be consistent with the desired energy of the business. The size, scale, shape, colors, and placement of signage are critical aspects and should be designed with the intention of contributing to the ease of reading and the clarity of the message that the client wants to convey. Although most of these concepts seem rather obvious, they are issues that we have addressed with every client.

Size and Scale of Signage

We often deal with either a stand-alone sign or a name on a wall. The size of the sign and the letters of a name communicate a message as to how the entity views itself.

In an office lobby where three corporations are listed on a wall, the name that is in the largest letters or on top will appear to be the most important. In many instances, the size of the lettering is determined by the total amount of space allotted per name, and the longer name has to be in a smaller type to fit in the designated space. In one situation, a corporation jumped at the idea of using the shortened name by which it was commonly known to maximize the size of its lettering. In another case, a firm insisted on using its long full name and continued to look insignificant. Although many other factors were clearly at work, the second entity was not as successful as the first. The order of the names may be unavoidable because of the landlord's determination that the companies be listed in alphabetical order, by floor, or by size of space. In such cases, the entity on the bottom might want to use a shortened version of its name to increase the size of its lettering. If its letters are larger than those in the names above it, the company on the bottom may well come across as the strong foundation on which everyone else rests.

Imagine the signage of a company in an elevator lobby on a single-tenant floor with control over the size of its name. One- to one-and-a-half-inch letters will convey an image of insignificance. Three- to four-inch letters will communicate importance. Eight- to ten-inch letters may appear "over the top." The distance from the viewer who is leaving the elevator and the length of the name will be relevant in determining the best size for the signage.

It should go without saying that the legibility of the particular choice of script is very important. The signage should be easily read at a distance. A fancy typeface may be elegant on the company's stationary but illegible on a sign. Remember that the purpose of the sign is information and image.

Shape and Colors of Signage

The shape of a sign can either attract attention because of its uniqueness or get lost in the crowd of many other signs. One of our clients was a town mayor who asked us to develop signage standards for the town. We picked a different shape that would quickly become recognizable as a sign that related to the town. Because we wanted to distinguish between the different locations of cultural sites, historical sites, and parking, we recommended that the basic background colors of the signs be different for the three types of locations, but that the shape and the color of the lettering be the same for all of the signs. In this case, we suggested using the same gold lettering on the active energy of a burgundy background for cultural sites, on the more calm and ancient purple for historical places, and on the most peaceful blue for parking. These colors differentiated the new signs from the very common green signs along the streets.

In front of a residential building, the nature of the sign and its condition will communicate a great deal about how the residents feel about themselves. A sign that is easy to read and well placed at the front of the walk conveys a very positive image to the residents themselves as well as to others. The faded sign that is hidden by weeds sends a very different message.

Placement of Signage

Residential signage often reveals the address rather than the name of the residents. As we approach a house, usually by car in much of today's society, the house numbers should be clear and easy to read from a distance. Where we tend to look for the numbers may vary somewhat on the nature of the location, but over the front door is an obvious place to start. Because most numbers will have been placed during the day, it is important to remember that the numbers should be well lit and easily visible at night. Another possible location for a multistory residence would be on both of the side corners at the front of the building, slightly above six feet. This placement will let people know where they are before they reach the front of the building, regardless of the direction from which they approach.

Because one of our goals in a business environment is to encourage people to come to our client for business, we should make it as easy as possible for the potential customer to find the building. The street address or the name of the building should be obvious as a person approaches the premises from either direction and not require any effort whatsoever for someone to find. In one instance, the only entrances to an office building were on the side streets that differed from the postal address. In addition, the street number for the building was on a sign on the side street that was the same color as the building. And a tree completely blocked the sign from the traffic on the main street. Talk about making it difficult for the prospective tenant or client!

An awning or portico that extends out over a sidewalk and has the name of the building on both sides is an effective way to raise the visi-

FIGURE 3.13 *Elevator Signage*

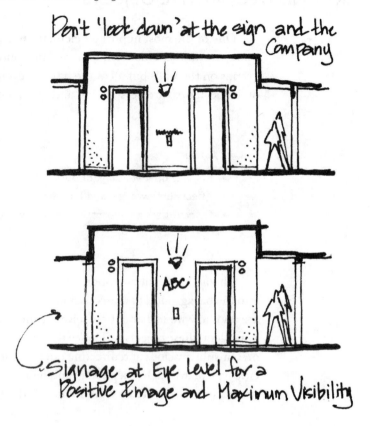

bility of the building and to convey that the owner cares about people by protecting them from the weather.

When you place a single name on a wall, keep in mind the average person's eye level. A sign that is six feet off the floor will require the average person to look slightly upward. This results in an individual looking up at the company, exactly the image that you want employees, clients, and others to have of the business. In one situation where our client's name and logo had been placed three feet from the floor, the sign was raised when we pointed out that everyone was physically and psychologically looking down on the company—not a positive image. See Figure 3.13.

G. ART AND DECORATIVE OBJECTS

One of the most important elements in a person's living or working space is *artwork*. This term includes not only the pictures and photographs on the walls but all of the sculpture and other decorative objects on bookshelves, dressers, tables, and other surfaces.

> **Our Artwork**
> - Reflects how we think of ourselves and others
> - Affects how we feel and how we act
> - Gives others an impression of who we are

The articles that surround us on a daily basis, often disappearing into the background in our conscious mind speak volumes about who we are and how we feel about ourselves at the present moment. Even more important, these objects influence the way we think and act by impinging on our subconscious and directing our behavior. Unless we refer to a specific type of art, such as a photograph or a sculpture, we will be including decorative objects of any medium in this discussion of artwork.

The Energy of Artwork

One of the most important Feng Shui concepts to remember in choosing art is that the emotions and feelings of the artist go onto the canvas or into the object in the creative process. However, the process does not stop there. Those same emotions reflect back at us every time we look at the art. If the artist was angry when he or she created the painting, we will experience that anger as if it were aimed directly at us every time we look at the picture *and* every time we merely enter the space in which the piece of art can affect our subconscious. It is critical to be aware of the emotions that a piece of art generates before selecting it for a particular spot. Fortunately, one can usually analyze the state of mind of the artist at the time of the creation. Ask yourself whether the energy of the artwork will reinforce the Primary Purpose of the space.

As a professional, be very careful about saying anything judgmental about the artwork in a client's space. I learned this the hard way by once reacting viscerally to a collage that happened to have been done by the client! The best approach is to ask the individuals to tell you about the piece of art they already own, or to ask them to tell you what attracts them to the work they are considering purchasing.

Let me give you a few of many examples from the homes of real clients, even though they may seem unbelievable.

George and Mary asked me to Feng Shui their home and focus on improving George's health. Above the dining room table, where they ate all of their meals, was a large portrait in black, gray, and white of a woman just before she committed suicide. The colors of the picture, the pose of the woman, and the energy that was coming off the canvas captured the depression that the young lady must have been experiencing at the time she posed for the portrait. Despite the excellence of the painting, this energy was not what this couple needed to have hovering over them as they were eating. Mary reluctantly acknowledged that maybe this was not a great place for the painting but said she did not want to give it up, so we had to find a new place for it. We finally placed it above the toilet in a downstairs powder room that was rarely used. The image that we created in their mind was that the woman was sitting like Rodin's Thinker and that all of her negativity was being flushed down the toilet. Although the picture was probably not ideal for a home, we moved it from a harmful location to a more innocuous position. I would not be surprised if they ultimately sold the picture after focusing on the negative energy of the painting and the effect it might be having on their health.

That, however, was not the end of this story. When I entered the master bedroom, I was struck by another black, gray, and white picture that hung just beside the bedroom door, the last thing that George saw before he went into the peace and quiet of his bedroom to rest. This was a self-portrait by a well-known artist just before he committed suicide. On his shoulder was a black raven and in the background were three dancing skeletons. This energy was clearly not beneficial to George. Once again, their question was, "Where can we hang this picture?" In this case, it would have been best to move it out of the house. I suggested that as long as they kept it, they could put it in the family room with the television, stereo, Ping-Pong table, and other highly yang activities that would act to balance the extremely yin energy of the painting.

Margaret and Henry invited me to help them Feng Shui their home to increase the passion in their relationship. When I looked at the art in their apartment, I discovered a wonderful collection of 18 sculptures and paintings. However, of the 18 works of art, 12 were of single women, 4 were of female couples, and the remaining 2 were landscapes devoid of people. When I pointed this out to Margaret, the collector in the family, she gasped, "Oh my, part of me must want to be a single woman." The large painting at the foot of their bed, which they gazed upon as they lay together, was of 2 women sitting apart having tea. The colors of the painting were cool greens, blues, and lilacs. In addition, the other colors in the room were also cool blues and greens, with white in great abundance. Not only was the bedroom lacking any passion in the colors, but this large painting was not about the passion and closeness of a couple but about a cool formality and distance. This was a perfect example of how the art did not create the environment that the inhabitants said they wanted.

These concepts are equally as relevant in a hospital, office, or any type of project. In one law firm, the lawyers avoided using one of the conference rooms where a large abstract painting with sharp contrasts and hard edges conveyed a chaotic and violent energy. This piece of art completely shifted the energy in the room away from a feeling of coming together in mutual agreement. In another office space, a somewhat surrealistic picture of a dark, clownlike figure with a missing eye hung in the hallway beside the door of one of the partners. Within several months after moving into this office, the partner incurred a very serious eye problem that required major surgery. We have frequently found in offices that the art was chosen for its commercial value without any thought of its impact on the occupants. Rarely does an office need artwork that conveys tension. That does not mean that the artwork needs to be bland and uninteresting, but it should be selected to create energy that is consistent with its Primary Purpose.

A professional must be circumspect in this area. Because the artwork is usually chosen by one of the occupants of the space, as opposed to being inherited or received as a gift, the art reflects, in some way, the personality of the one who chose it. Of course, the possibility always exists that an inherited piece or a gift was drawn to the recipient because of the recipient's energy. Our role is not to criticize a client's choices but to point out the various elements of the art and the effect the art may be having on the viewers. Once we have provided the client with the information, it is up to them to decide how to act. On some occasions, I will ask if the client would like to try a piece in a different location, and I will offer to help make the move, just to jumpstart the process of change. Do not be aggressive in this regard. If you detect any hesitation, let it go. It is extremely important to be sensitive to the client in this area.

Directional Artwork

Most pictures and some hanging art lead the viewer in a definite, and often subconscious, direction. In placing art, be very much aware of the direction in which the piece "reads." When entering a space, we would almost always prefer to have a person's energy directed in a particular direction, toward a living room or a reception desk, for instance. If we want an individual to go to the right, we do not want to hang a picture opposite the entrance that shows a boat moving to the left. Because we read from left to right in our culture, we tend to be more comfortable reading a picture to the right, while a picture that goes to the left tends to create some tension. This is also consistent with the preference of creating spaces where the energy of the people moves in a more natural direction to the right.

The "direction" of a picture can also be created by the placement of color or the movement of the lines of the painting. An abstract picture will probably have a focal point, such as a splash of more intense color, that leads the eye to a particular side of the canvas. This is apt to be the direction in which the viewer is being led. A picture with depth can be either an outdoor or interior scene. Keep in mind the image you want in the viewer's mind given the Primary Purpose of the particular space in which the painting will be hung. If we are just entering a building, an interior scene or a welcoming abstract may be more appropriate than a landscape, which may pull our subconscious back outdoors.

Wind sculptures also create a sense of the flow of energy. The motion of the sculpture can be a metaphor for movement in a person's life and can stimulate more yang energy in the environment at the same time.

Artwork That Ties Us to the Past

Photographs, paintings, objects, and even pieces of furniture often tie us to the past and prevent us from moving ahead, without our even realizing what is occurring. That does not mean that reminders of the past are bad and should be eliminated. They are an important part of who we are today, but we should be aware of the impact that an item is having on our subconscious and how it may be affecting our behavior and the way we appear and relate to others. The placement of these items is important.

It is very easy for us to hold on, through photographs or even furniture, to a part of our past more appropriately left behind. How many of us have kept pictures of an ex-boyfriend or girlfriend, even after we had a new relationship? I don't think I need to point out the issues here! Even retaining a photograph of an ex may make it more difficult to move on and find a new relationship. In one situation, Cate had kept several pieces of furniture that an ex-boyfriend had given her. She admitted that they kept her tied emotionally to him. When she finally was able to get rid of the furniture, she was able to let go of her attachment to him and move on to another relationship.

Jennifer asked me to help shift the energy in her apartment with the goal of enabling her to enter into a relationship. She was appalled when I pointed out that three feet away, on the wall next to the male side of her bed, was a large portrait of her father and that three feet away, on the wall directly opposite her bedroom door, was an even larger photograph of her grandfather with a shotgun. I am not making this up! She did not need to get rid of these images to change the messages they were sending to her and to others, only to move them to a less personal place in the apartment. Of course, one might question whether Jennifer really wanted a relationship. That was solely her choice. Our role as the professional is to point out the energies that are at work in the environment and how they may be affecting the particular situation.

In Janet's case, she had been divorced for ten years and, although she said that she wanted a new relationship, she was having trouble relating to men. When I looked at her home, I was immediately struck by a very large collage beside her bedroom door that emanated a tremendous amount of anger. When I asked her to tell me about the painting, she began to tell me, in a voice that became increasingly agitated and angry, that she had constructed the collage while she was going through the divorce. Every time Janet entered her bedroom, she subconsciously returned to a period in her life when she was filled with anger, and even hatred, toward the male. These emotions were with her as she went to sleep and were active on a subconscious level during a time that should have been calm and peaceful.

Objects on Shelves and Other Surfaces

Very commonly, a multitude of objects covers a shelf, mantle, piano, bookcase, dresser, desk, or other surface. This happens not only in homes and offices but also in retail stores. It is important for the professional to create surfaces, such as mantles or shelves, that are capable of holding objects but that are not so large as to encourage the placement of too many pieces. When faced with a preexisting large surface, the designer should discuss the following issues with clients.

The immediate impression when confronted with many items on a surface is one of chaos and clutter. Because our natural impulse is to avoid confusion, we often look away and try to ignore completely the group of conflicting images. However, that is not the intention of having objects on display, especially in a retail setting.

Having row upon row of items also makes a subconscious statement of importance. For instance, the people in the photographs in the front row will be considered by the viewer to be the most important to the person who arranged them, with the subsequent rows of pictures having decreasing importance. One family with whom I was working had three children, a girl and two boys. The two boys had developed illnesses, so I was looking for factors that might be adding to that situation. I noticed that on all of the surfaces in the house, the front row was always a series of photographs of the father and the daughter. The two boys had been relegated to the back rows. Although other aspects of the environment had added to the boys' conditions, the placement of the family photographs undoubtedly caused the boys to find ways to cry out for attention, including by becoming ill.

The scale of photographs that are near one another also communicates a statement of importance. Two people in an eight-by-ten-inch frame come across as being more important to the owner than are the people in the adjacent four-by-six-inch frame whose heads are tiny in comparison. Placing photographs near one another in which peoples' heads are approximately the same size eliminates this subtle message.

We often suggest that clients remove all of the objects from a surface and place them on a nearby table, then choose the one item that means the most to them, taking the time to think about the reason for the selection. If the reason enhances the Primary Purpose of that space, place that object on the surface. Continue this process until three or five items rest on the shelf. We pick the numbers *three* and *five* because they are yang numbers and will generally convey more energy than an even number of items. A group of items, such as two candle sticks that are placed together, can read as one item. Do not be bound by any rigid rules, however, but be very sensitive to the energy that the objects give off individually and as a group. A client often has trouble selecting even three or five items, because many of the objects have been placed there without any conscious thought or because "Aunt Erma gave it to me, and she will want to see it when she visits." It is usually revealed that Aunt Erma last visited three years ago.

Another common response to the suggestion that the number of photographs be reduced is that "We want to be able to see these pictures." Because we do not tend to "see" them when they are crowded together and blocking one another, a much more effective way to display photographs and avoid clutter and a hierarchy of importance is to place them in an attractive album that can be left out for easy viewing. The psychological difference between the group of crowded photographs and the neatly arranged album is great.

Broken Objects

Furniture, objects, or pieces of art that are broken or are not working well are a metaphor that the lives of the owners are not working well. That does not mean that you should get rid of the valuable art piece that is not perfect. It does mean, however, that you should be very aware of what is not functioning. The grandfather clock that no longer works may be a valuable heirloom, but it may also be creating issues for the owner about being mired in the past and not being able to move forward. The pretty pitcher with the missing handle, when seen with its damaged neighbors, may be holding the owner back and conveying an image of being stuck in place. The nature of the broken object and where it is located in the person's space, using the *Bagua* as a guideline, may have an impact on that individual's ability to move ahead in a particular area of life.

Antiques and Artwork from Other Countries

Artwork can include objects that are very old, as well as pieces that come from other countries and cultures. These items, which can include antique furniture as well as art, carry with them the energy of the people who made them and used them. A piece of art or furniture that was owned by someone whose energy is not healthy for the new owner can adversely affect the new owner. We have found that masks, sculptures, and other objects from parts of Africa and Indonesia, for example, which are often used in rituals indigenous to those particular areas, have energies that are not comfortable for many of us. As a result, antiques and artifacts from other countries occasionally are accompanied by energies that we may not want in our spaces. If you are considering the purchase of a piece for a client and have any uncomfortable feelings or second thoughts, move on to another object. Trust your intuition. In the event that a client already has the object or wants to purchase it, you may want to discuss why the client feels compelled to have this particular piece. If they must keep it or buy it, and you feel that it has an energy you want to disperse, it would be appropriate to clear the object with a transcendental technique.

Artwork as a Solution for Problem Areas

Artwork can be an effective way to shift the energy in spaces that have preexisting problems, such as blocking walls or unbalanced spaces. The traditional Feng Shui method of eliminating a blocking wall that is too close to an entrance into a house or that is directly opposite a doorway in a hallway is to hang a mirror directly opposite the entrance. We often find that this technique, however, creates more problems than it solves. When a person goes through a door, it is with the intention of entering a new space. The moment one sees oneself in a mirror that reflects both oneself and the environment one has just left, the individual's energy is directed back into that area rather than led into the new space.

FIGURE 3.14 *Blocking Wall*

to counter a 'Blocking Wall'...

Add a painting with depth and direction

In these situations, we have usually found that a more effective way of providing a feeling of depth to counter the blocking wall is to hang a picture. See Figure 3.14. The picture should not only have depth to it, but should also "read" in the direction that you want the energy and the person to flow. This approach can also be used when one passes through a doorway and is confronted with the corner of a wall. In this situation, a picture of an interior space on the near wall gives the illusion of equal depth to the opposing space.

Long corridors can create an unnatural feeling and pull us along at an ever-increasing speed to a point of discomfort. One way of creating a meandering feeling in a long hallway is to hang artwork that projects slightly from the walls, as shown in Figure 3.15. By alternating the spacing of the hangings on the opposing walls, the professional can create the sense of a meandering path and natural flow of energy. Similarly spaced wall sconces can create the same feeling.

One of the most effective uses of artwork is to bring a balance of color energy into spaces, as we discussed in Chapter 3, Section A.

FIGURE 3.15 *Meandering Corridor*

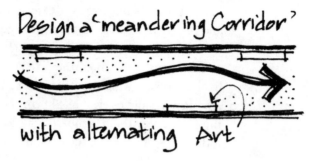

Vertical or Horizontal Artwork

The vertical or horizontal nature of artwork affects the energy of the viewer. A horizontal element that conveys the image of Earth will tend to create more of a sense of calmness and stability, whereas a vertical picture will convey more of a sense of the power and upward movement of the Wood element.

Humorous Artwork

Humor deserves special mention in a discussion of artwork. Most people's lives are extremely serious and high pressured. By adding pictures and objects that are humorous in almost any area, we can shift the energy of the viewer and reduce our client's stress level. A bathroom or restroom is a wonderful place to introduce humorous artwork because we begin and end our day there, and being as relaxed as possible to effectively eliminate some of our toxins is important.

Frame Materials and Locations

Employing the principles of the *Bagua* and the Five Elements, the colors and materials of the frames of pictures and mirrors are an easy way to add a balance of energy to a space.

Leaning a painting on a mantle against a wall or setting it on the floor rather than hanging it has occasionally been a popular decorative style. Because pictures in our culture are intended to be hung on the wall, both for protection and for ease of viewing, the propped-up picture conveys the image that the people in the space are there only temporarily. Even if that were the case, it would be better for their happiness and productivity to promote the image of permanence.

Be very careful about hanging pictures or mirrors over a bed or frequently used chair. In earthquake country, a professional would rarely hang an object with any weight or substance over a bed, but the same approach is valid elsewhere. Subconsciously, a client will feel uneasy that the object over the headboard may come crashing down in the middle if the night. As a result, the person's sleep patterns may not be as sound as they could be.

Mirrors

Mirrors can be an effective way to open up the energy in a space, especially in tight entrances and narrow hallways. Despite what you may have heard about Feng Shui, mirrors are not a panacea for every problem! They are frequently recommended as enhancements for the following problems:

- *Missing Areas*: Mounting a mirror on the wall separating an interior room from a missing section outside a house can visually "fill in" the missing section with the reflection of the room's interior.
- *Door Walls*: Mounting a mirror on the shared interior wall of a room that is outside the door wall will reflect and bring that room back inside the house or office.
- *Poison Arrows:* A mirror placed on an obtrusive column or beam makes the construction appear less obtrusive.

Several issues should be considered. As we previously discussed, it is important to visualize what will be reflected in the mirror, because those images will affect the viewer's subconscious.

Although antique mirrors are often highly valued, the glass is frequently cloudy or spotty, resulting in the viewer's face being incomplete or even distorted. Modern mirrors can also be made with "antique" glass. Try to avoid them. We want people to view themselves as whole, complete, and unblemished. If this type of mirror is a "must," place it in a location where people do not see it on a regular basis. You do not want this mirror in the bathroom, over the dining room table, or in the entry way as the first thing one sees upon entering one's private space or going out into the world.

Beveled edges are a finishing touch that can create a tension. If the mirror is less than 24 by 36 inches, the bevel will probably cause your image to splinter one or more times as you pass by and look into the glass. No one needs to be any more fractured than one is in normal daily life. Our goal is to create an environment in which people see themselves as complete. A well-known New York restaurant has an entire wall of 12-inch mirrored tiles with beveled edges in a hallway leading to several dining areas. Although the idea of opening up the narrow passageway with mirrors was a good one, the hundreds of beveled edges create a feeling of nausea as one passes by. In a restaurant?

The size and mounting height of an ordinary mirror is also important. See Figure 3.16. To make every occupant of the space feel like a complete person, select a mirror that is large enough and hung at a height that as many people in the space as possible are able to see their entire head in the mirror without having to stand on tiptoe or bend down in an awkward position. This situation might communicate a subliminal message that the person who does not appear complete in the mirror is not really welcome in the space.

FIGURE 3.16 *Mirror Height*

Artwork as an Enhancement Tool

Using the *Bagua* and the Five Elements, artwork can be added to an environment for the specific purpose of enhancing a particular aspect of one's life. In looking at art from this perspective, we take into consideration the subject matter of the art, the scale of the art, whether it is a vertical or horizontal shape, the colors of the piece, and the material and color of the frame of a picture. Because this technique is a way for the occupants of a space to change their subconscious belief system and the resulting behavior, it is most effective when combined with the transcendental methods described in Chapter 9. This method is a form of "the power of positive thinking."

Let us consider several examples in which we used artwork to shift the energy of the individual.

June was having difficulty moving ahead in her life and was constantly talking about the "old days." On the wall, immediately visible in June's home as the front door opened, hung a picture of June as a young child playing the cello. The neck of the cello pointed toward the door, and it appeared as if June were looking out the door. The door was in the Path in Life section of the *Bagua*. This picture looked to the past in both the subject matter and the direction it led the viewer. June really wanted a picture of herself on this wall. By replacing the cello picture with a current and friendly image of herself that conveyed the sensation of going into her home, June not only got the impression of moving forward into her own life but also welcomed her visitors into her space.

Marianne, a young teenager, called me shortly before she was headed off to a national swim meet. Marianne was very open to the transcendental approach of Feng Shui, because we had already worked with success on her room. After discussing her goals, we looked at the Reputation area of her bedroom. Using red, the color of that *gua*, we placed a red velvet cloth on the wall above a shelf in the Reputation area. On the shelf, she placed several of her best swim meet trophies, and on the red cloth she hung some of her first-place medals. Her intent in focusing on these objects was to know that she was a winner. You can imagine her elation when she came in over 100 places higher than she was ranked before the meet.

In Eloise's law office, the bookcase in the Path in Life area of the *Bagua* was filled with photographs of her children. When I asked her if she would rather be at home than practicing law, she looked at me as if I were crazy and said, "Of course." I pointed out that she was communicating this message to herself and to everyone entering her office on a daily basis. Because her goal at work was to be a successful attorney, we moved the family pictures to the less conspicuous Family area and placed the mementoes of her legal successes in the Path in Life *gua*.

The use of this technique to help individuals, and even a company, to shift energy and empower themselves is limitless and well within the ability of any professional who focuses on the energy of artwork.

H. PLANTS AND LANDSCAPING

Although a discussion of plants and landscaping from the Feng Shui perspective deserves a book of its own, we feel it is appropriate to raise some landscape issues related to project design. Your client may ask for everything from landscaping an entrance area to creating a front yard, a side yard, a backyard, a meditation garden, a pool area, a play area, a classical garden, an English garden, or a Japanese garden. We have even worked with people on situating labyrinths, on locating burial sites, and on creating landscaped areas that paid homage to deceased children or friends, their ancestors, or their predecessors on the land, such as the Indians who came before them.

The plant world is a very large and important part of our planet. We often lose sight of the fact that the plant kingdom is much larger than the human community. When nature is left alone, there is a natural cycle of generation, destruction, and regeneration that supports our human existence in many ways. The Western medical profession is increasingly joining other cultures in using nature as a healing tool. When we build our physical spaces, we frequently replace nature with man-made structures. In the world of Feng Shui, we often introduce plants to help restore a natural balance to our environments. This may involve adding trees, shrubs, or other vegetation to the property around our structures or using plants or flowers in our spaces to bring the energy of nature indoors.

Because plants take in various elements of the atmosphere, the use of certain plants can be an effective method of purifying an interior space of some of the toxins that exist because of the use of chemicals and synthetic materials. Moving existing plants around in a space is also an easy way to change the energy and stimulate the flow of chi in the environment.

Some clients may express concern about the fact that although plants give off oxygen during the day, they are said to take oxygen from the air at night. This is probably the reason that some hospitals permit only cut flowers in patients' rooms. We would never recommend that a bedroom begin to look like a plant nursery but have never found that one or two plants in a bedroom have affected a client's sleep. If a client has sleeping issues and a multitude of plants in the bedroom, however, you might want to reduce the number of plants.

The Yin and Yang Energy of Plants

Plants vary considerably in the type of energy they communicate. The professional must be aware of the energy that a plant sends out by virtue of it size, shape, leaves, and other attributes. Is that energy consistent with the Primary Purpose of the location of the plant? An entrance area is usually intended to welcome people. Placing a large cactus with very sharp thorns adjacent to the front door is probably not the best message for the homeowner to be giving to either family or guests. Unless a warning is intended, a more gentle plant, such as a sweet-smelling, flowering jasmine from the same climate, would be a much more welcoming plant at the entrance. A separate cactus garden to display the wonderful variety of cacti could be placed away from high-traffic areas and add a wonderful visual element to the property without creating tension in people.

Locating Outdoor Plants

Begin with dead or empty corners or locations on the property as a general starting point for where to plant. Filling in these areas will make the whole of the property, which is a metaphor for the life of the people who occupy the space, feel more complete. You can also use the *Bagua* as a guideline in determining where to place a plant and what type of plant to use. For example, if a home is out of balance in that the male side, the side to the right of the front door, is weak, we might suggest placing a strong tree with white blossoms in the front right corner of the property. A tree will draw attention to the male side of the house and make it feel more prominent; the upward shape of the tree will enhance the male image; and the white flowers will be consistent with the color of Metal, the element of the *gua* to the right of the entrance.

However, if you use the *Bagua*, you must look at everything else that is going on in the immediate environment. For instance, if the front of the house is relatively close to the street, placing a tree in that location might block the view of the house from the outside and make that side appear hidden and even less significant, as well as prevent light from entering the home. In that situation, a large urn with upright growing plants, a lamp post, or other strong image on the right side of the property might be more appropriate than a tree. Place trees and bushes far enough from a building that they will not touch the structure when they reach maturity or that they will still retain an attractive shape after they are trimmed back from the structure. A tree or large bush that touches a building acts as a highway for insects and other animals to find their way into a structure and is also considered in Feng Shui to drain the energy from the house. In this case, the health of one of the occupants may be affected, and a further analysis of the individual and the *Bagua* might be appropriate.

Trees, shrubs, and flowers that attract birds and other wildlife increase the energy of a property and make it feel even more vibrant. Bird-feeders also attract this type of energy, provided they are always full. An empty feeder is a symbol of something that is not working as intended, frequently a metaphor for the life of the people who inhabit the space. As simple as it may sound, remind your clients that the full birdfeeder is an image of the fullness of their own life.

Cutting Plants

Trees and plants are living things and clearly a form of energy. We are all aware of the many studies in which plants react positively to calming music and to a person's gentle voice and react badly to being roughly treated. Extending this concept only slightly, Feng Shui approaches the cutting or destruction of a plant as a form of killing that at times may have a negative effect on the health of the person who has cut down a tree or branch that is more than three inches in diameter or ripped up a bush. The stories are legend. There are transcendental methods for these situations, but even if a person cannot go this far in their thinking, part of the process makes common sense. In cutting a plant, have respect for the living energy of the plant and think of its energy as going back into the soil. Once the tree has been cut down and the building erected, place new plants in the area to replace the calming color, oxygen production, and other energies that the plant world supplies.

Locating Indoor Plants

Because interior space is usually at a premium and passageways between objects are narrow, it is generally best to use plants that have an overall round shape and round leaves, such as a philodendron, so that a person does not feel threatened by sharp pointed leaves and feel the need to stay farther away from it. Softer shapes are generally more effective in balancing the excessive Metal energy of many spaces. The nature of the Wood element of plants will blunt the harshness of the Metal element. The Wood element in the form of plants can also be used metaphorically to feed the energy of the Fire, either in general or in a specific aspect of one's space, read as "one's life."

Plants are also a good way to fill a corner that feels empty and collects dead energy. The plant in the corner will give a room a rounder shape, making it feel more in compliance with the roundness of nature and therefore more comfortable. The containers for indoor plants can create a color balance in a space and utilize the Five Elements. A red vase may begin to balance a green room and at the same time add the spirit and enthusiasm of the Fire element. A black pot increases the energy of the Water element and causes the creative Wood element to become stronger.

Using the *Bagua* to Locate Plants

We have discussed several ways in which you can use the *Bagua* to enhance a particular aspect of your client's life. Plants are an easy way to accomplish some of these transcendental goals and improve the visual impact and energy of a space at the same time. Let's use the example of a client whose general health is not great. First, we would look to the center of the space, the Essence, perhaps in the bedroom because the subject matter is very personal. Although we have not included the topic in this book, each section of the *Bagua* is also associated with particular body parts and health conditions. If a client had a specific health problem, we would also ascertain the particular *gua* with which the illness was associated. By placing in the appropriate *gua* a live, very green plant that conveys an image of being full and healthy, we have given the person a metaphor that the person can use to envision thriving health. We strongly recommend using the procedure described in Chapter 9. As people take care of a plant, they are psychologically nurturing themselves at the same time. Does the plant heal the person? Of course not. But because the plant is a thriving image, the people have begun to think of themselves as healing, as opposed to being ill. Even modern Western medicine recognizes the power of positive imaging in the healing process. The same psychological shift can occur in any aspect of a client's life, and the *Bagua* is a powerful tool in accessing that positive shift in behavior.

The Care of Plants

Because we are using plants to provide life, color, and other energy to our environment, it is extremely important that we keep plants healthy and thriving. This should seem obvious, but I have often found dead plants and plants with dead leaves in clients' homes. Immediately prune dead leaves and remove dead plants and flowers. If they have chosen a plant that is appropriate for the light conditions in a particular location, clients should not blame a dying plant on the lack of a green thumb. The plant has taken negative energy from the environment and has served its purpose. However, it is important to realize that the plant may not have been large enough or of the proper type for the space and its particular problem. With this in mind, replace the plant with one that is larger or is a more appropriate type for the needs of the space.

Cut Flowers and Silk Plants

Cut flowers are a wonderful way to add energy to a space, divert attention in a particular direction, and bring a color balance to the space, even to the point of completing the full color spectrum.

A common question is, "What about silk plants?" In view of the fact that the quality of silk plants has improved and they are often indistinguishable from live plants, they are frequently the best option. If a person travels a great deal and cannot tend to plants on a regular basis, or if the plant is to go in a dark area, it is better to add the color energy and image of a silk plant than to have a dying plant or nothing at all. The silk plant clearly will not remove the toxins from the air or smell as sweet as a live plant, but it will add color energy to a space and create an illusion of nature.

Dried Flowers

Avoid using dried flower and plant arrangements. Because these have generally lost their color and connote death and dying, they are highly inappropriate for most spaces. Clients often keep a bouquet or arrangement that reminds them of a person or past event. When the arrangement becomes dried and brittle, it is time to replace it with a more vibrant energy that is related to the present and not the past. The only time it is appropriate to have dried flowers in a space is when the flowers contain a strong energy because of their vibrant color or a strong smell. Once the color has begun to fade or the odor to disappear, remove the dried arrangement and replace it with something more lively.

I. WATER FEATURES

Water is critical for survival. The human body is 75 percent water, and we cannot live without it. Water is necessary to raise crops and animals, and throughout the centuries, civilizations have risen and fallen because of water's effect on commerce, defense, and other aspects of life. Every capital in the United States and every major city in the world is located on water. Because plentiful water signifies thriving commerce, it is not surprising that water has become a metaphor for success and prosperity. Water has a great deal of personal psychological significance to us, running the gamut from the fluid that was our initial source of existence, to our daily sustenance, to the source of economic success, to the lake or pool that is a place just to have fun. Water features, therefore, are a design tool that can add a sense of vital energy to a property or space. The best siting of a building in relationship to water and the specific placement of a water feature can add or detract from the image that people have of themselves and convey to others. Water features can also be used to enhance people's lives through the use of the *Bagua* or to create a better balance of the Five Elements of a space.

Siting a Building on Water

When a town is built near water, it always "faces" the water. Although the town center may have grown away from the water over the years, it undoubtedly began on the water's edge. There are numerous practical and psychological reasons for this. Feng Shui tradition teaches that facing the water and having the higher, or "mountain," image supporting your back is always better than facing away from the water. Turning a building around and having the land fall away behind you to the water creates a sense of vulnerability and lack of support. A view of the water also tends to be very calming, giving a sense of peace and connectedness with many different aspects of existence. In siting a building, try to place the primary entrance facing the water. As you approach the entry, you will feel yourself rising, a stronger feeling and image than walking down to arrive at your destination. Remember that castles were always located above the subjects' home in a Commanding Position. In addition, as you leave the home or office building, having the water in front and walking down toward the water will create a more comfortable and powerful sensation. The occupants will feel in control of the world that lies before them. A common problem with houses or offices located near water is that the road leading up to the site is often on one side of the building and the water is on the other side with the structure in between. In this case, the front door is often on the road or upper side of the building. This requires one to go down (sinking) in entering and to move up (climbing) when leaving, contrary to the ideal scenario. If possible, plan the approach in such a way that the main entrance to the space is from the water's side.

Having said this, there can be situations in which this principle conflicts with the concept we discussed in Chapter 2, Section C: Commanding Position. The Commanding Position would dictate that the front of a building should face the principal flow of energy so that the occupants will feel in control of the energy coming in their direction. Consider this principle when situating a building on water that is approached by a road on the other side. Feel the force of the two energies and place the entrance on the side of the greater flow of energy.

Consider these two extreme examples:

1. If a meandering country lane is on the upper side of the structure and a large lake or river is on the other, locate the main entrance on the more powerful water side.
2. If a major highway is on one side of the building and a creek is on the other, the front door will feel better on the roadside, facing the predominant flow of energy.

If there were no way to plan the space to accommodate both the Facing the Water and the Commanding Position concepts, we would give the Commanding Position the primary importance.

Locating a Water Feature at the Main Entrance

Because very few of us have the luxury of actually building on water, we can create the impression that the client is facing this psychologically powerful form of energy by placing a water feature in front of the main entrance. See Figure 3.17. The size, intensity, and motion of this outdoor feature will be an important metaphor for the activity inside the space. For example, a three-foot pool of inactive water in front of an office building will convey an insignificant and stagnant company image. A nine-foot pool with an active fountain that sends the water upward in a powerful, but controlled, flow of energy creates a dynamic business image. The scale of the water feature should be proportionate to the building and send the message that the occupants want to communicate to themselves and others about who they are and what is occurring inside their space.

FIGURE 3.17 *Water and Building Entrances*

Building Entrance with powerful Lake, River or Ocean

Building Entrance with powerful Road Energy.

Using the *Bagua* to Place a Water Feature

In applying the *Bagua* to a property or building, the Water element is an attribute of the Path in Life area. In addition, the Wood element, which is nurtured by Water, is one of the attributes of the *guas* of New Beginnings/Family and of Prosperity. These three areas are delineated in Figure 3.18. Placing a water feature in one or more of these sections can be an effective way to enhance the subconscious belief and behavior of the occupants in these areas of their life. However, using Water in one of the other *guas* may create a negative impact, because Water puts out the energy of the Fire in the Reputation gua, muddies the Earth element of the Primary Relationship, Essence, and Self-Knowledge sections, and drains the energy of the Metal of the Completion/Children and Helpful People areas.

FIGURE 3.18 *Bagua Water*

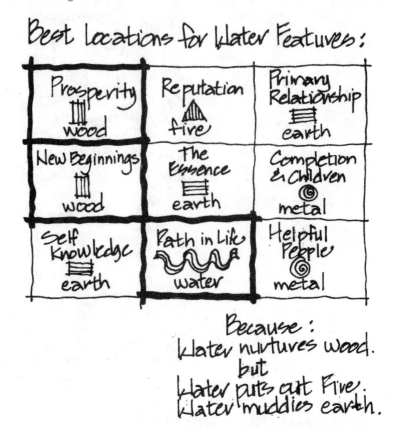

Best Locations for Water Features:

Prosperity ⫿ wood	Reputation ◮ fire	Primary Relationship ☰ earth
New Beginnings ⫿ wood	The Essence ☰ earth	Completion & Children ◎ metal
Self Knowledge ☰ earth	Path in Life 〜〜 water	Helpful People ◎ metal

Because:
Water nurtures wood.
but
Water puts out Fire.
Water muddies earth.

Path in Life *Gua*. If locating a water feature in front of the main entrance to a space is not possible, an indoor water fountain inside the entry can enhance the flow of the occupants' life and give them the sense they are moving forward in a clear and smooth direction in their Path in Life. If there is no room for a fountain in a tight entry, a picture of water that is visible as one leaves the space can be used to create the same feeling: The occupants are part of the successful flow of commerce out into the world. Be very aware of the content of the picture. A photograph of rapids will convey an image of a very rocky future in the world, whereas a powerful, but steady and unthreatening, stream will give the viewer a sense of power without apprehension. Let the clients select the picture. It is their space, and they must feel comfortable with the image. Using a black Metal frame on the picture may further enhance this image, because the Metal element creates Water and black is the color of Water and is associated with the Path in Life *gua*.

New Beginnings/Family *Gua*. When a client desires to focus on New Beginnings or Family, a water feature in this *gua* presents an opportunity for nurturing the young Wood of this section and enhancing this part of life. The appropriate image of water in this context is not one of a strong flow into the world, which would be suitable in one's Path in Life area, but one that gently nurtures the growth of the new shoots and young plants of spring (New Beginnings) and of one's Family. If a picture of water is used instead of a fountain, the picture could be framed in green wood to continue to use some of the other images associated with this *gua*.

Prosperity *Gua*. Because water is a metaphor for money, placing a fountain or an aquarium in the Prosperity *gua* is a way for an individual to activate a feeling of personal richness. The water feature should represent the type of energy that could enhance one's prosperity. A fountain that is still or merely dribbles may convey a feeling of inertness and lack of energy. A fountain where the water splashes over the edges may feel as if the person's life in this area is out of control. In an aquarium, the traditional fish to use are goldfish, with eight reddish gold and one black fish or two reddish gold and one black fish. The numbers are considered auspicious, nine being the most complete number and three representing the triumvirate of heaven, human, and earth. Gold is a metaphor for wealth and black is the color of the Path in Life. The combination represents success.

In the same way we have discussed above, a picture with an appropriate subject can also be used to enhance the feeling of Prosperity or Abundance. In this *gua*, a burgundy-colored, wooden frame would continue the element and color images associated with the Prosperity *gua*.

Bagua Locations for Water "Rooms" and Pools

Where is the best place for a swimming pool, hot tub, or rooms that contain water features, such as a bathroom or laundry room? A pool or hot tub is usually located at the back of a lot in the more private portion of the property. Keep in mind the elements that are related to each of these back sections of the *Bagua*. Placing the pool or hot tub in the Prosperity *gua* would feel the most auspicious, because the Water can be viewed as feeding the Wood image of that area. A pool or hot tub should not be placed in the Reputation area, where the Water puts out the Fire, or in the Relationship section, where the Water muddies the Earth.

This same approach, however, cannot be followed in connection with the placement of a bathroom or laundry room in the Prosperity *gua*. Even though no great sense of dynamic energy is found in the outdoor pool or hot tub, the water, read "prosperity," is being circulated on a regular basis as part of the system's mechanism. Indoors, however, the water in the bathroom and laundry room is leaving the building. Because water is a metaphor for prosperity, this symbolizes the owners' money literally going down the drain. Although we talked about placing a fountain in the Path in Life section, locating a water room in this area is considered to be an excess of refuse water that is going down rather than useful water that is flowing into the world of commerce. Another location that is not considered a good one for the water rooms is the center, or *Essence*, of a home. Having an excess of any type of energy in the center, whether Fire or Water, is felt to be too extreme, possibly resulting in an imbalance in the life, and particularly in the health, of the residents. So where should the water rooms in a house be placed? The traditional Feng Shui placement for these facilities is in an area that bridges two *guas* with different elements, as shown in Figure 3.19. The concept is that this placement will avoid the water's impacting completely any one specific *gua* or element. Area A bridges Earth and Wood, and Area B bridges Earth and Metal. Try to avoid the Reputation area, because the Water will extinguish the Fire. Each of the other pairs of *guas* that are adjacent to one another includes the same Element, and the escaping Water may throw those Elements out of balance. Because Area A is in the more public, forward area of the house, a more public facility, such as a powder room or shared bathroom, would feel better in this location, and a master bathroom would psychologically feel more private in Area B.

Adding Water Features to Balance the Five Elements

When an individual or business is out of balance, with either too much or too little of the Water Element, the use of water features or images can be used to add a balancing effect. The professional must determine what type of water energy is needed before guiding the client. If the existing energy is excessive, as in a kindergarten classroom, a calm lake with ducks would be a balancing image. If the client wants to improve the ability to interact with the outside world, such as a research scientist who wants to market a product, a strong and controlled river scene would convey the image of an easier, more fluid interchange with the world.

The Yin and Yang Energy of a Water Feature

We have discussed different types of water energies and specific placements. In general, the motion and sound of most water features will add yang energy. A picture of a water feature will add some water energy but will obviously not give the actual sensations of motion and sound. If a space is too yin, the addition of a water fountain may add yang energy for balance. It is possible that a large fountain with too much noise may be too yang for a space. As with any design choice, the scale of the water feature should be appropriate for the space and support the client's intention, conveying the desired psychological image of the occupants and their life or work.

FIGURE 3.19 *Water Features*

4

GUIDELINES FOR SITE SELECTION

A. GENERAL GUIDELINES

"Location, location, location." Although everyone in the real estate business is familiar with that phrase, I never realized the extent of its significance until Feng Shui expanded my knowledge. Ideally, we are involved in reviewing various properties during the site selection process to anticipate potential issues, helping to save time, effort, and money and increasing the potential for success. This process would apply to land for a new building site, as well as an existing building, facility, office space, residence, or apartment that the client wants to rent or purchase. As always, the analysis of various sites will be based on what we have learned during the information-gathering meeting about the client and the Primary Purpose of the building or space. In that context, here are some of the issues we consider.

The Energy of the Surrounding Area

A traditional Feng Shui analysis of a building location might look at the topography of the surrounding area and describe the specific site as a positive or negative part of an animal or natural feature. The site might be called the eye of a dragon, the muscle of a clam, or the nose of a tiger. Although these references are metaphors for the energy of the site, they are unfamiliar in our culture, and you will be more comfortable with a logical analysis of a site's energy.

The approach to a site and the neighborhood in which it is located begins to establish a psychological image of the destination. Often without our realizing it, our state of mind has been altered as we near the property. If we have gone through a beautiful pastoral countryside, we will enter the site itself in a very different mood than we would if we had just walked through an industrial area or down a very crowded street. Even the method we use to arrive, whether by car, foot, or snowshoes, affects us.

Be aware of the environment as you approach. What is the nature of the energy of the land? How does it feel to you? Do not be lured into a false sense of peace but be aware of *every* nuance. Just because the property is in the country does not necessarily make it peaceful. We recently reviewed a parcel of vacant land in a beautiful hilly area as a potential building site, and the property felt as if a devastating force had gone through and killed much of the vegetation. The soil was wet and hard, and the energy of the land was very low, even though we were on a hillside. The client puzzled, "This land doesn't feel very good. It feels sad." Adjacent to the parcel was a small cemetery.

Chapter 1, Table 1.1, lists some of the elements on which you may want to focus. The surrounding environment sets the tone for a particular site that your client is considering. In addition to noting the psychological impression that the neighborhood will have on residents, employees, clients, and customers, you will want to analyze whether the energy of the area is very yin, very yang, or in balance. If the energy of an area is yin or too low for the prospective use by the client, this issue should be addressed. Envision having a residence surrounded by a church on one side, a school on the other, and a cemetery across the street. A number of issues are at work here, but the basic one is that all of these man-made sites will be empty most of the time the house is occupied, surrounding the home with very yin, low, energy. Even when these neighboring areas are occupied, their energies will not be compatible with the Primary Purpose of the residence. On the other hand, large and "threatening" structures or objects can create a feeling of too much hostile or overwhelming yang energy. An old, dark, large bridge that looms over an apartment building will create an uneasy feeling in the residents, and the sharp corner of a nearby building or a major road that is aimed directly at an office building will disturb the productivity of the employees.

Roads are a major source of energy for a property. Unless the site is being chosen as a hideaway, most buildings should be located so that the maximum amount of energy is coming in the direction of the site. For instance, if a building is facing a one-way road that is taking energy toward the town, then it is not bringing energy from the town toward the building. An example is the office building in Figure 4.1, which is surrounded by three one-way streets. When the building was built, the original front entrance was in Area A. Note the directions of the traffic. The two streets on the Area A side of the building come from the main sources of energy in the town and are both aimed toward the entrance, whereas the traffic on the two streets on the Area B side is moving away from the building. When new owners purchased the building, they moved the main entrance from Area A to Area B. Very soon thereafter, the fortunes of the building took a downturn, reflecting the fact that the primary energy was now moving away from the site. As strange as this occurrence may seem, it is not unusual and should be considered as part of the overall review of a property.

FIGURE 4.1 *Traffic Area*

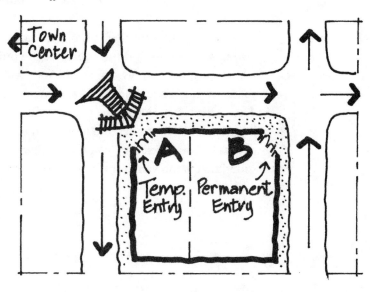

The Direction of the Flow of Energy to and from the Property

The eight road configurations shown in Figure 4.2 influence the same office building positively or negatively as they either bring energy toward the property or lead energy away from the property.

1. Roads go straight by the building and bring energy to the property from both directions, a very positive energy flow.
2. Roads curve around the building, creating the feeling that the energy encompasses the structure, the most auspicious energy flow.
3. Roads curve toward the building and appear to bring the energy toward the building, but then take the energy away.
4. Roads approach the building head-on at the T-intersection and are confrontational, bringing energy too forcefully to the property.
5. Roads create a Y-intersection in which the building is in the crux of the Y, giving the feeling that the energy comes too forcefully toward the building and then bypasses it.
6. The building is on a cul-de-sac where the energy is low or, depending upon the location on the cul-de-sac, is confrontational.
7. The building is on a dead-end street where the energy is stagnant and building is on a one-way street that sends only half of the road's energy moving toward the building or away from it.

Access roads or driveways on the sides or back of a building may also have an impact on the energy of the building. These avenues may add a sense that energy can escape too easily from the building. If the roads are busy, a feeling of chaotic energy may surround the property. The "private" spaces in the Commanding Position at the back of the building may feel vulnerable if exposed to the energy of an active back street. Although roads bring positive energy to a site, they can also bring sound that is too yang for the property's Primary Purpose.

FIGURE 4.2 *Eight Roads*

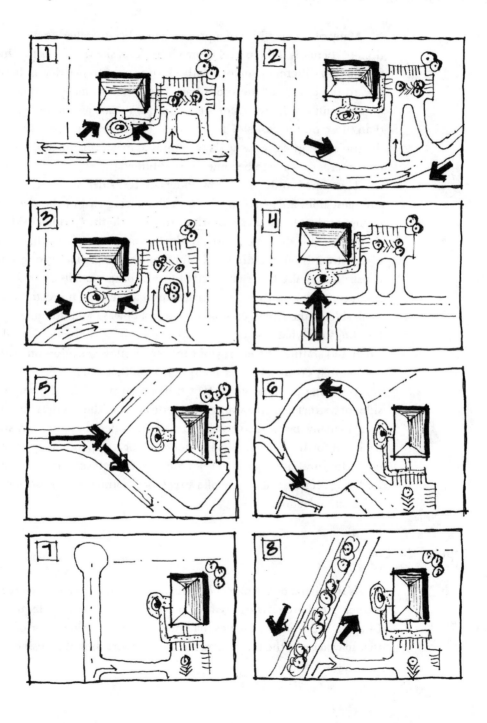

The Orientation of the Building

Many of the qualities of a property may be attributed to its orientation, particularly if the parcel is on a hillside. A site that faces northwest will be very different from one with a southeast entrance that is directed toward the energy of the sun. I have found that in many instances the houses built on the west side of a lake facing east are more expensive than those on the east side facing west. The western properties receive the sun's energy early in the day as opposed to later in the day, when human energy is ready to become more subdued.

The same is often true of buildings on two sides of a road. The two strongest sides are generally the west side facing east or the north side facing south. The Chinese call the stronger side the "mother" side and the weaker side the "child" side. In the business area of a town, one side of the street is often more successful than the other. The strong side of the street may also be determined by factors other than its direction. For instance, a new and very tall structure may have been erected on the weak side of the street, completely overshadowing and dominating the buildings on what was once the stronger, more energetic side of the street and shifting the energy of the area. A subway exit on one side of a street may create a greater energy flow on that side.

Watching the amount of foot traffic that passes by the respective sides of a street can give a very good indication of the energy flow in the area. In many towns, the stronger and weaker sides of a street may switch back and forth as one goes from block to block, depending upon inherent factors and subsequent development. Although you can compensate for being on the weaker side of a street, positioning is an important factor in site selection.

The Shape of the Lot

Is the shape of the parcel on which the building is located a regular shape? Are there missing areas or projections? As we have discussed in Chapter 3, Section B: Shapes, irregularity can be a precursor of issues that may arise in the life of a resident or the fortunes of a business.

The Topography of the Lot

Is the property located on the downward-sloping side of a street, creating the feeling that the property and the people occupying the space are less important than those on the upward side of the street? Does the property fall off at the back, creating a feeling of a lack of support? These answers establish the image the land is communicating to the subconscious about the importance of the occupants and the support and protection they will have. Similarly, if a building is located above others on a hill, it will feel more powerful and convey the image that the occupants are more important than those below. However, if the structure is sitting on top of the hill and is unsupported at the back, the inhabitants may feel vulnerable. The preferred location is generally on the upside of a road and partway up the hill with the support of the hill at the back of the structure. In traditional Feng Shui, there ideally would be smaller hills to the left and right of the building to create a "protective armchair." In our urban culture, smaller structures on either side of your client's building would create a similar image. See Figure 4.3.

The Shape and Height of the Building

Does the building have a regular shape? As we discussed in Chapter 3, Section B: Shapes, missing sections from the basic structure may predict possible issues that will affect certain aspects of the occupants' life or the future of a business. Using the *Bagua* as a tool to determine vulnerable areas may lead the client to select another property.

If the building under consideration is lower in height than the buildings on either side, it immediately communicates that the people

Tools to Raise a Building's Low Image
- Design a structure that creates the image of upward movement.
- Use the Five Elements to select colors for the elevations in relationship to the buildings in the neighborhood.
- Raise the energy of the property with flags or upward lighting on the rooftop.

FIGURE 4.3 *Topography*

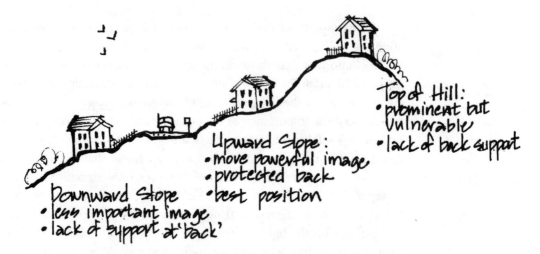

Top of Hill:
• prominent but vulnerable
• lack of back support

Upward Slope:
• more powerful image
• protected back
• best position

Downward Slope
• less important image
• lack of support at 'back'

or business is less important or prestigious than their neighbors. Although this lower image can be overcome by the following techniques, your client should be told of the potential problem.

The Arrangement of Rooms

Are the rooms within the structure arranged in a way that creates a natural flow of energy from one space to another and from one purpose to the next in a logical manner? Are the more private spaces, such as the CEO's office or the master bedroom, in the more distant, private areas of the structure that reinforce their Primary Purpose, or are they in the public areas near the main entrance? It is possible that in your client's particular business, it is important for the CEO to be "out front," in which case that office by the front door is exactly what the client wants.

The Arrangement of Furniture

Is the layout of the rooms conducive to arranging the furniture so that the residents or employees can be in the Commanding Position and be the most productive? Even though we can always compensate for designs that are not optimal for the Primary Purpose of a space, being aware of the potential issues helps the client make a more informed decision.

The Previous Owners or Occupants

The history of the prior owners or occupants of a building or space is often a dramatic clue to the problem areas of the environment or of a particular building.

I have consulted on a number of cases in which the property's history was rather dramatic. In one instance, the prior two owners had become seriously ill within a year of moving into the house. In another, the last three couples that had lived in the residence had gotten divorced. In a third, the three previous occupants of the home had experienced serious financial difficulties, even bankruptcy. In one major office building, a succession of tenants repeatedly had financial problems. How often have we all seen the tenants in that one retail location on the block turn over after the free rent period has ended? That location undoubtedly has poor Feng Shui as well as a buildup of negative energy from a succession of failed businesses. In all of these cases, the poor Feng Shui can be identified and remedied and the negative energies cleared, but clients may be well advised to select a more beneficial site.

In an office building, you may find that the turnover rate of the tenants in certain spaces is much higher than the average rate of turnover for the building or the industry as a whole. Usually an aspect of the space or its immediately surrounding area indicates the reason for the frequent change. In addition to the physical problems with the environment, a negative residue of failing energy from a prior business may permeate the space. Both of these situations can be dealt with if the client decides to occupy the space despite these concerns. On the other hand, if turnover has been because tenants consistently have outgrown the space, this would be a positive factor.

In an office complex, you frequently find that the turnover rate in a small number of offices is much higher than the average rate of turnover for the company. This is generally not the consequence of the losers being relegated to a bad office. Something in the individual office or the surrounding area invariably indicates the reason for the frequent change. If the turnover is the result of the occupants' being promoted, you may want to repeat the elements that have created the positive environment. Otherwise, it may be time to correct the problems within the space.

In reviewing the history of the predecessors in a space, as well as in the properties in the neighborhood, we will probe, to the extent possible, into the following conditions that may cause predecessor energy issues, realizing that some of these questions may be rather delicate ones.

- Health, illness, or death
- Marital relationship
- Size of family or company
- Family or business relationships
- Prosperity or financial problems
- Business successes or failures
- Upward or downward mobility
- Duration of ownership or occupancy
- Other

In addition to these issues, we are always aware of possible historical factors that do not fall into one of these categories. These points are not necessarily negative ones. If a family or company is moving because they have been successful and outgrown a space, the energy is undoubtedly positive. Be conscious of everything that you see. The most important aspect of the space may be something that is not on this list.

B. RESIDENTIAL SITE SELECTION GUIDELINES

Purchasing a house or renting an apartment is an important decision in everyone's life. Do not wait until you are inside a space before you begin to feel what is happening in the environment.

Be aware of the neighborhood as you approach the potential home. Observe the nature of the properties in the area, especially those directly on either side, in back, and in front of the house or apartment building. Listen to the sounds around you. Are there birds and other animals? Wildlife is attracted to areas with good energy. Be aware of all of the sensations you experience as you approach the site. Are they energies that will benefit the client? Consider the direction from which you would be approaching your home on a regular basis, and focus on what you will see that will be affecting your energy.

A positive example is the approach to my apartment in New York that is two-thirds of the way down a block. As I enter the block, the first building that greets me is a florist shop that always has beautiful windows. The displays range from exotic orchids fancifully arranged on antique wooden school desks to groups of small pigs, puppies, rabbits, or other adorable live creatures. The windows never fail to stop me for a moment and bring a smile to my face and lightness to my soul, no matter how overwhelming the day has been. This same florist has planted flowers around the trees that line the street, adding life and color to the "path" that leads me home. My well-kept front door and a friendly doorman add to the feeling: "I'm glad to be coming home."

A house in a suburban neighborhood has the same issues. You probably arrive by car. Is the street wide and lined with trees that give you the feeling of being in a natural setting? Or is the road narrow and lined with parked cars that make you feel tense as you swing your car wide to navigate the narrow entrance into the driveway? Is the road filled with potholes, conveying the image of a rundown neighborhood? The important point is to be sensitive to your feelings as you approach the site. After you have approached the area several times, you will begin to block out the elements that affect you in a negative way. Remember, however, those elements have not disappeared. You have shoved them into your subconscious. They will continue to affect you. The easiest time to spot these environmental issues is during the first few visits when you are not familiar with the neighborhood.

As you leave your car and approach the house, be aware of everything you feel and see. Is the vegetation flourishing? Are there signs of decay and peeling paint? Are there burned-out light bulbs or broken objects? Although these may be indications of sloppy housekeeping, they may tell you something about the energy, or lack thereof, in the property. These signs may also be clues to other aspects of the environment. If you or the client has a dog or an infant, take one with you to the potential home prior to signing a contract or lease. Animals are very sensitive to the energies in their environment. How often have we seen an animal growl at something unseen or unheard by us or seen a dog dash to the door and growl long before we are aware of any external noise or presence? If you are very tense when you enter a room in which there is an animal, the animal will pick up on the energy emanating from you and react accordingly.

Similarly, if you a take a dog into an unfamiliar home, the dog may pick up on energies of which you may not be consciously aware. If the dog does not want to go into the house or apartment, or if the dog growls at something once inside the space, assume that the animal has sensed an unseen energy, and trust your animal's instincts. A young child also has sensitive instincts that may reveal a certain type of energy. Young children have not yet been "educated" to distrust their instincts. Do not tell the crying child to be quiet, but watch how the child reacts as you go through the house. Notice whether the child reacts differently in various parts of the space. Oh, yes. Please feed and change the baby before you visit the home. You want to have your barometer as peaceful as possible!

Be aware of the position of the building with respect to the view, as well as the view from the particular apartment that is being considered. A view of a light shaft will diminish your self-esteem, whereas a view over a park, trees, or other natural features will bring a greater sense of balance and raise your self-image. The floor on which an apartment is located also has an impact on you. The apartment on the ninth floor will make you feel more important than one on the lower floors.

Avoid using a very yin basement space for any activity other than a temporary one that is accompanied with high energy, such as a family room. A basement will not have the appropriate energy for a home office or bedroom. Be very aware of bedrooms that are built over garages. Because a garage is void of human activity and is usually filled with objects that are primarily metal, they are very yin spaces that contain non-human energy. We frequently find that a person whose bedroom is over a garage has health problems. Plan to use this room as you would a basement for high-energy activities like those in a family room or for nonregular occurrences, such as a guest room.

C. BUSINESS SITE SELECTION GUIDELINES

The building entrance and lobby areas communicate a strong message about the tenants in the building to the staff and clients. As we discussed in Chapter 3, Section F: Signage, the exterior signage for the building and the interior signage for the tenants convey an image about the strength and success of your client's business.

Be aware of the floor on which the business will be located and which companies are above your client's prospective space. These facts may impact the client's self-esteem. For example, if your law firm client is leasing three floors beneath a five-floor law firm, your client's employees and clients may feel that your client is not as good as the larger firm on the higher floor. Being the largest tenant in the building or being above the competition conveys the opposite impression.

If the entrance to the reception area of the business is in the middle of the floor plate, a common occurrence in high-rise office buildings, a large percentage of the personnel will be "outside the door wall." See Figure 4.4. This building feature should be mentioned to your client, because this can lead to non-business-related activities being carried out by those employees who are outside the door wall. It can also result in those employees leaving the company sooner than might be expected or desired. See Figure 4.4 for a comparison of two office spaces, one where the majority of the firm is inside the door wall and the other where most of the firm is outside the door wall. We will discuss this issue in greater detail in Chapter 7, Section B: Office Buildings.

The site selection guidelines in this chapter will benefit all types of projects and clients by focusing in advance on issues that will impact your client's success. The energy of the neighborhood, the direction of the flow of energy to or from the property, the history of the prior owners and occupants, and the other issues we have discussed are factors that clients may not think to consider in their deliberations. Although the cost of the property or the lease rate is critical, the actual cost to your client will be greatly increased if the property is not energetically conducive to a satisfying residence or a successful business experience and needs to be dramatically altered to make it as productive as possible.

FIGURE 4.4 *Corporate Office Door Wall Examples*

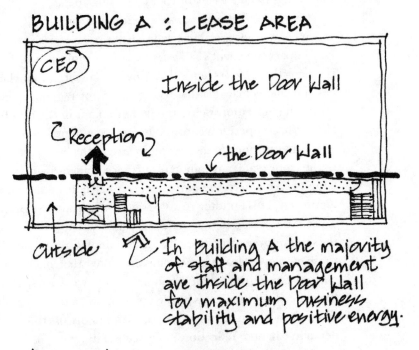

BUILDING A : LEASE AREA

CEO

Inside the Door Wall

Reception

the Door Wall

Outside

In Building A the majority of staff and management are Inside the Door Wall for maximum business stability and positive energy.

BUILDING B: LEASE AREA

Inside   Reception   the Door Wall

Outside the Door Wall

CEO

5

AN INTRODUCTION TO FENG SHUI SOLUTIONS FOR ARCHITECTURAL AND DESIGN PROJECTS

We have discussed some of the principles and design elements involved in incorporating Feng Shui into your project designs; and in the next chapters we will apply those elements to different project types, from single-family residences to office buildings. Feng Shui solutions are applicable to all project types because successful businesses of every kind strive to present a consistent image to the world through their name, logo, signage, Web site, and office design. This message reinforces the company's particular purpose and goal. With increasing competition in the marketplace, it is important for businesses to use every tool at their disposal to enhance their properties, including Feng Shui.

A. INFORMATION GATHERING

During this process, you learn about your client's history, existing facilities, operational needs, business goals, and corporate image before you begin a schematic design. An analysis of the company's current space and its existing issues often provides useful information about the psychological state of the company and its employees. This process often requires a great deal of very careful listening to what is *not* being said verbally. "Listen" to the body language and the facial expressions. Do not hesitate to ask questions, but do so in a sensitive manner that will continue the dialog, not turn it off. The information you obtain drives everything that follows. The primary goal of Feng Shui is not to create a dramatic space that will photograph well for a brochure or Web site but to create a space that will do the following:

- Maximize the personal and professional potential of everyone in the company
- Enhance the experience of customers, guests, patients, and others
- Retain employees and lower absenteeism
- Improve the company's financial position

A design that accomplishes these goals will produce a happy and successful client, who will undoubtedly ask you to design its next project and will refer you to others.

During the information-gathering phase, some businesses focus primarily on features that will impress their clients, although an increasing number of firms acknowledge that keeping and attracting good employees is their top priority. In most cases, emphasis should be placed on the employees and how they interact with one another, because the company's people are its most important asset. If the employees are not "comfortable" and as free from stress as possible, they will not produce up to their capacity, and your clients will not be as successful as they could be.

The information-gathering meeting is the time to ask your clients about the type of energy they want in each space. What is the Primary Purpose of each area, and do they want that space to be creative, stimulating, peaceful, or something else? Designers normally ask about the function of a room but often do not consider the best way to create the desired type of energy for the space. The energy of each area can enhance its Primary Purpose through particular choices of colors, shapes, materials, and other features. Remember that every employee, from CEO to mailroom clerk, contributes to a company's success. When the environment keeps employees in a good place psychologically, productivity will be higher, the turnover rate and absenteeism will be lower, clients will be more satisfied, and the result will be a substantial addition to the company's bottom line. The role of Feng Shui is to help create a space that will maximize each person's contribution and experience.

B. METAPHORS

Every aspect of your design is a metaphor, and every choice should be consistent with the Primary Purpose of the space. During the design process, take a step back to look at the subconscious psychological metaphor that you have created and eliminate choices that are not consistent with that Purpose. Consider these examples.

- A reception desk sits beneath colorful banners that hang from wooden rods and look like axes suspended over the receptionist's head—not a positive "reception" into a building.
- A two-story hospital atrium has dramatic exposed trusses that appear to be sharply pointed swords and glass shards hanging over the patients waiting to be admitted, like many swords of Damocles.
- In an office building lobby, the paving pattern design includes accent bands running perpendicularly to the desired traffic flow, saying, "Stop!" rather than running parallel to and reinforcing the flow of energy toward the elevators.

In each of these instances, the architectural elements create a metaphor that runs counter to the desired intent. Step back and evaluate how each aspect of your design will function on the occupants' subconscious mind and whether the choices you have made will create the best design for the well-being of the occupants.

C. CHECKLISTS: SITE PLANNING AND SCHEMATIC DESIGN

Before we begin to analyze individual types of facilities, and at the risk of oversimplifying, we will summarize a few of the basic Feng Shui guidelines we have previously discussed that are applicable to all project types. Remember that these are guidelines. You may well have strong reasons for going in a different direction, but be certain that the reason will enhance the Primary Purpose of the space for the goals of the client. In Addition, you will often find that the following guidelines will save money. No matter what choices you make, be certain to "live" in the space, experiencing all of the sensations that people will have when they approach, enter, and occupy the environment you create.

Site Planning Checklist

❏ Be aware of traffic patterns and energy flow and position the buildings to receive the best energy.
❏ Locate the building above the road, if possible.
❏ Avoid missing areas on the property or in the buildings.
❏ Locate the building entrance facing the most important and energetic roadway or water feature.
❏ Use regular and complete shapes for the building outline, preferably the Golden Rectangle.
❏ Raise the energy of the building as much as possible with color, lighting, and other architectural features.

Schematic Design Checklist

❏ Use regular and complete shapes for floors, departments, housing units, and rooms, preferably the Golden Rectangle. Although non-orthogonal structures may look more interesting from the outside, they inevitably create problems for the occupants of the building. The interest quotient can be supplied instead by porches, projecting entrances, decorative facades, landscaping, and other design elements.
❏ Place the main entrance of the building in the center to create a feeling of balance.
❏ Be aware of the impact of the first view upon entering a building, residence, or office space. Avoid a view of a bathroom, bedroom, or kitchen.
❏ Create entrances that are open and visually clear and that direct you to your destination, whether to a living room, a reception desk, or an elevator.

❏ Locate the public spaces of the residence or business in the front portion of the structure and the more private or intimate activities farthest from the entrance.

❏ Locate only nonessential functions "outside the door wall."

❏ Avoid having columns and other protruding or blocking elements inside entrances, corridors, or rooms.

❏ Create corridors that are wide enough for two people to pass one another without any sense of contact but are not long enough to make you feel you are in a tunnel, which creates a sense of speed and pressure.

❏ "Curve" straight corridors and features as much as possible with artwork, furniture, light sconces, and other architectural details.

❏ Use closed risers on all staircases and do not center stairs on the entry door.

❏ Do not plan doors or workstations at the end of long corridors.

❏ Provide right-handed doors where possible.

❏ Be aware of the effect of the placement of doors in relationship to one another and to partial or blocking walls.

❏ Design all spaces and their furniture layout with the Commanding Position in relation to the room and, if possible, to the main entrance.

❏ Do not locate the bathroom against a kitchen wall or a headboard wall of a bedroom.

❏ Avoid having any door open directly on to the side or foot of a bed.

❏ Avoid locating a door directly opposite windows.

❏ Avoid angled walls, sloped ceilings, and overhead beams in standard height ceilings.

❏ Specify a dark floor color value, medium wall and furniture color values, and a light ceiling color value.

❏ Select materials and finishes with the Primary Purpose in mind.

❏ Whenever possible, use natural and sustainable materials. From a Feng Shui prospective, these materials will create an environment that contains fewer toxins and is more balanced and more comfortable.

These guidelines are based on principles whose goal is human comfort and lower stress. Now let's take a look at specific types of projects.

6

RESIDENTIAL PROJECTS

A. SINGLE FAMILY RESIDENCES

A person's home has a tremendous impact on the person's psychological, physiological, and behavioral conditions and attitudes. Home is where we relax, nourish ourselves, rest, propagate, and often work, and every design choice should enhance these activities. The professional's responsibility is to be aware of the impact these choices will have on the residents and to make decisions and recommendations that will improve their lives. If you create a space for a particular client, the information-gathering phase is a critical part of the design process. If the residence is on spec or part of a development, following general guidelines will increase the possibility that the home will be a positive experience for its future occupants. We assume in this chapter that you will incorporate the concepts discussed in Chapter 3. Underlying every choice should be an awareness of the Primary Purpose of that particular space and the intention of creating a flow of energy and balance in the home that will make the environment feel "natural." Try to apply as many of the same guidelines as possible when planning a house, an apartment, or a condominium unit.

Schematic Design

Always begin with three basic tools.

1. Start with the Golden Rectangle or other regular shape for the house footprint and for each room.
2. Place the public spaces in the front portion of the home or on the first floor of a multilevel house, and put the private spaces in the back part of the residence or on the second floor.
3. Superimpose the *Bagua* as a starting point for locating specific rooms within the home.

Because Tools 1 and 2 are self-evident, we will focus on the *Bagua*. Using the *Bagua* grid, Figures 6.1 and 6.2A and B are very simple layouts that place the various rooms in a manner that is consistent with the *Bagua*, as well as with Tools 1 and 2. Obviously, variations on the rooms' locations will also work, and you do not need to be rigid, so long as the placement of the major spaces makes sense. We have also placed the primary pieces of furniture in accordance with the Commanding Position, discussed in Chapter 2, Section C.

In Figure 6.1, a one-story plan, the living room is in the Helpful People area, the master bedroom is in the Primary Relationship *gua*, and the office is in the Reputation section.

In Figure 6.2, a two-story layout, the living room is in the Helpful People section, the kitchen is in the Primary Relationship area, which is also the *gua* that is related to nourishing the occupants, and the office is in the Prosperity part of the *Bagua*. On the more private level of the second floor, the master bedroom is placed in the Primary Relationship area. In both figures, we

- swing the main entrance door to reveal the most public area, the living room, and swing the doors to each room to disclose the majority of the space.
- do not place doors opposite one another, unless the two rooms are both public spaces, such as the living room and dining room in Figure 6.1, so that the energy of a person who is leaving a room will not be pulled into someone else's private space.

FIGURE 6.1 *Bagua Grid Applied to the Second Floor of a Two Story Residence*

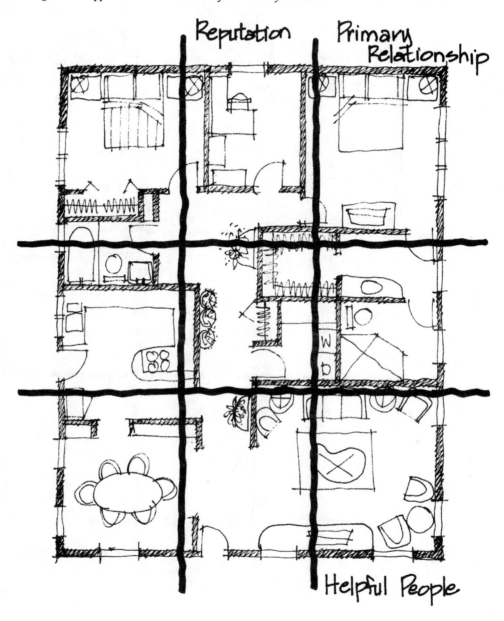

- do not locate doors opposite windows so that when people enter a room, their energy stays in the room and is not pulled out the window immediately.

FIGURE 6.2A *Bagua Grid Applied to a One Story Residence*

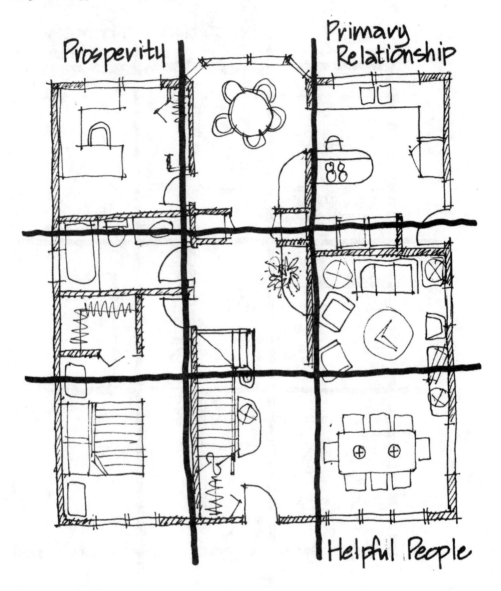

- plan bedrooms with the Commanding Position in mind for the bed so it is not necessary to place a bed under a window and have the energy from the outdoors directly behind the headboard. This situation can cause an uneasy feeling of not knowing what is behind you, thereby making it more difficult to sleep well.

FIGURE 6.2B *Bagua Grid Applied to the First Floor of a Two Story Residence*

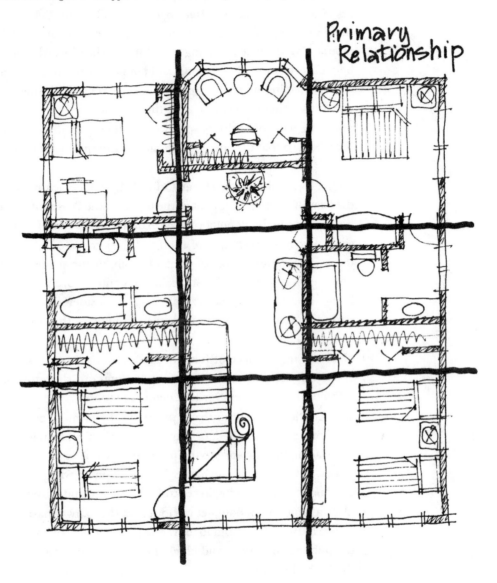

- locate the bathrooms so that they do not share the same common wall with a headboard wall in a bedroom. If the head of a bed is against a bathroom wall, especially a wall with plumbing in it, the people sleeping in that bed may have problems, particularly health issues. The noise of the plumbing, the temperature of the wall, and the psychological proximity of the bathroom fixtures to one's head create an energy that is not conducive to a good night's rest. This situation can affect people's health and behavior in their work and with their family. If this design is unavoidable, mount a large fabric wall hanging behind the headboard. This will help absorb some of the sound and temperature differential and create a feeling of separation. Traditional Feng Shui would also use transcendental techniques in this situation.

- place the bathroom doors somewhere other than directly opposite a bed, so that the energy from the bathroom will not be aimed at the occupant of the bed.
- do not locate the Water element of a bathroom, which represents the flow of money energy out of the home, in the Prosperity area of the home or in the Reputation area to diminish the Fire of that *gua*.
- avoid placing the strong Fire energy of the kitchen or a fireplace, the exiting Water energy of the bathroom, or the strong up-and-down energy flow of the stairs in the central core area of the home, because all of these attributes are considered to have too strong an energy to be located in the center of the occupants' home and life.
- place the major piece of furniture in a room so that it is not directly opposite the entrance to the room and therefore confronted with all the energy that enters the room.
- arrange the furniture so that a person in the primary position in the living room, in a bed, or at a desk is in the Commanding Position, facing the entrance to the room in which he or she is located as well as the front of the house. This positioning will give people a stronger sense of being in control of the space and of their life.
- place a table with a bouquet of flowers in the hallway past the entrance to the living room to move the primary flow of energy into the public living room and block the flow to the private areas in the back of the house.

If you must put bedrooms on both floors of a two-story house, avoid placing the children's rooms on the second floor and the parent's room on the first level. This hierarchy of levels may lead to an imbalance in the family dynamics, with the children acting as though they are in charge. Locate a guest room, rather than a child's room, on the first floor to avoid a child's leaving without the parents on the second floor knowing. Parents generally do not care if the guests leave but do want to feel in control of their children's activities.

In designing a home, be aware of the traffic patterns throughout the house and the placement of the furniture. Focus on the paths that will be used on a daily basis as well as intermittently. To create an open flow of energy, allow at least 36 inches between the walls and furniture or between pieces of furniture—even more if the furniture or objects on the walls have sharp corners.

Because basements are usually at least partially below ground level, a person's energy drops when going into the basement. This sinking feeling can create low energy and low self-esteem in a person who sleeps or works there. Use a basement space for storage or for high-energy activities, such as those occurring in a family room, which will balance the lower energy. Garages are yin spaces because they are devoid of active human energy and are often filled with automobiles, machinery, and other Metal elements. Avoid placing important rooms, especially bedrooms, over a garage. We have frequently seen the occupants of bedrooms over garages adversely affected, particularly in the areas of health and primary relationships. If a room must go over a garage, make it a high-energy room, such as a family room that has a great deal of *yang* energy and will only be used for short stretches of time, or make it an infrequently used guestroom.

Approaching the House

Being conscious of the surrounding area will give the professional some direction as to the design of the approach to the house itself. See Figure 6.3. Some forms of energy around the house may be inconsistent with its intent, such as a warehouse neighborhood, or may be too strong, such as a road that is aimed directly at the house. Several mundane, as well as transcendental, techniques can balance these unwanted or unneeded energies. For instance, a row of trees or hedges may be sufficient to block the energy from the road and give the occupants a feeling of being more protected. A row of trees can similarly help absorb unwanted energies from the cemetery next door and visually block it out.

When planting trees in a front yard, avoid placing a tree in the area immediately in front of the main entrance. Not only does this placement block the view of the house and give the impression that the residents

FIGURE 6.3 *At a 'T' Intersection*

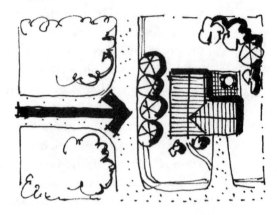

are hiding from the world but the tree in front of the door will block the occupants as they leave the house, possibly causing them to feel as if their path in the world is difficult. See Figure 6.4.

Entrances

Entrances are one of the most important, but often overlooked, aspects of a home. The transition from the energy of the open sky to the closed-in space of the home is dramatic. Porches and porticos are wonderful transitional areas from the outdoors to the indoors. Although their "ceiling" height is lower, the openness of the space

FIGURE 6.4 *Tree Centered on the Main Entrance*

makes the transition less extreme. Strong lighting also increases the energy of the porch or portico.

Recessed entrances usually create a missing area in the home—and perhaps in the lives of the residents. These entry areas are also apt to be dark and lacking in energy and may feel as though they are closing in on the residents, especially as people enter from the outdoors. Placing plants in the ground or in pots on either side of the entrance at the main front wall line can visually "push out" the entrance to the house. Adding lights and wind chimes in the hidden or missing area will also increase the energy and welcoming feeling of the entrance. As the energy increases, the corresponding *gua* of Self-Knowledge, Path in Life, or Helpful People will also improve.

If stairs lead up to the front door, consider having them in sets of three steps, with a landing between each set that is deep enough for the average person to take one comfortable step. Three is an auspicious Feng Shui number representing the trinity of heaven, earth, and human. Railings should be built on both sides of the stairs to create a feeling of support. With respect to all outdoor and indoor stairs, the risers should be closed so that energy does not "leak" through. The treads of each step should be deep enough and the risers shallow enough that anyone who climbs the steps will feel comfortable and not off balance. The front steps should be wider than the front door. A 36- to 48-inch door should open up to steps that are at least 48 to 60 inches wide or more than 12 inches wider than the doorway.

A solid front door conveys a sense of strength as well as separation and protection from the outside world: the definition of a home. We have discussed different types of doors in detail in Chapter 2, Section A: The Flow of Energy. Lighting above the door is usually designed and installed during the day, so the impact of the lighting at night is sometimes forgotten. Lights on both sides of the door usually will ensure that the keyhole and doorknob are not in the dark.

Entry Halls

When a person or family enters a home, they are entering their private world, a place that reflects who they are and what they think about themselves. Making the entry as open, light, and welcoming as possible conveys a positive image to the occupants and guests. The entry is the

Path in Life area and the most public part of the house. Select images for this space that are consistent with the residents and how they want to feel about themselves and be viewed by the outside world. Putting chimes on the inside of the front door will add a welcoming sound energy to the entry and will add a feeling of security, because they can be heard throughout the house if someone enters unannounced.

Design the entrance hall so that the occupants will not be encouraged to place objects or furniture behind the front door. This concept applies equally to doors into any room. Placing something behind a door increases the likelihood that the door will not be able to open all the way, thereby creating a feeling that the entrance is closed down and people cannot move easily into the room and through life. In addition, having an object behind a door increases the tension level because of the persistent fear of hitting and damaging the item. If a piece of furniture must be behind the door, make certain that the door can open a little more than 90 degrees and that a substantial doorstop protects the item from the door's swing.

The first room or area of the residence that people see as they step over the threshold creates an immediate need or desire, whether it is a bathroom, a kitchen, or a bedroom. The ideal first view is of the living room, a place for relaxing and enjoying family and friends. If the bedroom is visible from the entrance, the occupants may always feel tired. An immediate view of the kitchen may make food the priority and result in eating disorders.

If the entrance does reveal a less than desirable space, consider changing the swing of the door to redirect the view. If this tactic does not improve the situation, find a way to divert attention immediately away from the poorer view. Color most easily accomplishes this objective. A very energetic flower arrangement or a picture with bright colors can often be the answer. Because empty spaces are yin and tend to lack energy, especially compared to the yang energy of the outside world, our attention is immediately drawn to the yang energy of reds, oranges, and golds to fulfill our physiological and psychological need for balance.

Kitchens

Experienced kitchen designers discuss the five- to six-foot-triangulation of the refrigerator, the sink, and the stove and usually place the sink in front of the window, but rarely discuss the location of the range rela-

FIGURE 6.5 *Kitchens*

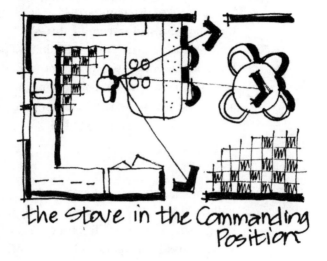

the Stove in the Commanding Position

tive to the door. The Commanding Position and Feng Shui tradition place the stove so that the cook has a view of the entrance to the kitchen. Because the energy of the cook is thought to affect the energy of the food, having a relaxed chef is positive for the entire family. Locating the range on an island or peninsula can easily accomplish this. Because of the issues of space and of venting, many people are forced to place the stove against a wall. In this case, mirror the backsplash above the stove to give the cook some feeling of control over the kitchen entrance and avoid the uneasy foreboding of surprises. See Figure 6.5.

Staircases

If you are designing a two-story home, focus on the psychological placement of the stairs. Remember that the first thing we see when entering a space has an impulsive effect on us. If the staircase, grand or otherwise, is right in front of us, our energies are immediately pulled upstairs, which is usually the private bedroom area of the house. For the residents, thinking of bed may make them feel more exhausted than they might otherwise be. For guests, having the private part of the home thrust upon their subconscious is generally not the optimum greeting.

Spiral staircases are an example of extreme yang energy because energy accelerates with the spiral. Because spiral stairs rarely have risers, they also encourage energy to drop through the stairs back to the lower level instead of rising upward. Placing plants, hangings, or other items behind the spiral can ameliorate this effect to some degree. Spiral staircases can also feel as if they are closing in on a person and increase the tension level, because the passageway is often fairly narrow. Design a spiral staircase with an abundance of light from every direction, especially from above to focus attention and draw energy up to the higher levels.

Hallways

Colors, lighting, and artwork are the most important features in a hallway. These pathways are generally narrow areas that lead from one open space to another. To minimize the feeling of suddenly being constricted, use light colors and good lighting to heighten the energy. Any representational art in this space should feel comfortable when viewed from close range and should have depth, which adds a feeling of width to the hall.

Bedrooms in General

Our bedrooms are our truly private spaces. Because we spend more time in them than almost any other space, they are critical to our well-being. Even when we are asleep, the energies of the room continue to affect us. When we enter a room and are immediately confronted by the end of a dresser or other piece of furniture that blocks us, we become tense rather than relaxed.

Bedroom Ceilings. A very large bedroom with high ceilings may look dramatic but fails to confine the energy in the room needed for rest, relaxation, and intimacy. Let the drama occur elsewhere than with the ceiling. A normal height throughout the bedroom will be the most comfortable. Any uneven height over the bed, such as a partial cathedral ceiling, a slanted ceiling, a fan, or a beam, may create a "compression" over the body and be detrimental to a person's sleep and health. As the energy flows around the room, these elements cause the energy to be pushed down on to the individual, creating an unnatural pressure.

Beds. It is best to have the box springs and mattress at least three to four inches off the floor so that energy circulates freely over and under the bed without being blocked. For the energy to flow around the occupant smoothly, it is also advisable not to have objects stored under the bed. The nature and energy of an object that is under a bed can affect the individuals in the bed. For example, I had a client who was having severe back problems. When we surveyed the bedroom and looked under the bed, we discovered a box filled with beautiful, antique hunting knives. This is not the place for harsh instruments of violence! If you must place objects under a bed, store items such as bed linens that are conducive to sleep and leave enough space for the energy to pass under the bed without blockage.

Four-poster and canopy beds create rooms within rooms and allow energy to flow around the bed, a good combination. The bed frame and the poster material and shape are important in light of the individuals who sleep in the bed. Wooden posts are generally preferable to metal ones, and a rounded shape will be more conducive to a peaceful night's rest than a post with hard corners. The size of the post and the crossbars of a canopy bed should be light enough not to create a feeling of heaviness next to the occupant of the bed or the uneasy subconscious feeling that the crosspieces might fall on the sleeper.

A waterbed tends to feel unstable. The Water element may also be too strong for the occupant and cause health problems. It is thought that a waterbed may be a contributive factor for asthma. In addition, these beds usually have a solid platform that goes to the floor to support the weight of the water, instead of having four legs that will allow the energy to circulate under and around the bed.

A futon gives a sense of being temporary. Therefore, it is preferable not to use a futon as a permanent bed but only as an occasional bed for guests who are staying for a short period. If the bed is being placed in front of a window, move the bed far enough from the wall that a curtain or drapery may be hung at the window and fall to the floor. This will add to the sense of support behind the sleeping person.

Headboards. Headboards are a very important element in the bedroom. See Figure 6.6. The headboard is one of the last objects you see when you climb into bed. The headboard is the mountain at your back, the support that protects you as you lie in bed in your most vulnerable

FIGURE 6.6 *Headboards*

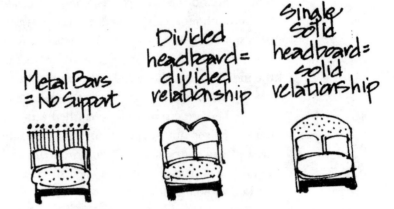

state. The headboard should be strong and stable to nurture a strong and stable person and relationship.

The headboard should be a solid piece. One with metal bars, such as in a brass bed, does not create the sense of being supported. A good way to select the headboard material is to consider the appropriate elements to help balance the bed's occupants. A person may need more of the strength of Wood or a stronger sense of the grounded Earth, a feeling that could be conveyed with an earth-tone fabric.

If a couple's headboard is divided or creates the illusion of two individuals, as opposed to a single unity, they should replace the headboard or psychologically connect the two sides with an image or symbol that clearly connotes for them a union of the two halves, then reinforce it with the technique described in Chapter 9.

Bedside Tables. Bedside tables with lamps on both sides of the bed add energy to the bed and to the person's development by creating a balance on both sides of the body. The image and the reality are both aimed at developing the right brain and left brain and the yin and yang sides of the body. In addition, two bedside tables ensure that the bed will be at least the width of the table away from the wall.

Bedside tables convey the image that a couple has of themselves and of one another. I have seen many master bedrooms in which only one member of the couple had a bedside table or in which the scale of the two tables was completely disproportionate. It is invariably possible to tell who sleeps on which side of the bed by relating the behavior of the two individuals to what you see when you look at the comparative bedside tables. The two tables and lamps do not need to be identical but should be of the same scale. Different pieces can be more interesting and can reflect the different personalities of the two people. The important question to ask here is whether the two sides of the bed are in balance when you are standing at the foot of the bed. A unified and balanced bed and bedside arrangement will enhance a unified and balanced relationship.

Master Bedrooms

As strange as it may sound, every couple I have known who later divorced or had a very difficult marriage had a major problem in the Feng Shui of their bedroom. In most instances, it has been the location of the bed. See Figure 6.7. As we discussed in Chapter Two, Section C: The Commanding Position, design the room to place the bed on a wall other than the "door wall," so the entrance to the room can be easily seen from the bed. If this is impossible, which it rarely is with a little bit of ingenuity, place a standing mirror on the opposite wall turned at the correct angle to give people a view of the entrance to the bedroom and some feeling of control over the space. Also try to avoid the energies directed at the bed through bathroom and closet doors and from "poison arrow" columns and corners.

The "doorkeeper" position in a bedroom is the side of the bed closest to the principal door into the bedroom. The person in this position may feel more responsible for the family, which can create an imbalance in a couple's relationship. If one person is feeling more overwhelmed than the other, focus on their positions in the bed. If the bed is on the door wall, the person in the doorkeeper position has an added level of stress that may produce high blood pressure, nervousness, or centerline problems in the body. At a subconscious, if not conscious, level, this person will be uneasy.

A double or queen-size bed, not a king-size, is generally more conducive to a good relationship. A king-size bed has a division line down the middle created by the two box springs. At a subliminal level, the couple will feel separated, as if a thin curtain has been drawn between them. A double or queen-size bed also brings the couple closer together, creating a greater sense of intimacy. If someone has managed to have a single-unit box spring constructed that is raised off the floor, the problem of sepa-

FIGURE 6.7 *Master Bedroom*

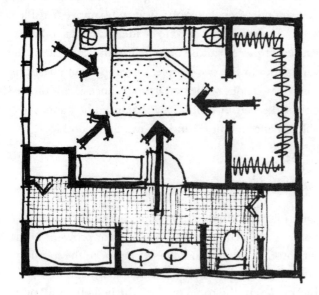

Energy from the Bathroom, Closet and Poison Arrow corner overwhelm the sleepers in this layout.

The bed is in a vulnerable position next to the door.

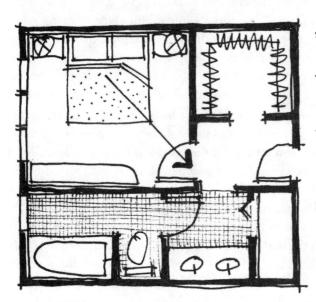

This is a peaceful Bedroom.
The bed is in the Commanding Position.
The Bathroom and Closet doors do not open onto the bed.
The Bedroom is a complete shape without poison arrow corners.

rating the couple no longer exists. If the intimacy factor of the relationship is less than 100 percent, however, a couple may still want to consider replacing their king-size bed. In the event the couple strongly resists replacing the bed, a traditional transcendental adjustment exists.

Colors. The Religious Society of Shakers was well known for the simplicity and beauty of the furniture that its members designed for themselves. Such furniture is popular to this day. One of the tenets of the Shaker religion was celibacy. As a consequence, the members of each sex slept apart from those of the other sex. It is interesting to note that the 1845 Millennial Laws adopted by the Shakers required that bedsteads were to be painted green and were to be covered with blue and white linens. These color choices were very appropriate in a room where thoughts of passion were discouraged. Most of the time when we are asked to help a couple bring more passion into their relationship, the colors in the room are out of balance. Introducing warm yang colors of reds and golds can shift the energy and make the relationship more balanced and complete. Because this is a bedroom, use dark, restful window treatments to enable the room to be dark or at least muted on the brightest of days.

Children's Bedrooms

At the risk of being redundant, we'll say it again: please place a child's bed in a Commanding Position and avoid placing its side against a wall. Our children are our future, and we want to do everything in our power to maximize their potential. By placing the bed out in the room with a solid headboard against the wall for a feeling of support and stability and two bedside tables with lamps, we are increasing the likelihood that the child will develop in a balanced way to fulfill his or her capabilities.

Although bunk beds are a way to save space for two children or to give Johnny a bed for his friend to stay over, a bunk bed establishes a hierarchy and is also apt to create a feeling of pressure. The person on the top bunk is clearly "over" the one below. Very few of us would feel comfortable if the ceiling over our bed were as close as the bottom of the upper bunk or the actual ceiling above the upper bed.

It is often necessary to place a desk in a child's room. Ideally, both the bed and the desk should be in a Commanding Position. If one of the pieces cannot be well located, give the bed preference, because it will have more effect on the child's development. Try to avoid having the desk face a wall, because the wall may act as a block to the child's ability to think as freely as possible. And don't place the desk against the window. Looking out the window is not the Primary Purpose of sitting at

FIGURE 6.8 *Childrens Bedroom*

Childrens Bedrooms:

Which is the calmer environment?
Would You sleep better with clouds, clowns &
bright colors?

the desk. If a child has a desk in the bedroom and does not use it, the reason is often because the placement is blocking or otherwise uncomfortable. If the desk must face a wall, open up the wall and the child's thought process by mirroring as much of the wall as possible.

Be aware of the impact of wall coverings and colors on the sleep patterns and behavior of a child. See Figure 6.8. Wallpapers, especially those with stripes and contrasting, bright colors, can have an adverse effect on a child's sleep and behavior. Children are extremely sensitive to energies. Listen to the child's ideas. It is not the parent's or the designer's environment. Children, especially young ones, intuitively know what they need. When five-year-old Sammy told his parents he wanted to paint his room dark green, they laughed. But when I sat with him in his room, what was happening was apparent. Sammy's room was covered with a "child's" wallpaper with clowns and balloons in primary colors on a stark white background. Using the Squint Test, I quickly saw the chaotic effect that the numerous shapes and value distinctions were having on him as he tried to fall asleep. Sammy knew at some level that he needed the calmness of the dark green. The night after the room was painted Sammy's color, he slept peacefully through the night, and he became a much less hyper young boy.

FIGURE 6.9 *Bathroom*

Less Privacy...
Less Relaxing...

More Privacy...
More Relaxing...

Bathrooms

The placement of bathroom fixtures is very important. See Figure 6.9. Avoid seeing the toilet as you enter the bathroom. Walking in toward the sink is a much more comfortable feeling. Place the toilet off to the side or behind the door swing so that it is as hidden as possible to provide a greater feeling of privacy. If space is available, locating the toilet behind a partition or in a separate closet is an even better choice. By being relaxed, one will be more physically able to eliminate toxins from the body.

Because the bathroom is where we begin and end our day, light colors and humorous artwork will add to a feeling of relaxation and balanced energy. If a person has trouble sleeping, focus on whether the colors in the bathroom are too invigorating and should be calmer to facilitate the transition to rest.

Private Spaces within a Home

In any residence, whether a one-bedroom apartment or a large home, giving each person a space or area that is entirely his or hers will enhance each person's life. To the extent that you can keep this in mind during the information-gathering phase and explore the interests of the family members, fulfilling this often unspoken need will be easier. Frequently, the children have their own room to which they can escape, one person has an office or den, and the other partner has the master bedroom, the kitchen, and the laundry room, all of which are shared with other people. Providing a quiet private retreat for everyone can greatly affect the dynamics of the entire family in a very positive way. This may be a workshop, exercise room, sewing room, meditation space, or studio.

The concept of "my space" frequently becomes a major issue when someone moves into a residence that is already occupied. The existing occupant has invariably filled the home with his or her own life, and not much space is left for the newcomer. As the professional, it is important to point out the need for a balance of both individuals' energies in the living space if it is to be the home for both people. To begin with, focus on the need for convenient storage of the newcomer's personal belongings. The attic is not the answer, unless some of both people's effects are stored there jointly. The next level is to encourage the existing resident to make some changes in the home that will reflect the personality of the incoming resident. These alterations may be as simple as new paint colors on the walls to add some yang energy to a very yin environment, or vice versa, or the purchase of a new piece of furniture that the couple selects together. A new addition or renovation is the other end of the spectrum in this regard! At the risk of being politically incorrect, we'll note our experience that the nesting instinct of women is more apt to express a need for putting an imprint on a space into which they are moving than the instincts of most men. Do not assume, however, that men do not have the same need. At a subconscious level they do but in many cases are not as capable as women of expressing it.

Furniture

As we have mentioned repeatedly, try to design or select counters, mantles, tables, and other furniture with rounded edges and corners. Rounding creates a more natural and comfortable feeling as well as additional space by allowing the passageways between pieces of furniture and walls to be several inches narrower. Although five or six inches may not seem like much, these dimensions are significant when multiplied by 3 or 6 or 18 times for all of those passageways in the house.

In this era, many couples are in a second marriage. In working with these couples, be very conscious of furniture that may be a holdover from the prior marriage. Even if you cannot appreciate that these pieces of furniture contain energies from the past, you can certainly understand that the bed from the prior marriage will have a subconscious effect on both of the newlyweds. This happens more often than you would imagine. Purchase a new bed and bed linens.

Always keep your clients' energies in mind, not just your own design preferences, when looking for furniture. In purchasing old furniture for clients, inquire as to its origin and history. If you have any unusual feelings about a piece, move on. Even though you may not be able to explain your reaction, do not dismiss it. If the object is from a foreign country and is part of a tradition that is alien to your clients' culture, such as a ceremonial mask, encourage them to find another object.

Avoid any indications that the occupants are only in the house temporarily. This would include such common decorating touches as pictures that are propped against a wall, on a mantle piece, or on the floor. Everyone should feel that this is *home* at this point, not just a stop along the way.

Do not include in your design any feature that could convey the sense of being "dead" or "broken" or not working as well as it once did, because the goal is to make the entire environment convey the image that it and the people residing there are operating at maximum capacity. For example, dried flower arrangements convey a dead image. Some antique pieces, intended to look chic by having broken corners or old glass in which you cannot see anything clearly, may not be the best image for allowing the residents to move forward effectively.

Design mantles and shelves that are narrow and do not encourage the placement of too many objects. Excessive accumulation creates an overwhelming sense of clutter. If the proportions of the design do require a large surface, explain to the clients the importance of keeping the surface reasonably simple to avoid adding to the feeling of chaos that probably already exists in their life. Teaching them the Squint Test and explaining the impact that the visual image has on the subconscious is often an effective way to communicate this point.

Feng Shui Enhancement and Client Psychology

In practicing Feng Shui with an individual, it is important for the consultant to focus on enhancement. Our role is not to enter people's life and begin to point out all of their problems but to assist them in the specific areas in which they have asked for help. The Feng Shui consultant must develop a great sensitivity and be extremely aware of the potential consequences of pointing out a possible problem that the clients might not be ready to discuss at that point.

The effectiveness of a Feng Shui adjustment will depend on the person's ability to deal with the subject. There is a definite connection between the individual's need and their ability to receive. If a client resists making a change in the environment, that person is, at the moment, comfortable with the problem. The consultant should tread carefully. Our role as a Feng Shui consultant is to assist the client. Sometimes the most helpful action at this particular moment is just to be understanding of the process through which the person may be going. For example, if a client has a weight problem and is clearly not ready to talk about it openly, the Feng Shui consultant may want to allude to an element in the space that is conducive to overeating in a nonthreatening manner. In many cases, the oblique reference is enough for the individual to broach the subject openly so the exploration can begin.If a client has several homes or offices, that client should consider adjusting each space, because every environment will impact their life. The most important spaces, however, are those in which he or she spends the most time.

B. MULTIFAMILY HOUSING

Multifamily housing developments include single-family homes, town houses, condominiums, and apartments. In addition to all of the issues discussed in the previous section, each of these types of residences involves other concerns, particularly with respect to the public areas of the development.

Be very conscious of the energy in the neighborhood. The surrounding environment will have an impact on the residents. We are currently working on a housing complex that will be located on the site of an old hospital and is surrounded by medical and hospital facilities in a neighborhood that has seen better days. This environment needs to be recognized and dealt with, not ignored. Planting very hardy trees around the perimeter of the property will help create the feeling of a natural and healing barrier between the residences and the neighboring hospital facilities. Although the trees may block out some natural light, the energy and view of the hospitals will not have a positive effect on the residents. The management of the facility will need to be aware of the health of the trees, which will absorb a great deal of negative energy from the neighborhood, and immediately replace any that die.

We have also recommended painting the complex the healing color of green. Applying the concepts of the Five Elements, the green of the Wood will metaphorically take up or overcome some of the Earth element that is symbolized in the brown colors of the surrounding medical buildings. In addition to providing these practical tools, I also suggest some of the techniques described in Chapter 9: The Transcendental Aspects of Feng Shui.

Residential Signage

Signage creates the first impression of residential housing. Suggest that the developer of the units name the project rather than using only a street address. A name gives the complex an identity and adds to the feeling that this is a unique place to live.

The location, size, and colors of the signage on the street depend upon the image that the developer wants to convey. Are these homes "very private, restful, and secluded?" Or is this "an exciting, active, and hip place to be?" Once inside the development, make certain that the name or number of each individual building is clearly visible from a distance to reduce the aggravation of trying to locate a unit. Number the buildings and units in a logical sequence, remembering that we read from left to right. Having the numbers jump back and forth with odds on one side and evens on the other may be okay if the area is set up like a city street, but in other situations sequential numbers may be easier to read.

Use the same colors and style of lettering for the signs at the entrance and throughout the complex. Although the lettering can be an interesting font, be certain that it can be read from a distance. Some fonts can be difficult to read. Although you should consider the particular market for the housing, a general guideline is to use colors that are calm and peaceful, because a home is a respite from the high energy of the outside world. If the effect is to be one of calmness, use the cooler colors as the background color. Light-value lettering on a darker-value background usually reads more clearly than the reverse. A mixed color for the background will look more sophisticated than will a primary color. A good example of a calm and elegant color combination that stands out and looks successful is gold lettering on a darker blue-green background.

FIGURE 6.10 *Road Entrance and Site Planning Alternates*

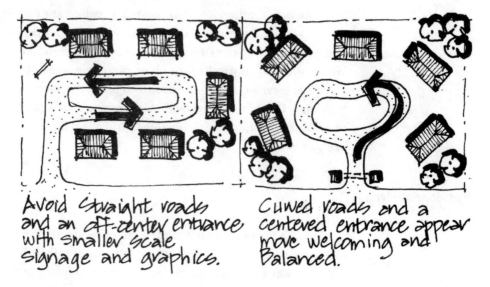

Avoid straight roads and an off-center entrance with smaller scale signage and graphics.

Curved roads and a centered entrance appear more welcoming and balanced.

Main Entrance to the Site

If possible, place the main entrance to the property in the center of the front line of the property. See Figure 6.10. This gives the development a greater feeling of being balanced. Think about historic sites. This aesthetic "feels right" to people and the entrance gates create an immediate image of the complex and the residents.

Having no markers at all except for a street sign communicates a very different message than do stone columns with a solid iron gate. Nine-foot, round columns on either side of the entrance with an arch over the driveway, all of which are well lit and carry the name and address of the complex, conveys the message that you are entering a different world that is special and welcoming.

If a driveway leads to the homes, town houses, or other buildings, avoid long straight roads with right-angled turns that feel rigid. Roads and adjoining sidewalks with a very gentle curve will feel more natural, more comfortable, and more elegant.

Building and Property Shapes

Whether the residential complex consists of single family homes, town houses, or buildings of multiple units, use the Golden Rectangle as the ba-

FIGURE 6.11 *Bagua Applied to Building and Property Shapes*

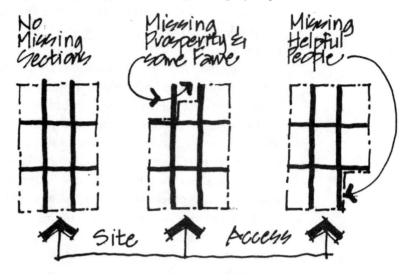

sic shape for each of the buildings. This will make it considerably easier to plan interior units and rooms that will benefit the residents by eliminating any "missing" sections that could result in problems. See Figure 6.11 for examples of property and unit shapes resulting in missing areas.

Exterior details can prevent bland building designs. Landscaping and porches or decks with awnings of a color different from the building itself can break up the massing. A portico or awning over the front entrance adds visual variety, creates a feeling of protection from the elements, and gives a sense of importance to the building and its residents. Awning signage also raises the visibility of the name or address. The awning also appears to be an extension of the building and therefore enhances the Path in Life of the building's residents.

Exterior Building Colors

In selecting building colors, focus on both the intended energies for the development and the energies in the surrounding areas. If the developer is building a complex of single-family units and is selecting the colors for the homes, be aware that the use of different colors for adjacent homes may well create an unintentional relationship that is not productive for some of the residents. Because fire overcomes Metal, a red house next to a white home creates the image of the red house being more powerful and "melting" the metal. Using the colors of the Five Elements described in Chapter 2, Section E, and in Chapter 3, Section A: Colors, place the colors along the streetscape in a way that will enhance everyone's life. One method of accomplishing this would be to order the colors of the houses sequentially in the constructive cycle of the elements, with each color representative of an element. Being aware that we are talking about color groups, not specific hues, the red of Fire creates the yellow of Earth creates the white of Metal creates the blue or black of Water creates the green of Wood. Repeating the colors in the cycle throughout the development will also add individuality to the homes that may otherwise be very similar in style.

In a high-rise condominium building, select a color that will enhance the metaphorical image of the complex and reflect its relationship to the community. As an example, recall the housing complex surrounded by medical facilities described earlier. In addition to planting the buffer of trees, I recommended painting the buildings a medium to dark value of green to add a healing and peaceful feeling to the complex. On the other hand, the condominium building mentioned in an earlier chapter, which was in a gray and metal environment and targeted at a younger market, was more appropriately colored a reddish hue to raise its visibility. The Fire of the red overcoming the Metal of the surrounding grayness will make this complex stand out as an exception in the neighborhood.

Building Entrances and Lobbies

Center the main entrance to the building in the front line of the structure to create a feeling of balance. Because our aim is to make coming home an easy experience, have the front doors swing in, if legally permitted, or, if not, have them swing both in and out. Automatic sliding doors are another way to accomplish the goal of reducing the effort of entering a building. Good lighting, both outside and immediately inside the entrance area, also creates a welcoming environment after a long day.

The size and shape of the lobby in a multifamily building creates a strong impression. Use the Golden Rectangle as a guideline and proportion the size and ceiling height to the human scale. We do not want residents to feel as if they have just entered an office building.

If a reception desk is in the lobby, place the desk to the right as people enter, because the most natural movement is a curve to the right. By locating the desk as far from the entrance as possible, residents have an opportunity to become accustomed to the lobby area before arriving at the desk. If the desk is too close to the entry doors, they are on top of it or past it at once, creating an uncomfortable feeling. Angle the desk so that the doorman has a Commanding Position with respect to both the front door and the elevators. Placing the desk directly in front of the entry doors creates a confrontational relationship and often places the doorman's back to the elevators, a vulnerable position, increasing the degree of stress, illness, and resulting absenteeism.

Mailboxes are often tucked away in an inconvenient "extra" space. Try to locate them so that the natural flow of a person's path from the entrance to the elevator does not become a journey of twists, turns, and backtracking.

The use of warm temperature lighting in the lobby further enhances the residential feeling. Adding large plants and several comfortable seating arrangements in the lobby gives the building a feeling of comfort and elegance. Including table lamps in the arrangements will add an inviting energy. Round the corners of the reception desk and all of the furniture in the lobby to create a softer, more comfortable environment. The choice of chair fabric is another way to balance the Elements and colors and add energy in what is often an impersonal space.

Public Areas

Stairs. Stairs with open risers either cause residents to look into a dead space behind the stairway or into the open area on the lower level. Design stairs with solid risers so that people going up the stairs will have a greater feeling of security and stability and their energy will go up the stairs and not through them. They will be led upward, not psychologically pulled back to the level they are leaving. If the stairs double back in a stairwell, avoid solid walls as dividers between the two sections and use open railings that allow a person to see someone on the stairs around the corner, thereby reducing tension.

Corridors. The corridors in a condominium can greatly enhance, or detract from, the environment. Avoid placing doors directly opposite

FIGURE 6.12 *Corridors*

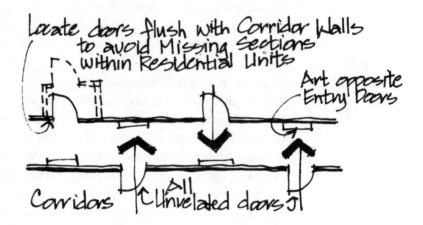

one another in the corridor. See Figure 6.12. When a person leaves an apartment, their energy should not be directed into the unit across the hall. A piece of art that is hung in the hallway opposite their door and reads in the direction of the elevators or staircase is the optimum view for a person leaving an apartment.

Lighting. Lighting in the lobby, corridors, and other public spaces is usually surface mounted in the ceiling, recessed, or provided by wall sconces. The two most important factors here are that the lighting is warm in temperature and creates a balanced light throughout the entire area. Warm lighting will help compensate for the transition of coming from the outdoors into an interior space. Almost everyone prefers the warmth of the sun to the blue coolness of the standard fluorescent bulb. Frequently, high ceiling lights will create an imbalance of light and dark areas on the floor that is disconcerting. Use warm lighting and create an even light throughout the entire area.

Flooring. The color and the texture of the floor in the lobby convey an immediate feeling as a person enters a residence. The darker the flooring, the more natural and grounded people feel. Light-colored flooring can seem unsettling and unstable. Earth-tone colors generally feel more relaxing and stable. Because the darker shades of blue subconsciously remind us of water, we may not feel as comfortable stepping on blue flooring. In residential buildings, a highly patterned floor, such as tiles with a great deal of color variation or with geometric shapes in strong contrasting colors, is apt to feel somewhat chaotic and disturbing rather than comforting.

The texture of the floor also creates an immediate physical and psychological sensation. Because one is coming in from the outdoors, practical issues limit the range of feasible surfaces in the lobby. Even though stone tile is often specified, a shiny surface may be too slippery and dangerous. A matte finish with a slight texture will feel less dangerous. Wood, cork, high-quality vinyl, or rubber flooring can run the gamut from casual to elegant, look less dangerous, be less noisy than stone, and convey a feeling of nature and stability. Although the warmth of carpet may not be practical in the lobby and elevators in certain geographical areas, when people step from an elevator onto a carpeted corridor, they will experience a further feeling of transition from the harshness of the outside world to the comfort of home.

Wall Color. In a residential environment, the colors in the public areas should usually reflect both a feeling of tranquility and a subtle sense of upbeat energy. Although the full color spectrum should be included in some way throughout the building, especially in the lobby, the safest colors are relaxing blues and greens, with the more energetic warm roses and creams in those spaces that will naturally have the lowest energy, such as the hallways.

The color value will depend on the scale of the space. Although medium color values can be used in a large space to make it feel somewhat smaller, it is inadvisable to use dark wall colors that may feel heavy and oppressive, especially if the ceilings are relatively high. A discussion of the impact of the various colors and their different energies is set forth in Chapter 3, Section A: Colors.

Art. Artwork provides a finishing touch and offers an easy way to balance the color, energy, and vitality of public spaces. A painting in the lobby represents and reinforces the building's image and, as a consequence, the image that the residents will have of themselves. A harsh, cold picture behind the reception desk is probably not the appropriate greeting for the residents and their guests. Make certain that the art and the desired impression are consistent. We have elaborated on these concepts in detail in Chapter 3, Section G: Art and Decorative Objects.

Private Spaces

The design of apartment and condominium units should follow the guidelines set forth for single family residences in Section A of this chapter. Some of the most prevalent Feng Shui problems we see in multifamily projects include the following:

- Unit entry doors that are at the end of a long corridor
- Recessed entry doorways and irregularly shaped units that create missing areas
- "First views" from the entry door of bathrooms, bedrooms, and kitchens
- Doors that hit one another when opening, especially in the entryway
- Living room seating, stoves, and beds that are not in the Commanding Position
- Bedroom doors that are placed directly opposite balcony doors or windows
- Bedroom doors that are centered on another door, especially a bathroom door
- Bathrooms that share the same wall with a kitchen or bedroom
- Closet or bathroom doors that open onto the side or foot of a bed
- Columns near a headboard
- Electrical outlets that are placed behind beds or other major pieces of furniture

These issues are not difficult to avoid if you keep basic Feng Shui principles in mind during the design process.

7

OFFICE PROJECTS

A. OFFICE PARKS

In designing either a single building or a complex, you may be involved with a multiuse structure or a single-purpose office building. I will first discuss the general layout of buildings within a complex and then treat the individual structures primarily as office buildings. Throughout this process, the designer must be aware of the psychological impact that all of the design features have on the occupants, their clients, and visitors.

When multiple buildings are being developed, it is important to establish an image for the complex and to make all of the buildings and their individual purposes easily identifiable and accessible. Our goal is to create a natural pathway to the entrance of each building.

Building Locations. Place the buildings as far back on the property as possible, with the parking areas in front. This will place the buildings in the Commanding Positions of the property and make the occupants feel more in control than if parking or other large and relatively empty spaces were behind their building. Although delivery and other service entrances can be placed at the back, parking for both employees and visitors in front of the building will make them feel more important than if they enter through the back door. In addition, the flow of energy will be a consistently forward motion as a person enters the property, proceeds to park, and continues forward to the main entrance.

Design as many slight curves as practical in the driveways, rather than long straight lines with right-angle turns. These gentle curves, combined with plantings, soften the visual harshness of the cars in the driveways and parking areas. Avenues of trees along either side of the sidewalk to the front door add a natural feeling and create a sense of importance to the building and the individual.

An odd, or yang, number of buildings in the complex will feel more powerful and less static than an even yin number. Three buildings in the park will also feel more complete than two and less overwhelming than four. By arranging these buildings in an arch, as depicted in Figure 7.1, the main doors to all of the buildings are visible from the entrance to the property and are opened up toward the street to receive the energy that is headed toward the buildings. The visual image is that of open arms and is less rigid than if the buildings were at right angles to one another.

FIGURE 7.1 *Single Entrance to an Office Park*

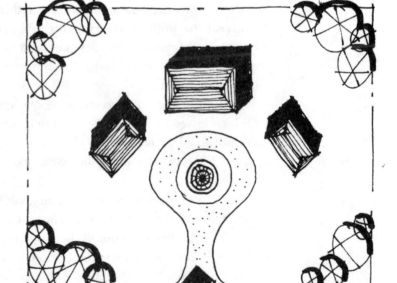

In the middle of the arc formed by the three structures, place a water fountain. This Water feature, a metaphor for the financial success of the buildings and their occupants, will be directly in front of everyone who enters from the street as well as anyone leaving the buildings.

If buildings will be of different heights, place the tallest building in the middle toward the back of the property to even out the visual height of the buildings from the street entrance. Emphasizing the height of one building over the others states that the businesses and people in the tallest building are more important than those in the smaller structures. In addition, having the smaller buildings toward the front on either side of the tallest building will visually create a smooth upward motion from the ground level of the front entrance to the lower-height structures up to the tallest building at the back.

When multiple buildings are identified by numbers, remember that we read from left to right. Numbering the structures in any other sequence can be confusing and irritating.

Building Entrances. Orienting the buildings toward the street and centering them on the property will make the complex feel more balanced. The water fountain described above will stop the harshness of the automobile traffic from flowing directly toward the lobby entrance of the center building. An alternative, as shown in Figure 7.2, would be to place the primary visual entrance in the center to create the feeling of balance but to make it a wide walkway, and place the traffic entrances in the middle of the spaces on either side of the visual center. See Figure 7.2. This would divide the front line of the property into thirds and could help drivers avoid the feeling of having passed by the property and give them a second chance to enter. The two driveways would also make it easy to create some curves in the interior roads.

Building Signage. Critical, as always. Our first view of a complex is often its signage. If it is small and difficult to find or to read, our reaction is that this place is not very impressive. Place the signage so a driver can easily see it before getting too close to slow down and turn into the driveway. This usually means placing it 10 to 15 feet off the ground. When approaching in a car, a comfortable signage height is actually slightly higher than eye level. Standing next to the sign and looking "up" at the sign is a metaphor for looking up to the businesses that occupy

FIGURE 7.2 *Double Entrance to an Office Park*

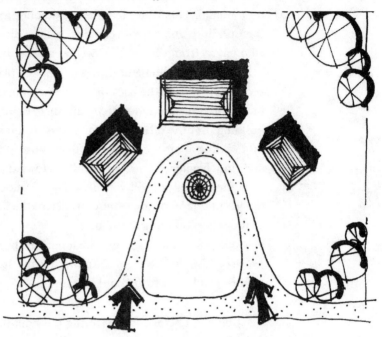

the buildings. Make certain that the name or number of each individual building is clearly visible from a distance to reduce further the aggravation of finding the way.

Although the market may dictate certain color choices, a general guideline for most complexes would be to use colors that are energetic and visible from a distance. In most cases, using warm colors will create the impression that the businesses are exciting and energetic. A cool color as the background color will create a more calming effect. Light-value lettering on a darker-value background will usually read more clearly than the reverse.

Building Shapes. Use the Golden Rectangle as the basic shape for each of the buildings. This will make it considerably easier to lay out internal office spaces that are beneficial for the occupants. Create the external visual interest through architectural materials, finishes, and details. Depending upon the height of the buildings, landscaping may be enough to break up the massing. A portico or awning over the front entrance is an effective way to add variety and create the feeling that those in the building are concerned about protecting people from the elements. You can also raise the visibility of the name or address of that building by placing the identification on the sides and front of the protruding element, which also becomes an extension and therefore an enhancement of the Path in Life aspect of the building's owners and occupants.

Exterior Building Colors. In selecting colors for the buildings, be aware of both the intended energies for the complex and the other energies in the surrounding areas. Different colors for the buildings in a complex may well create an unintentional relationship that is not productive for some of the tenants. Using the colors of the Five Elements described in Chapter 2, Section E: The Five Elements, and Chapter 3, Section A: Colors, pick colors that will enhance the metaphorical image of the complex. For example, we recently worked on a medical facility that was surrounded by taller buildings all in a cream color, representative of the Earth element. Our goal was to make the energy of the complex seem stronger than its neighbors and at the same time create a peaceful feeling consistent with the Primary Purpose of the buildings. A red exterior (Fire) would have been too extreme for the patients. Black or dark blue seemed too somber, and Water colors would have muddied the Earth and vice versa. Although the white of Metal would receive a creative energy from the Earth tones of the surrounding cream structures, the white seemed too harsh and would gray quickly in the urban setting. We recommended using green. The green of Wood takes the energy from the Earth and brings a balance to the street. At the same time, the green buildings in a world of earth tones stand out in the neighborhood and enhance the desired atmosphere of calm.

B. OFFICE BUILDINGS

Many of the issues that I have just discussed with respect to office parks are equally applicable to a single office building. Rectangular shapes, clear signage, porticos, appropriate colors, landscaping, and possible water features are all key elements to a building that feels and works effectively. As a person approaches a single building, however, additional factors will create an energetic feeling.

FIGURE 7.3 *Building Height*

Building Height. Frequently, you will feel the low energy of a smaller building that is sandwiched in between two taller buildings as in Figure 7.3. Using the Five Elements, select the appropriate color for your building based on the colors of the neighboring structures so that the taller buildings metaphorically enhance the smaller one. You may also lift the chi, or energy, of the building by placing lights on the four corners of the rooftop, with each light pointing upward toward the center and creating a spire of energy leading to the sky. Another solution is to place flags on the roof. This type of treatment is often seen with the flags angled out along the front edge of the roof. The energy of the waving flags extending over the sidewalk brings attention to the property. Be certain that the flags are kept in good repair and are not faded or torn. That is not the image you want to convey.

Building Entrance. Occasionally you see an office building with its main entrance on a street other than its actual street address. This sense of "hiding" from the flow of commerce is generally not a good idea and is often reflected in the poor economics of the building and its occupants. Placing the main entrance in the center of the primary street elevation will create a highly visible and balanced image for the building. If that is not possible, recommend changing the street address to that of the main entrance. A more "prestigious" address does not counteract the image of being hidden.

FIGURE 7.4 *Stairs*

In traditional Feng Shui, a recessed front door creates a missing area in the front wall and signifies missing opportunities, because the main entrance is a metaphor for the Path in Life of the building's owners and occupants. Placing trees and lights on both sides of the entry doors and filling in the missing area with energy will add balance to the space and symbolically create a flush doorway.

If there are stairs outside the main entrance or immediately inside the front doors, the direction of the steps can affect the energy and self-image of the people who work in the building. See Figure 7.4. Stairs that go down give you a sinking feeling and can decrease self-esteem, whereas rising steps make you feel you are going up in the world. Would you rather work in a basement or on the top floor? The number of steps also has an impact. Even though the staircase may go up, a long flight may make the journey feel arduous and exhausting.

Because our goal is to make the entrance into the building as easy as possible, have the entry doors swing in, or both ways, whenever it is permitted. Revolving doors are easier to handle than a door that swings out, and automatic sliding doors make the entry even smoother.

FIGURE 7.5 *Building Lobby*

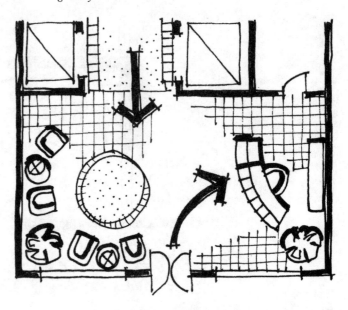

Lobby Plan. The size and shape of the lobby create an immediate impression. A very large space or a very high ceiling makes a person feel less significant. Begin with the Golden Rectangle as a guideline and proportion the size and ceiling height to the human scale. If this lobby will handle many people at one time on a regular basis, it should be larger than an area with less traffic. You do not want people to feel either crowded or lost in the space.

In Figure 7.5, the reception desk is to the right as people enter, because the most natural movement of a person is a curve to the right. Placing the desk directly in front of the entrance creates an uncomfortable and confrontational feeling. The receptionist still has command of the entrance and is far enough away from the door to feel secure. In addition, the visitor has an opportunity to become accustomed to the lighting and scale of the lobby before arriving at the desk. If the desk is too close to the entrance, a person is on top of, or immediately past, it at once, creating an uncomfortable feeling. By angling the desk slightly in the direction of the lobby entrance, the receptionist appears even more welcoming, and the angle helps break up the many inevitable straight lines in the space. This placement still gives the receptionist some control over, and a feeling of security with respect to, the secondary entrances into the lobby area from the elevators.

Preferably, locate the elevators close to the front of the building to create a side-loaded core rather than a central core. This configuration results in an office floor where the primary entrance to the reception desk is headed in the same direction as the main entrance to the building, and as much of the office floor as possible is in front of that main door line, as opposed to being behind, or outside, the entrance door wall. See the section on Space Planning later in this chapter for examples of locating the "door wall." Traditional Feng Shui strongly advises against placing stairs (elevators in our modern society) or toilets in the center of the building. The concept is that both of these activities create too strong an energy pull out of the center, or Essence, of the occupant's premises. If the elevators are forward in the building, these facilities are more apt to be located outside the center of the building.

Lobby Flooring. The darker the lobby flooring, the more natural and grounded people are apt to feel, because they subconsciously think of dark earth. Light-colored flooring is apt to be unsettling and unstable, like sand. Earth-tone colors generally feel more comfortable. Because the darker shades of blue subconsciously remind us of water, we may not feel as comfortable stepping on to blue flooring. A highly patterned floor may feel chaotic and disturbing rather than inviting.

Lobby Wall Color. The colors in the lobby should reflect the energy you want to convey. Is the building filled with young, high-tech companies or established law firms? What have people experienced prior to arriving on the premises? Did they walk through a dull gray warehouse district or a vibrant area of bars and restaurants? The initial impression of the lobby creates a strong expectation as to what awaits in the offices above. In most instances, we find that the best colors are those that are slightly warm and create an exciting energy. The color value will depend on the scale of the lobby. Although medium-color values can be used in a large space to make it feel somewhat smaller, dark wall colors may feel heavy and oppressive, especially if the ceilings are relatively high. A discussion of the impact of the various colors and their different energies is set forth in Chapter 3: Section A: Colors.

Lobby Lighting. Lobby lighting usually includes recessed down lights and wall washers. Ceiling lighting should be:

1. Warm in temperature
2. Evenly spread throughout the entire area

Warm lighting helps to compensate for the transition of coming from the outdoors into a darker interior space. Almost everyone prefers the warmth of the sun to the blue coolness of the standard fluorescent bulb. Frequently, high ceiling lights create an imbalance of light and dark pools on the floor that are disconcerting.

Lobby Plants and Furniture. To make the lobby feel less sterile, place trees in the two dead corners at the front of the building and two intimate seating arrangements with round tables between them. Table lamps add warmth to the space and bring energy to eye level. Rounding the corners and edges of the reception desk and the furniture in the lobby creates a softer and more inviting environment. You can also balance the colors and elements in this impersonal space with interesting materials, finishes, and fabrics.

Lobby Signage. Directional signage to the elevators and to the tenant spaces should be simple, easy to locate, and easy to read. A signage kiosk that requires multiple actions or signage that is too small to read comfortably adds unnecessary irritation instead of making the process as easy as possible. The process of going to an office is often filled with more than enough stress. Number the elevators in sequence from left to right, because that is the way we read and what you expect. For further discussion, see Chapter 3, Section F: Signage.

Lobby Art. Artwork is a finishing touch in the lobby and can add color, energy, and vitality. Unfortunately, the art too often reflects the taste and personality of the building's owner instead of focusing on the type of energy or mood that is best for the building's occupants. A painting behind the receptionist reinforces the building's image. A lobby sculpture is a statement about the building. Make certain the two are consistent. One high-rise office building opened with an etched glass panel in the elevator lobby that depicted a naked woman. Many floors remained unleased until the "woman" was replaced with an etched scene of flying birds. We have elaborated on these concepts in detail in Chapter 3, Section G: Art and Decorative Objects.

C. OFFICE SPACES

Before We Reach the Office Floor

We always begin a Feng Shui analysis outside a company's space, experiencing the energies in the neighborhood and the building that impact the employees and clients before they step across the threshold into the company's offices.

Why do we spend so much time on the outside world? There is clearly nothing we can do about the neighborhood or the building's façade, signage, lobby, or elevators after our client has negotiated a lease. Once we are aware, however, of the effect that various outside energies have on people before they enter the company's premises, we will know how to shift the energies in the office space to attain the result the company wants. For instance, if the first-floor lobby's energies are very intense, with a great deal of noise, lots of people, bright colors, sharp angles, large objects, and chaotic art work, and an accounting firm wants an image saying, "You are safe and secure with us," it will be important to shift the energy dramatically as soon as the elevator doors open on the company's floor or someone steps into the reception area. Similarly, if the neighborhood is dirty and depressed and the building lobby is dark, gray, and ill lit, then we want everyone to know when they enter an advertising office space that they have entered a new world filled with excitement. The outside world may dictate how extreme the first impression of the company space should be and what design direction it should take.

Tenant Elevator Lobby

In general, the most important aspects of the elevator lobby area on the company's image are the flooring, wall color, lighting, and signage.

Elevator Lobby Flooring. The color, materials, and texture of the elevator lobby floor communicate an immediate feeling when a person first steps into the company's space. As I have discussed before, dark earth tones without a strong pattern feel more natural and more grounding. To a certain degree, the texture of the floor can also support the intended image of the company, whether it is warm and soft and traditional or cold and hard and modern.

Keep in mind, however, the subliminal messages that are being created. Even though a glossy stone tile may look elegant, the shiny surface may be, or appear, slippery and dangerous. A hard surface may be noisy and make people self-conscious, especially those in heels. If the client wants a hard surface, then recommend a slightly textured matte finish that will make the surface feel less slippery and safer. In one instance, we worked with a client who insisted on exposed concrete floors with a clear sealant. After moving in, they were not pleased with the coldness or noise of the flooring. In addition, the inevitable cracks in the concrete conveyed the subconscious image of a company in which things were coming apart. Covering the area with carpet eliminated both the noise and the negative visual image.

Although wood flooring can look and feel less dangerous than marble, it can also be somewhat noisy. A frequent flooring combination is to use 12-by-12 stone tiles surrounding a carpet inset. Although this hard/soft image may be appropriate for the business, the carpeted area should be wide enough to accommodate the traffic and should flow uninterrupted into the reception area, because people will subconsciously want to walk on the more comfortable carpet without transitioning from one surface to another and back again. Stepping over a different surface to reach the carpet, especially if the color value is clearly delineated, creates an uncomfortable interruption in the natural subconscious flow of energy. Carpet clearly has a softer feel and can convey almost any design image, from Spartan to opulent. A carpet with a geometric pattern, even a subtle one, may feel busy and lead in a particular direction, often unintentionally and undesirably. A carpet with some variety of dark- and medium- value color and no strong pattern will generally feel calmer.

Elevator Lobby Finishes. Because an elevator lobby is interior space and is often fairly narrow for the number of people who will pass through it, the color of the walls and elevator doors should probably be a light or medium value, and the lighting should be warm and strong enough to raise the energy and people's spirits. The actual color and finish material should reflect the energy that you want to convey, given your analysis of the company and its desired message about itself, as well as what people have experienced prior to arriving at this point. Remember that the elevator lobby forms one of the first impressions of the company and will create a very strong image. A discussion of the impact of the various colors and their different energies is set forth in Chapter 3, Section A: Colors.

Elevator Lobby Signage. Signage is often the first image people have of a company. Some of the signage issues we've encountered in the elevator lobby are the following:

- *Very small 1- to 1½-inch-high letters.* Up close, this may be fine, but at a distance across the elevator lobby, this size is usually too small and can create the feeling for both the employees and clients that the company does not think of itself as being very important. In fact, it conveys insignificance.
- *Letters that are in a material or color similar to the wall color.* Again, the company is not one that "stands out" in its industry.
- *Letters that are below five feet, the average person's eye level.* This conveys low self-esteem to both the employees and clients. Lettering slightly above eye level has one "looking up at the company," always an important factor.
- *Letters and back panels that are cold and harsh, such as stainless steel letters on glass.* This may be appropriate if "modern technology" is the image that the company wants to portray. Be careful that the overall effect of the lobby is balanced. Small stainless lettering on a gray/white wall with gray flooring, stainless elevator doors, glass entry doors, and low lighting will feel cold, impersonal, and unwelcoming because it is out of balance in being primarily Metal.
- *Letters that are difficult to read.* A signage font or logo that is hard to decipher creates unnecessary tension.
- *Signage on only one side of the elevator lobby when there are elevators on both sides.* When people get off an elevator, we want them to know immediately that they are on the correct floor. Having the elevator doors open and face a blank wall does not deliver that information and is uninviting. Our goal is to make the journey as easy as possible.

- *Oversized letters that scream at you in size or color and are close to the ceiling line.* Such signage undoubtedly conveys an unfavorable image.
- *Inconsistent signage placement.* Be aware of the direction in which the name reads. Our signs obviously read from left to right. As we get off the elevator and read the name of the company, this carries our energy to the right.
- The easy case is when there is a single elevator bank and people get off the elevator, read the organization's name, and indeed find the receptionist to the right. It does happen, occasionally!
- Subconsciously, we expect the reception area to be in that direction. If a person turns to the right, finds a wall or closed door, and has to reverse direction to locate the receptionist, we have made that person's journey just a little bit more difficult.

We can shift this energy in several ways.

- When there is a single elevator bank and the reception area is to the left, we can immediately begin shifting people's energy by having the lighting at the left slightly brighter, drawing attention to that direction. That does not mean you should lower the lighting in the balance of the area so that it becomes uncomfortable. Other techniques are to have the name on a plate that, in a subtly creative way, points toward the left or to have a sign just below the name that says "Reception" in smaller type, with an arrow pointing in the direction of the receptionist. I will leave other methods to your creative imagination.
- When the elevators open up opposite each other, one side works well and the other less well. Have signage on both walls. On the side that reads in the wrong direction, find a natural way to redirect a person's energy.

SPACE PLANNING: USING THE *BAGUA*

Single and Multitenant Floors

In Chapter 7, Section B: Office Buildings, I discussed selecting a space where the main entrance to the reception area is as close to the street as possible. Because the main entrance establishes the "door wall," this minimizes the office space outside the door wall. Locate the less important aspects of the business outside the door wall. Because the people in these areas may subconsciously feel they are "outside" the company, they may be more likely to resign or transfer than will those who are inside the door wall. See Figure 7.6 for examples.

Now it is time to apply the *Bagua* to the footprint of the office space in order to locate people and departments. In most instances, the position of the main entry doors into the reception area determines the location of the nine *Bagua* areas. See Figure 7.7. Superimposing the *Bagua* grid over the floor plan tells us what type of energy will be magnified positively in these areas. Based upon the knowledge of business operations and relationships you learned during the information-gathering phase, determine where people and departments should be located to maximize productivity.

The ideal floor plan layout set forth in Figure 7.7 would locate people as follows:

Position	Location	Bagua Area
Chief Executive Officer	far right	Relationship corner
Chief Financial Officer	far left	Prosperity corner
Marketing Director	far center	Reputation area
Library or Research Department	near left	Knowledge area
Public Relations	near right	Helpful People area

The *Bagua* isn't the only Feng Shui tool suggesting the location of the CEO and CFO, the two people controlling the fate of the business. As you recall from Chapter 2, Section C: the Commanding Position, the power positions in any space are the farthest from the main entrance. These are the same two far corners that the *Bagua* template would select for these functions.

Conference Room Placement. Although the tendency is to place offices and conference rooms on the perimeter window walls and locate the service areas, such as the lunchroom or staff workstations, in the interior, this idea should be challenged for each business.

FIGURE 7.6 *Door Wall Examples in Office Spaces*

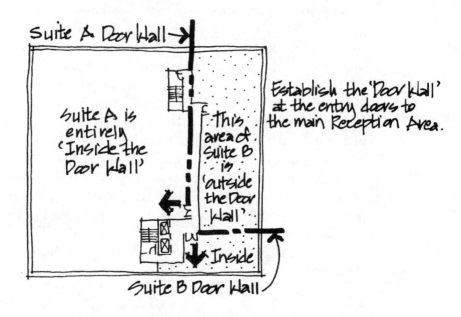

Suite A Door Wall →

Suite A is entirely 'Inside the Door Wall'

This area of Suite B is 'outside the Door Wall'

Inside

Suite B Door Wall

Establish the 'Door Wall' at the entry doors to the main Reception Area.

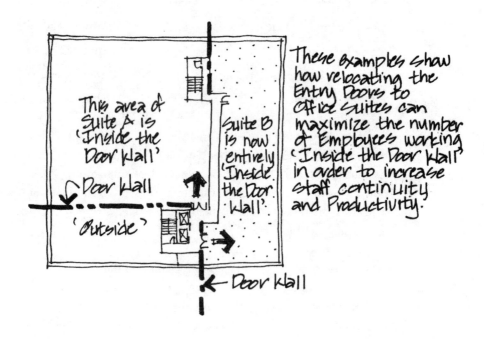

This area of Suite A is 'Inside the Door Wall'

Door Wall

'Outside'

Suite B is now entirely 'Inside the Door Wall'

Door Wall

These examples show how relocating the Entry Doors to Office Suites can maximize the number of Employees working 'Inside the Door Wall' in order to increase staff continuity and Productivity.

FIGURE 7.7 *Locating Offices Using the Bagua*

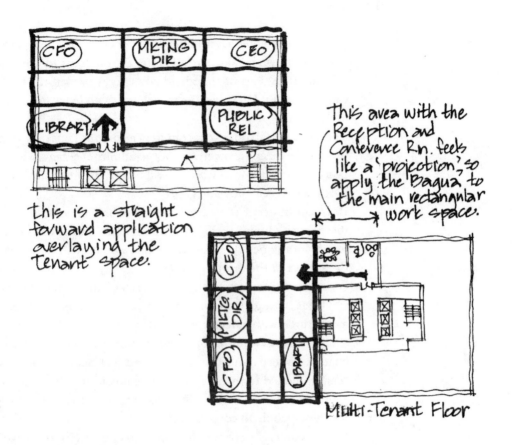

This is a straight forward application overlaying the Tenant space.

This area with the Reception and Conference Rm. feels like a 'projection', so apply the 'Bagua' to the main rectangular work space.

Multi-Tenant Floor

This area is both the 20th floor Reception area and the location of the 1st Floor Main Entry Lobby on the busiest street. Below. People 'feel' their relationship to this entrance so overlay the Bagua on the entire floor.

Conference rooms are often best placed in an interior space for these reasons:

- When people enter a perimeter conference room, their personal energy is drawn outside. We all prefer the outdoors to working inside an office. Part of an individual's energy has left the room. It can be brought back, but the view has just added a small hurdle to productivity.
- The Primary Purpose of a conference room is generally to hold productive business meetings, not to admire the view, which can be a distraction from the business at hand. An impressive meeting location is rarely the main goal.
- Distractions occur whenever a bird, a plane, a person moving in the opposite building, or other movement outside draws the attention of the people facing the window. Energy shifts away from the subject of the meeting.
- Perimeter conference rooms often become uncomfortable as the sun beats through large windows, causing glare and rising temperatures, even with a dedicated HVAC zone.
- The coating on windows often turns them into mirrors, reflecting chaotic patterns and overlapping and distracting images. This "chaos," added to the fact that the people facing the window are probably not in a Commanding Position, is apt to make it difficult for these people to concentrate.
- Placing conference rooms in the interior allows window space and natural light for open office staff areas. The company's executives gain a great deal of good will by conveying to employees that they are important enough to deserve natural lighting and not be stuck in interior rooms.

If a conference room must be located on the perimeter, it can be designed to provide "borrowed" natural light to interior spaces. Both workstations and small interior offices can benefit by sharing the natural light coming through glass conference walls. Later in this chapter I discuss conference room design and the importance of maintaining the privacy of the meeting space and the use of draperies and blinds to alleviate some of the issues described above.

Door Placement. Doors are important elements in Feng Shui. When space planning, be conscious of the location of doors and the way doors open into offices and conference rooms. See Figure 7.8. Avoid having an office door at the end of a long corridor. This is one of the office locations that frequently has a higher turnover rate than the average. Doors on opposite sides of a corridor that don't overlap at all are the best. Doors in direct alignment with each other are acceptable, but consider the room functions. A copy room door aligned with a file room door saves steps and provides a direct path. A copy room door aligned with a private office door makes the occupant feel that everyone leaving the copy room is headed into his or her office. We even had one situation where an individual's door was directly opposite a restroom door. Enough said! Overlapping, but unaligned doors, are considered a problem because they cause an uneven view and an equally unbalanced office relationship between the occupants. As discussed in Chapter 2, Section A: The Flow of Energy, a door should open inward to expose the greater part of the room. As also described in that chapter, be aware of the right-handed door versus the left-handed door concept, and make it as easy as possible for a person to enter every room.

Tenants with Multiple Floors

When office tenants occupy several floors, the psychology of "hierarchy" comes into play. The reception area should generally be located on the lowest floor. When clients arrive, they will either stay on the same floor or be taken to a higher floor. They will never go down. "Ivory tower" status is associated with higher floors, so both clients and employees feel subconscious pride and positive energy when they move upward.

We also recommend placing the officers of the company on the top floor in a superior position to the other employees. If executives make the decision to empower their employees and position staff above themselves, they must be strong enough to do so without losing control. Because people naturally feel more or less important depending upon their position on a higher or lower floor, you will want to discuss these psychological dynamics before locating various personalities and departments within the space. Executives should be advised to remain aware of the dynamics this spatial relationship may create. Remember: The goal is to maximize

FIGURE 7.8 *Door Placement and Corridor Energy*

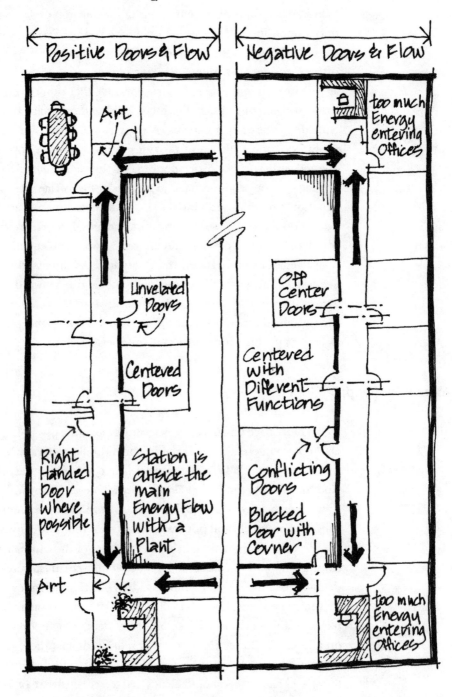

the potential of every individual to the greatest extent possible and to improve each person's life and the company's bottom line.

Reception Area

In Figure 7.9 there are a number of reception area issues. The layout shown in Figure 7.10 creates better energy in the space and a more comfortable experience for the receptionist, employees, and clients.

First, let's look at the issues in Figure 7.9.

- The entry doors open out, causing a person to step back.
- The receptionist is aligned with the main entrance to the space, creating a confrontational relationship. The longer the distance from the elevator to the reception desk, the more uncomfortable people will feel. The hard edges and sharp corners of the desk also contribute to a lack of harmony.

FIGURES 7.9 and 7.10   *Reception Areas*

7.9   7.10

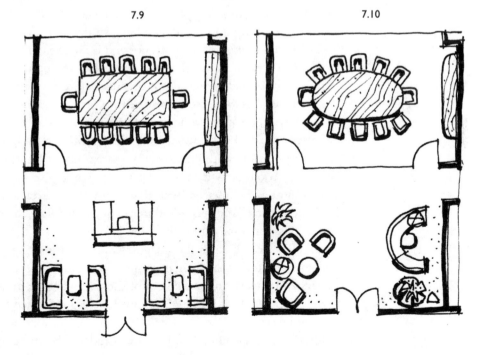

- The glass wall of the conference room pulls attention and energy past the receptionist toward the bright light and outdoors. Natural curiosity focuses attention on any people in the conference room. If the space is vacant, then it gives the impression the company is not busy and therefore not successful. Warm and inviting furniture, colors, art, and lighting that communicate success may overcome this reaction to some degree.
- Each seating area has been arranged so that the first thing people see is the back of a chair with hard edges and sharp corners, not a welcoming feature. In addition, sitting in a chair with its back to the door is a "defenseless" position that makes the occupant feel uneasy.
- All of the lighting in this space comes from recessed fluorescent ceiling fixtures, creating a cold, impersonal wash of light that often results in uneven lighting and light and dark areas on the floor.

Now consider the improvements in Figure 7.10.

- The entry doors invite a person "in" to the office.
- This plan relocates the reception desk to the Helpful People area, which is to the right as people enter. The most natural movement is a curve to the right rather than a long, straight line. The receptionist still has control of the entrance and is far enough from the door to feel secure. In addition, the visitor has an opportunity to become accustomed to the reception area before arriving at the desk. If the desk is too close to the entrance, you are on top of it or past it at once, creating an uncomfortable feeling. The reception desk itself is curved to create a softer and more inviting approach.
- Some corporations with busy reception areas prefer locating the conference room away from the reception area to give more privacy to those who enter and exit that room. A conference room that is adjacent to the reception area requires window covering, frosted glass, or some other treatment for privacy.
- This seating area creates the image of open and inviting arms, welcoming visitors to sit down in comfortable chairs with rounded corners and edges. The placement of the tables and an area rug makes people feel "at home." You now have a good place to put your coffee cup.
- In addition to the ceiling lighting, this plan includes three incandescent lamps to make the space warmer and more inviting. The lamp on the corner of the reception desk provides warm task

lighting. The lamp in the seating area adds an inviting energy to the visitor's part of the room. To create a better balance in the overall space, a small green tree is illuminated from below in the otherwise dead corner, providing natural energy.

If the floor is occupied by a single tenant, a sense of flow and continuity can be created by continuing the same floor and wall finishes from the elevator lobby into the reception area. In a partial floor situation, you will want to apply the concepts for the walls and flooring that was discussed above in entrance areas. Remember to include a coat closet in the reception area for the convenience of visitors.

Office Corridors

Corridors are the rivers that travel throughout office spaces. Employees may never enter all the rooms in an office space, but everyone uses corridors. Wider corridors make people feel more comfortable, so try to maintain a five-foot clearance, expanding wherever possible, because a long, straight corridor creates a sense of both speed and pressure. Think about strong, straight river channels versus winding rivers. Nature, including humanity, does not move naturally in a straight line.

There are several ways to break up a long corridor in an office space. See Figure 7.11:

- Maintain at least a 48-inch clearance between walls and objects, including low potted plants, wall console tables, wall sconces, or art. Alternating the objects on both sides of the corridor creates the illusion of a gently curved pathway.
- Design a strong curve in the flooring pattern and/or in the ceiling plane to create the sense of a natural flow. Subtly curving patterns in the flooring can give the same effect.
- Expand the corridor visually into glass-walled conference rooms and workstation areas with low partitions that are no higher than 48 inches. Extend the same flooring, lighting, and wall colors into these areas to create a consistent feeling. Be careful about invading the privacy of the conference room. Frosting the bottom two-thirds of the glass conference wall still creates a feeling of increased width at that point in the corridor. Widening the corridor at workstation areas also creates the feeling of a curved passageway.

FIGURE 7.11 *Long Office Corridors*

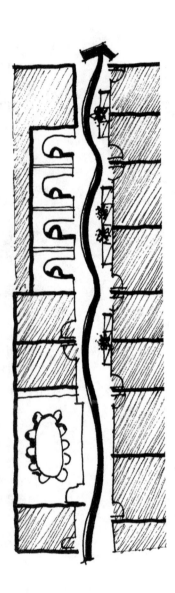

Be aware of the energy created by moving from a narrow corridor into an open office area, back to a corridor, into another open area, and so on. Frequent and extreme transitions may create more discomfort than will the corridor alone.

- Increase the corridor width to allow files along perimeter office walls. Group office doors in pairs and position the files between the pairs. The corridor will expand 20 inches at the paired doorways and create a natural flow. If you use this technique, do not locate the files within 24 inches of a doorway, and place plants on the files to add balancing Wood energy to reduce the negative energy of the sharp cabinet corners and to eliminate the inevitable clutter that will otherwise occur.

I am not recommending jogging the corridor intentionally with repeated right-angled turns, because that generally creates a "rabbit warren" office layout. Simple ring corridors provide a clean circulation path.

Some office designs include corridor flooring with borders of a different color or material along one or both sides. This visually and physically shrinks the corridor width, because our inclination is not to walk on two surfaces at the same time. Using different textures on the two walls can also narrow the hallway, because one wall will have a more comfortable feel and people will edge away from the less comfortable side. Painting each side of a long corridor a different color, however, may make it feel less like a tunnel if the walls are of the same color value and material.

Because corridors are generally interior spaces, they are often dark. Extending a light wall color value from the reception area onto the corridor walls creates a sense of openness and continuity. We can always shift the color energies for variety when we enter other areas of the company. It's best if the corridor lighting level equals that in the reception area so people don't feel the energy decreasing. This effect often requires higher corridor lamping to match the natural light or more open area of the reception area.

When space planning, try to avoid having a corridor lead directly into a workstation or into the door of an office, as shown in Figure 7.8. The turnover rate in these stations and offices will likely be higher than is the norm. The force of energy channeled down a long, straight corridor directly into a person's workspace can be unsettling. We suggest that you not take a chance on your client's behalf.

If a workstation is already located at the end of a corridor, place a large plant, silk if necessary, between the corridor and the individual to block and absorb the force of the energy. If an office door is at the end of a corridor, do not place the desk directly in line with the corridor and the doorway. This is one of the few situations in which we have actually used a transcendental Feng Shui adjustment in a corporate environment. Our corporate client acknowledged that a problem existed with the office at the end of the corridor and hung a crystal in the corridor outside that office at a height below the top of the door. Visualizing the crystal catching and dispersing this strong energy, the occupant of the office felt more comfortable. See Chapter 9 to read more about this transcendental Feng Shui adjustment.

Hanging art with accent lighting at the end of a corridor will create a point of interest and can subtly direct the viewer in a particular direction. Remember from Chapter 3, Section G: Art, that we can intentionally lead people in a specific direction with the content, color, and composition of art.

Conference Room Design

Typically, the Primary Purpose of a conference room is to facilitate the development of creative ideas and to exchange information in an agreeable, calm, yet slightly stimulating environment. Let's take a look at some of elements that make a conference room successful for the people who meet in it.

Flooring in Conference Rooms. Even if the company's image is sharp and modern, carpet creates a feeling of warmth and comfort conducive to conversation. If the corridor flooring is not carpet, then the change to carpet conveys a change in mood. Changing the color of the carpet will communicate a shift in energy. We recently visited a law firm's conference room with bright red carpet and more than enough confrontational energy already coming in the door. We recommended replacing the red carpet with a cool dark color to produce more balance during the meetings. Dark colors typically make people feel more grounded and lead to calmer conversations. Feng Shui associates blue with Knowledge, green with Growth, and purple with Wealth. These are all good choices for a conference room. Remember, however, that blue also is associated with Water and might create a less stable feeling than green.

Glass Walls in Conference Rooms. Conference rooms with glass walls frequently cause a number of privacy and clutter issues and require special features to provide a private, productive meeting environment.

- The most effective method is to add film to the bottom two-thirds of the glass. The two-thirds dimension is the "natural" division. If the film covers only the middle portion, the horizontal stripes create a feeling of busyness that is not productive. The open view below the film stripe also reveals whatever is visible—and distracting—from both inside and outside the conference room.
- A generally less desirable method is to install vertical louver drapes with small-dot perforations that transmit light but don't reveal faces. Make certain that the drapes cover the full expanse of glass and are always in good condition.
- Horizontal miniblinds aren't recommended at glass walls, because blinds rarely line up, they can be bent, and the wall often looks cluttered. They can be used for narrow sidelights where they are either opened or closed and never partially raised.

Providing total visual privacy is absolutely required at secondary conference rooms that are often "temporarily" used as computer training centers or workrooms. The chaos of computer wires, monitor backs, and file boxes conveys a bad impression of the company.

Perimeter Windows in Conference Rooms. As we discussed above, having a conference room on the perimeter may not be the best use of that space. We recommend that window draperies be drawn prior to, and during, the meeting and only be opened during a break to look at that spectacular view.

Conference Room Wall and Ceiling Colors. A dark, cool color on the floor and a slightly warmer but much lighter color on the walls help balance the energy in the room. A wall color of warm cream with some yellow adds a creative energy without becoming too intense. This subtle color communicates the warmth of the sun, always a stimulating feeling. In most cases, avoid white or gray walls. Both colors are associated with the harshness of Metal, and gray can lower energy to the point of depression. Office environments usually have many Metal elements, both outside and inside the building, including vehicles, harsh people, elevator doors, file cabinets, computer equipment, and so on. These Metal elements need to be balanced with objects, textures, and colors that represent the other elements of Water, Wood, Fire, and Earth to create a psychologically balanced and pleasant environment. A white ceiling completes the balance of the natural progression from the light ceiling (the sky) to the medium value of the walls (the plants) to the dark floor (the earth).

Conference Room Furniture Selection and Placement. Conference room furniture typically includes a table, chairs, credenza, and visual aid materials, such as a projection screen or white board. A round or oval table encourages people to work together. A square or rectangular table creates a more confrontational atmosphere. Rectangular tables also establish a power hierarchy regardless of the overall shape, curved corners and bull-nose edges around the entire table reduce edgy feelings in the room.

We always discuss with our clients the dynamics of sitting in the various seats at a table. The strongest positions are those in the Commanding Position. See Figure 7.12 for furniture layouts for large and small conference rooms and the most powerful chair locations. Chairs 2 and 3 are the strongest positions in larger conference rooms with two doors. Chair 5 is the most powerful position in a large conference room with one door. In the small conference room, Chairs 4 and 5 are both in a Commanding Position. Shifting these two chairs slightly could change the dynamic. Once we are aware of this concept, we can place ourselves or our clients in the positions that will create the desired result in the meeting.

FIGURE 7.12 *Commanding Positions in a Conference Room*

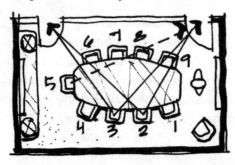 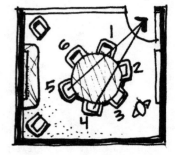

Dark- or medium-colored chair fabrics give a greater sense of support than light colors. If the predominant color feeling in the room is cool, then warm it up with the chair fabric color or vice versa. Use the chair color to balance the elements in the room. For instance, to balance a green carpet (Wood), cream walls (Earth), and white ceiling (Metal), use fabrics and accessories that include black or navy blue (Water) and red (Fire) to help make the room feel complete. I am not suggesting these particular color choices, but am using them as an example of the way color choices can balance the Five Elements.

Place a credenza at the end of the room opposite the door. When a credenza is placed right inside the door, it can create an unfriendly feeling of blockage, especially if it has sharp corners and edges. Locating a credenza here also makes food immediately visible. In most instances, people do not enter a conference room to eat, so food should not be the first thing they see. Remember, the first thing you see upon entering a room becomes the most important to the subconscious mind, or in the case of food probably to the conscious mind!

Adding table lamps with ceramic bases on either end of the credenza is a good way to add warm energy and balance color. Because most, if not all, of the conference lighting is in the ceiling, table lamps will create a more intimate feeling. Pendant light fixtures above the conference table will also add both warm light and interest at eye level, but these obviously are not possible if projection screens or white boards are used for presentations because they would block the view. In using pendant fixtures over the conference room table, be very aware of the metaphor of the light fixture. Does it consist of harsh metal pieces that are aimed at the people in the room, or does it convey a message that is conducive to the Primary Purpose of the room? People often ask where to install a projection screen. The guidelines of the Commanding Position place the screen at the main entry end of the room so that people will not feel uncomfortable if someone enters the room behind them while they are watching a presentation.

Conference Room Art. Art and other decorative objects, like wall hangings, have a strong impact on a room's occupants. One law firm's conference room we viewed was "the last choice" of the lawyers, solely because it contained a large, colorful, abstract painting that conveyed a chaotic, almost angry energy. Although valuable, this painting did not belong in a space that often held adversarial energy. Conference room art should contain colors, shapes, and images that are positive and stimulating in a gentle way. A balance of mixed warm and cool colors rather than primary colors and a predominance of round shapes and curved lines rather than sharp edges and straight lines are more appropriate for the conference room's Primary Purpose of consensus building.

Private Offices

See Figure 7.13 and Figure 7.14 for two midsized private office layouts. Figure 7.13 violates most Feng Shui and good design principles, whereas Figure 7.14 enhances the productivity of the occupant. Many of the concepts that drive the good office relate to the Commanding Position, which we discussed in Chapter 2. Do not let electrical and computer wiring dictate the placement of furniture. Office layout is about enhancing the productivity of the individual, not the wiring.

The layout in Figure 7.13 subconsciously reduces the self-esteem and productivity of the office occupant.

- The energy coming in the door and from the eyes of everyone walking past is aimed directly at the person at the desk. This intense flow of energy can be overstimulating and fracture con-

FIGURES 7.13 and 7.14   *Private Offices*

7.13   7.14

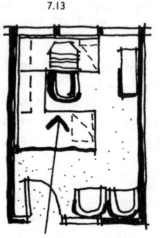

centration. With this layout, the turnover rate tends to be higher than the company norm, perhaps because the person is trying to escape this intense energy.

- To block out the distractions from the corridor, the occupant's back is to the door while working at the computer. This increases tension and may have a negative effect on performance. When visitors enter, they will be in control of the space, not the person occupying the office. If this arrangement exists and cannot be changed, place a mirror on the desk so that the occupant can at least see who is entering the room.
- The first office view is the uninviting back of a chair. The occupant must then walk around sharp desk corners and through a narrow passage to reach the desk chair. I discuss narrow passageways in detail in Chapter 2, Section A: The Flow of Energy.
- The ceiling lighting is cold, impersonal, and not at eye level. Because the needs for adequate computer lighting versus adequate task lighting are different, the ceiling lighting will not be appropriate for both functions.

The layout in Figure 7.14 feels better, even before we analyze its various components.

- By moving the desk to the other side of the room, the occupant and guests are no longer directly in the path of energy, making it more protected and inviting to everyone.
- Relocating the computer forces the person to sit in a more Commanding Position. It is now clear who is in control of this office.
- This plan causes the occupant to move in a natural curve through a wider passageway between rounded corners to the primary chair. Note that the corners of all of the furniture are rounded.
- In addition to the ceiling lighting, this layout includes three light fixtures to create a warmth and balance of energy. The lamp on the desk provides good task lighting. The guest area lamp makes that area more inviting. A light in the corner adds the third point of energy we discussed in Chapter 2, Section B: The Balance. Plants and silk flowers add life energy, often absent from an office, and fill the dead spaces.

Make certain that office furniture is suitable for the specific office plan. Sometimes offices hold desks meant for larger rooms or rooms with a different door handing. An inappropriate desk will impede movement and reduce comfort and productivity. Most people greatly prefer desks with returns and attached credenzas that create an L-shape or U-shape. Furniture with these components allows people to swivel into a variety of ergonomic working positions for different tasks, improving employee health.

Be very careful about using moveable modular components that the occupant can easily rearrange. These can produce good or bad layouts. Once an individual office has been arranged, make certain that the components are attached firmly to one another and do not wobble or move in the slightest. Any instability in part of the desk will create a feeling of instability in the user. The desk chair should be fully ergonomic, preferably with a high back so the occupant feels more important and projects that impression. Think "CEO!"

We frequently hear people say, "But I want to have my desk facing the window so that I can look at the great view I finally have." However, when we point out that the Primary Purpose of the office is not the view, but for them to be productive, in control, and successful and that they can always take a break and relish the scenery, they almost always relent. The general principles we have discussed for the good midsized office have also been applied to the small and large private offices shown in Figures 7.15 A and B.

Now let's consider some of the other design elements that can make a private office successful for its occupant.

Private Office Flooring. A change in the color of the carpet or other flooring from the corridor creates the sensation that one is entering a different world. This could be a positive feeling for the occupant, if this change occurs uniformly in all offices. If the flooring for the executive offices differs, however, such a distinction in hierarchy will probably not enhance the performance of the nonexecutives. Carpet seems more comfortable and is quieter than a wood or tile floor. An earth tone adds an elemental aspect that will make the occupant feel more grounded and stable.

FIGURES 7.15A AND 7.15B *Small and Large Offices*

7.15A

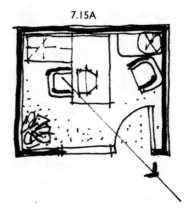

7.15B

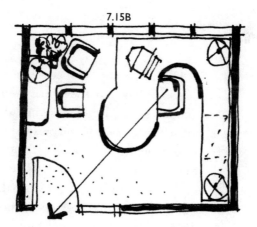

Private Office Windows. Window blinds that pull down are recommended, although the building owner often selects the window covering. We strongly recommend that people lower and close the blinds or pull the curtains shut when leaving for the day. The next morning when they arrive at work, their energy and thoughts will be contained within the room and will not immediately fly out the window to a place they would rather be. Remember that the first thing we see when we enter a space is where our subconscious takes us. People can raise blinds later to let in natural light or look at the view. We also suggest lowering the blinds when visitors are expected so that they, too, remain highly focused.

Private Office Wall and Ceiling Colors. Because everyone's personality and needs are somewhat different, the ideal situation is for each employee to choose the color for his or her own office or for one accent wall from a preselected group of colors based on the elements that we discussed in Chapter 2, Section E: The Five Elements, and your design scheme. If one color is selected for use in all the offices, then a change from the color in the public areas may create a feeling of importance and enhance the productivity of employees. The colors you select will also depend upon the desired effect you want the space to have on the employees, using the approach we discussed in Chapter 3, Section A: Colors. In almost every case, we strongly recommend that the default color be a warm cream, not a white or light gray. The energy of the cream color is a subconscious reminder of the energy of the sun and will raise the energy level of the room's occupant.

Shared Offices

When a shared office arrangement is required, it is best to lay out the desks with both of the primary work surfaces facing the door. This may require a slightly larger office but will give both occupants a greater sense of ease and control. If one person sits farther from the door, that individual will be in the Commanding Position and will subconsciously feel more important and be more comfortable than the person sitting closer to the door.

If a shared office is too small to allow both desks to face the door, make certain that both employees sit away from the direct energy coming through the door opening. If people face a wall, place a mirror on the wall in front of them that is large enough to open up their space and their thinking process and allows them to feel more in control by giving them a view of the door.

Open Office Workstation Areas

When an open office area is designed to include workstations, the most important guideline is to position the computer or most frequently used desk surface so the occupant faces the main entrance to the open office area. This gives individuals at least some sense of being in command of their world. See Figure 7.16.

FIGURE 7.16 *Workstations*

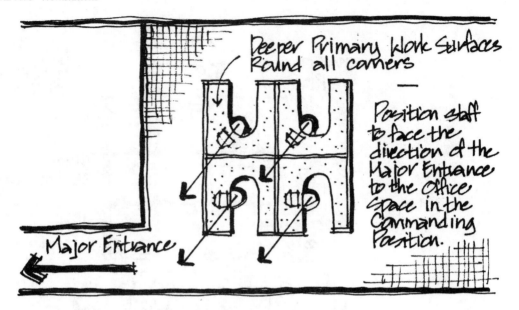

Because people like privacy, the workstation panels should usually be high enough to block the view of adjacent workstation staff when sitting. Although most employees prefer high partitions for privacy and acoustical reasons, lower partitions contribute to a light and open office feeling that employees also appreciate. One solution is to group high-partition workstations together in interior areas with low-partition workstations fronting the corridor. Another is to divide workstations into linear groupings, with high back spines, medium height panels between stations, and low panels at the corridor.

Unless the excitement of a noisy office is considered a positive aspect of the office environment, acoustic partitions with sound deadening material should be provided. Carpet and plants throughout the space will also absorb some of the sound. Workstation counters are typically plastic laminate but can come in a variety of wood patterns that appear natural. Employees will benefit from the feeling that warm wood patterns convey, and they will enjoy working on surfaces that are visually similar to the real wood desks in most private offices.

We often give a lecture to the employees of a corporate client when the space has been completed to explain what we have done and why. Because workstations are less private than offices are, we explain some

FIGURE 7.17 Bagua *as Applied to Workstations*

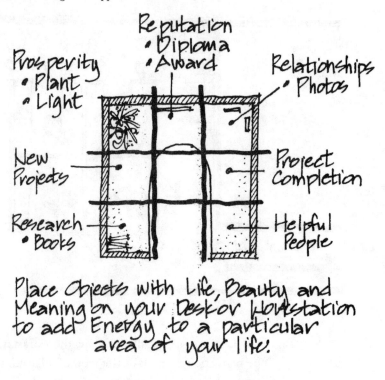

Reputation
• Diploma
• Award

Prosperity
• Plant
• Light

Relationships
• Photos

New Projects

Project Completion

Research
• Books

Helpful People

Place Objects with Life, Beauty and Meaning on your Desk or Workstation to add Energy to a particular area of your life.

of the techniques, including the *Bagua* and other tools, they can use to personalize their space and make themselves feel less anonymous.

Open Desk Areas

In an open floor plan, the most important feature is to have all of the desks facing the main entrance to the space. Remember that the placement of people will create a natural hierarchy, with those who are farthest from the entrance appearing to have the most authority. An employer who is aware of these dynamics can place some of the naturally stronger people in a weaker position to even out the dynamics within the company. The important thing is to be cognizant of the effect of the placement of people within the open area.

In some open office layouts, particularly in the financial industry where people constantly need to interact with one another, rows of desks often face one another. In addition to the issues mentioned above, the people with their backs to the main entrance are more exposed and vulnerable. The people at those desks clearly should be the strongest and calmest personalities in the company.

Lunchrooms

The break and lunchroom areas are for the purpose of relaxing and becoming reinvigorated. In most businesses where stress is apt to have been building over the day, the calmness of cool colors, especially greens, will have the desired effect. We would not recommend using gray or blue in these areas, because gray is apt to depress one's energy and blue tends to kill the appetite. The furniture in the break areas should look and be comfortable and substantial. Cheap-looking pieces, poor lighting, and bad artwork will communicate a message to the employees about how important, or not, management views them to be. Round tables will enhance a feeling of collegiality.

Staff areas are vital to a successful business and should be designed accordingly. We have previously discussed the benefits of locating open office staff areas and break rooms on the perimeter walls instead of rarely used conference rooms. Follow the same concepts discussed for Individual Offices and Workstations. Using plants throughout the office space will visually and psychologically connect the various departments. Select plants of the same size and shape and place them in groupings of three, six, or nine, auspicious numbers in traditional Feng Shui.

Chapter

8

OTHER PROJECT TYPES

A. HOSPITALITY

Even though most guests are not consciously aware of it, the energy that pervades a hotel, casino, or any other space in the hospitality industry significantly influences their experience and satisfaction. Feng Shui is one of the tools many companies in the hospitality industry use to attract more guests and keep them coming back.

We recently talked with the CEO of a casino about the psychological effects of differently shaped interior spaces. "Amazing," he said. "We expanded one of our most successful casinos, but people still seem to prefer the old portion more than the new. Now I know why. The new space is shaped differently, and the old space really does feel more comfortable." Casinos, more than most businesses, intuitively apply some of the Feng Shui concepts to create energies that promote the specific feelings and behaviors of optimism and enthusiasm.

Although every room in a hotel has an impact on the guest, each space is not intended to have the same effect. During the initial information-gathering meeting, you will need to ask, "What is the Primary Purpose of your hotel? Is it for families, business executives, long-term stays?" Frequently the basic answer is: "To make the guest feel at home and leave the next day rested and relaxed." Ask the same Primary Purpose question about each space through which the individual passes during a stay. The answers will vary, and you can then design spaces with the energy to enhance each area's Primary Purpose to benefit both guests and employees.

Begin by looking at what the guests have probably experienced prior to arriving at the hotel. In all likelihood, they have dealt with a long business day, crowds at the airport, or a similarly difficult experience. The environment as they approach the hotel is also an important factor and establishes a subliminal feeling as to the kind of experience they expect to have. If the neighborhood is beautiful, then the transition from the chaos of the day has already begun to shift. If arriving has not been an easy or pleasant journey, then the moment the guest approaches the hotel, the energy must completely shift, literally screaming out, "Welcome! You have finally arrived home, a place that will be very peaceful and easy and where you can escape all of the chaos of your day."

Signage

The ultimate goal is to make the guest's flow of energy very smooth. Effective signage is often the first guest experience that we can control. Issues include exterior signage showing where the hotel is located, where to park, where to enter, and where the front desk is located, as well as interior signage indicating where the front desk is located, where the elevators are, where the banquet rooms and health facilities are, and last, but certainly not least, the direction of the rooms on each floor. In numbering the guest rooms, remember that we read from left to right. If the low numbers take people to the right when they exit the elevator, the sequence will feel more natural. Because many people will not remember the correct direction to the elevators when they leave their room, include frequent directional signs to the elevators throughout the individual floors to avoid any confusion. A picture opposite a room door that reads in the correct direction is a subtle way to reduce the elevator signage and accomplish the same effect.

As discussed in Chapter 3, Section F, signage should be of a size and font that makes it easy to read. Placing the signage just slightly above eye level makes it more prominent and easier to find. We have seen exterior "Hotel" signs with an arrow pointing to the entrance that were only two feet high and partially covered by landscaping. Talk about making it difficult! Signage within an elevator cab should be hung slightly higher than six feet so that it is visible to the person at the back of the elevator. Make the guest's journey as easy as possible.

Main Entrance

When a guest has trouble finding the hotel because of poor outside signage, has trouble opening the door because the first one was locked, or has trouble finding the reception desk, the experience has already become a stressful one, creating an unpleasant impression of the hotel. If, on top of these difficulties, the color energies of the lobby, the shapes of the furniture, and the finishes in the elevators are out of balance and lower their energy, you have designed a hill for the guests to climb. Even the more subtle elements, such as the roughness of the stone columns at the outside entrance, the low lighting at the front door, and other seemingly minor aspects of the entrance area can have a cumulative negative effect. By this time, the guests may have already decided that they dislike the hotel—and they haven't yet reached their room.

Let's discuss two specific examples relating to the hotel entrance. We often see deep and dark porticos with low clearances of eight to nine feet. These create too extreme a change from the very high "ceiling" of the outdoor sky and immediately cause a feeling of compression. Figure 8.1 shows the dramatic contrast between sky and entry. The gradual sloping transition in height shown in Figure 8.2 creates a more natural and comfortable flow of energy. If a gradual transition isn't possible, then flood the low ceiling area with a great deal of light, using ceiling, sconce, and landscape uplighting to fill the area with energy in order to balance the compression of the low ceiling.

As a guest approaches the entrance doors with a suitcase in one hand and a purse or briefcase in the other, opening a door outward is awkward and requires the person to take a step backward. We realize that fire codes usually dictate that an entrance door swing out. Using doors that slide open automatically, revolving doors that are large enough to comfortably include a person and at least one large suitcase, or doors that swing both ways are good alternatives to make it easy for the guest to enter the lobby smoothly.

FIGURE 8.1 *Hotel Entrance Without Transition*

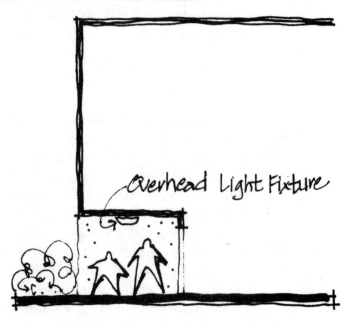

FIGURE 8.2 *Hotel Entrance With Transition*

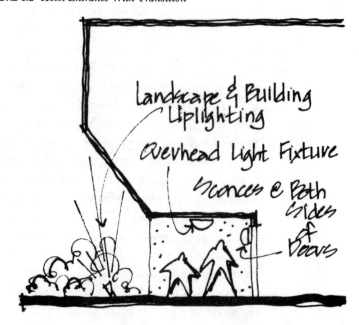

Lobby and Front Desk

The transition from the outdoors into the lobby should also be effortless. A dramatic change in the intensity in lighting will cause the body to tense. Going from bright daylight into a darker lobby forces the eyes and brain to adjust to the new light level. Similarly, going from the dark of night into the bright light of a lobby is also a shock. Provide dimmers on the lights in the portico and lobby areas that can be separately adjusted throughout the day to create a more natural shift in a guest's energy.

The textures in the lobby area convey an immediate message to a guest. Is this going to be a hard, noisy place or a gentle and cozy environment? Your design decisions should always go back to the hotel's Primary Purpose. Marble lobby floors with chrome, steel, and glass fixtures and furnishings convey a message of coldness that the guest immediately expects to be reflected in the front desk personnel and the entire stay. As a result, the energy of the guest who is coming from a chaotic world has not begun to shift from the harshness of the outside environment. Stepping onto a soft carpet in an environment that is balanced in color but leans towards the cooler colors with soft music subtly playing in the background will shift the guest's energy fairly quickly to a more relaxed state. On the other hand, if the hotel is located in a very hot, sultry climate, the coolness of the marble, white, and chrome may be exactly the relief that the guest is seeking.

The location of the reception desk also affects the guest's flow of energy. Guests should not have to search for the front desk. The placement of the reception desk directly opposite the entrance, as is commonly done, may create a confrontational feeling.

So where should you locate the reception desk? Because the majority of people are right-footed and right-handed, our natural inclination when entering a space is to go to the right. In addition, people are more comfortable moving in a curved manner. Nature is composed of curves, not straight lines. Place the reception desk to the right of the door and far enough from the entrance so the guest has a chance to adjust to the change in the energy inside the hotel without either walking past the desk and having to backtrack to reach it or having to stop in the doorway to find it. Figure 8.3 shows two variations using this principle. A reception desk that is to the right in a lobby will also be in the Helpful People section of the *Bagua*, a highly appropriate location.

FIGURE 8.3   *Hotel Lobby Plans*

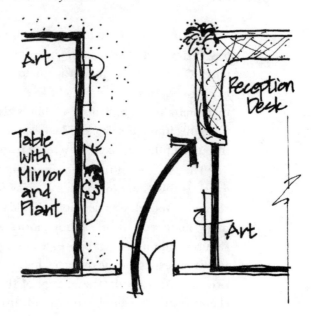

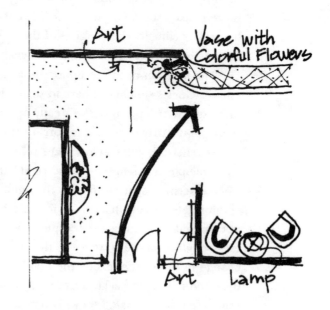

If the lobby area has ample room, a round table with a bouquet of flowers in the middle of the entrance area and 15 to 25 feet back from the entrance will be a colorful and welcoming greeting to the guests. Placing a bouquet of flowers on the far end of the front desk from the entrance will draw the eye to the front desk, add both nature and color energies to the lobby, and not block the front desk personnel's view of the entrance.

One of the first hotel representatives a guest may see is a front desk staffer. Provide the front desk personnel with enough space so they can move freely to perform their duties. Place the computers and all of the required equipment in such a way that the staff can use them without having to turn their backs to the guests. Turning around repeatedly and frequently having their backs to the guests will increase the employees' tension level and make them less pleasant. Reducing the stress level will result in the staff's being more relaxed, courteous, and healthy in a sometimes inherently stressful job.

Elevators and Corridors

Elevators are very close spaces in which strangers often feel crowded together. Although more expensive, a larger elevator cab feels more comfortable. Mirroring the walls of the cab "enlarges" the space and gives everyone a sense of more control over those unknown people behind them. Light, cool colors with warm wood or color accents will open up the space, make the walls recede, and calm the environment.

Stepping off an elevator and facing a wall with small, or no, room numbers is not inviting or informative and adds to the guest's tension. Make certain that the directional signs are very easy to read. Incorporate a table with rounded corners on the facing wall, and a bouquet of real or silk flowers or a picture of a relaxing scene above to add a welcoming energy. If you use a picture opposite the elevator, make certain that it pulls viewers into the space and doesn't send them in a specific direction, because the guest's room may be in the other direction, adding to the tension. Avoid placing a mirror over the table, because it would reflect the guest back into the elevators. For further discussion, see Chapter 3, Section G: Art.

The long corridors that seem to stretch on forever can be very uncomfortable preludes to a guest's room. Uneven lighting, bland colors, and the unbroken stretch of two straight walls often create a feeling of sterility. Specify warm and even lighting throughout each corridor to avoid the feeling of repeatedly going from one level of energy to another.

If the colors in the corridor are very neutral and moving toward gray, the effect can be depressing rather than calming. Using the principle of the three basic values of nature, use the darkest value on the floor. A medium-value carpet in cool earth tones, with touches of warmer colors to create a balance, is generally the most appropriate energy. Save the darker flooring for the guest rooms. Select a lighter side of the medium range on the walls to avoid making the corridor seem even narrower than it is. A pale yellow or rose on the walls is reminiscent of natural energy and will add a warm color balance to the cooler carpet. Because yellow is in the middle of the visual color spectrum, both men and women are apt to be comfortable with it. The other colors of the spectrum can then be introduced in the artwork. A white or extremely light ceiling completes the range of color values.

The most effective way to create the meandering feeling of nature in a long, straight corridor is to place semicircular tables with silk flowers or plants at regular intervals on alternating sides. See Figure 8.4. Mirrors over the tables will also widen the passageway, create a feeling of motion and variation in the width of the space, and magnify the color energy of the flowers or plants on the table. The color of vases or pots can complete the full color spectrum and add energy to the corridor.

Sconces on alternating sides of the corridor also create a sense of motion in the corridor. The depth of the sconces into the passageway, as well as the additional light energy, adds variety to a straight wall. Artwork and projecting wall panels or door frames alternating down the corridor can also give a slight variation in the visual feel of its width. In selecting artwork for a corridor, choose images with depth. Pictures should have a calming effect, and images should be viewed easily from two to three feet, because the corridor is probably only five to six feet wide.

Another technique for creating a "meandering" corridor is to use a carpet with a wavy pattern. The best way to create this feeling is to have a very subtle and quiet motion in the overall carpet or to have a narrow wavy border on both sides on which no one will be walking. The wave will bring an image of water to the subconscious. If the border is wavy, have the basic central carpet pattern turn into the door of each room so that the guest is neither walking on nor stepping over the wave.

FIGURE 8.4 *Hotel Corridor*

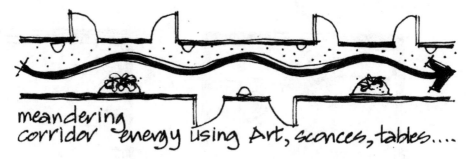

Doorways are occasionally recessed, often creating a feeling of inse-curity because people cannot see what is happening in the rest of the corridor as they try to enter their room.

Be conscious of the light fixture location in the area around a guest room entry door. The light should be above or on the keyhole side of the door, so the guest can easily find and use the room key, not behind the guest or on the other side of the door, where the guest's body can block out the light.

Guest Rooms

A good night's sleep is obviously the Primary Purpose for a hotel room. To make us feel safe and secure, the Commanding Position is an important principle in guest room design. Figures 8.5 and 8.6 show two commonly designed guest rooms, one of which is much more likely to accomplish the intended goal than is the other.

Beginning at the entrance to the room, the door swing in Figure 8.5 immediately reveals the bathroom door, not the most welcoming sight or most positive psychological imprint for a guest. By changing the swing in Figure 8.6, the guest first sees the closet, a neutral image. If these doors are mirrored, the guest will see the restful image of a bed-room and be pulled visually into what appears to be a larger room than it actually is. If the room is large enough, avoid having the bathroom door open into the entryway. In every case, avoid having the bathroom door open onto any part of the bed itself. Because we often recommend to individual clients that they carry small door chimes to hang on the door to create a welcoming greeting as they enter the room, as well as a

FIGURES 8.5 and 8.6   *Hotel Rooms*

8.5   8.6

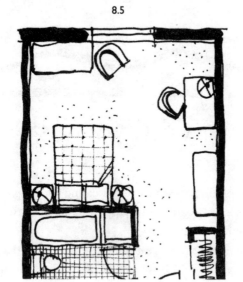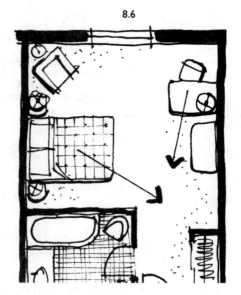

subtle alarm system that will enable the subconscious to relax even more, incorporating door chimes in your design would be a wonderful feature.

The placement of the bed on the bathroom wall in Figure 8.5 violates several basic principles. One side of the bed is too close to the wall, making it uncomfortable for the person on that side of the bed. The message is almost one of not being welcome. This positioning also prevents guests from feeling in control of the space, because they do not face the entrance to the room and are not in a Commanding Position. It is not necessary for people to be able to see the door so long as they are looking in the direction of the entrance. The third major issue with the bed in Figure 8.5 is that the headboard is on the bathroom wall. This can make sleeping more difficult than it would be if the bed were located in the position in Figure 8.6. Placing a headboard so that plumbing noises echo in the tiled space behind it poses potential acoustical problems. The subtle psychological effect of having one's head near a bathroom may also be unhealthy.

We have changed the locations of the toilet and the sink in the two diagrams. In Figure 8.5, the toilet is directly in line with the door instead of in a more private location. In Figure 8.6, the toilet is shielded by a 42-inch-high wall, providing the feeling of greater privacy. This layout also provides a "first impression" of the artwork opposite the door, instead of the toilet.

If the toilet has to be located behind the door, add a doorstop so that the individual using the toilet will feel secure that the door cannot hit them if it swings open. In addition, a mirror over the sink that reflects the door to the bathroom will give a feeling of psychological control over the entrance.

The desk in Figure 8.5 shows the occupant directly in line with the energy from the entrance and with his or her back to the majority of the room. By turning the desk 90 degrees, we put the guest out of the line of the door and into the Commanding Position. Place a lamp behind the easy chair to add light energy to a dead space and to warm up the room.

Because we subconsciously avoid potentially painful sharp corners, rounded corners and edges on the bed, chairs, dresser, desk, and bedside tables create a more calming environment. To the extent that the corners of the bathroom and the closet that project into the room have round molding edges, the flow of energy will also feel more comfortable.

Your choice of colors and fabrics will also affect the energy of the room. Change to a differently colored, plusher carpet to enhance the feeling of personal comfort and separation from the outside world. Large patterns, stripes, and other geometrical wall covering and fabric patterns may give the room a busy feeling that is not conducive to sleeping well. In general, cooler colors are more relaxing but should be balanced throughout the room with some warm hues. The balancing of the colors can occur in the furniture fabrics, accessories, and artwork, which should also be calming images rather than chaotic or "dark."

We often recommend that clients carry a personal item, such as a picture or personal icon, so they can create a sense of familiarity and a feeling that the space is theirs, not just a strange room in a strange locale. Some hotels are beginning to realize the importance of making a person feel at home and are providing guests with a choice of objects to personalize their room.

Conference and Banquet Rooms

Conference and banquet rooms are frequently empty and located in areas of the hotel that lack regular traffic, so no consistent human energy passes through these spaces. In addition, the scale of banquet rooms is often very large, subconsciously overwhelming the smaller scale of a person. The high ceilings, which often contain most of the lighting for the space, also create a sense of human insignificance and diminishing energy on our human level.

Beginning with the approach to these facilities, make certain that the signage is clear. Place trees, chairs, and round tables with table lamps in the expansive hallways outside the meeting rooms to add energy and to make the areas more user friendly. Avoid recessing the entrances to these spaces so that they do not feel at all hidden.

In designing these rooms, use the Golden Rectangle as a guideline for both the plan and the volume. A deep room that is considerably longer than those proportions will feel even more immense than it really is.

Use warmer colors throughout these areas, because high energy and excitement is generally the goal of these spaces. Wall sconces will also bring more energy to the human level and make the space feel more welcoming.

Employee Spaces

Employee offices, break rooms, and restroom facilities are often treated as "second cousins" during the design process. These rooms are just as important as every other space in the facility, because one of our primary goals is to maximize the productivity of the employees. Avoid placing employee facilities in the basement or in areas that seem out of the way. Such placement communicates a message of low esteem, and the individual who feels treated like a second-class citizen certainly will not give a first-class performance.

With respect to all of these employee spaces, the corridors should have the same feeling as the other corridors in the hotel. This would include good lighting, peaceful colors, and artwork. In summary, to keep the person's energy in the room, place the employee in a Commanding Position with ergonomic and comfortable furniture, and provide storage space that will help the individual avoid clutter. All of the furnishings and fixtures in staff areas should be good quality. Table lamps and comfortable furniture will add to the feeling that employees' work is appreciated. Through good design, communicate the message that each employee is as important as each guest.

B. HEALTH CARE

Each of us knows what it feels like to walk into a doctor's office, a hospital, or a nursing home. Even if we are healthy and just visiting a patient, our anxiety level increases dramatically. Many of us know the even greater stress level of being a patient. As we approach a health care facility, we experience the following:

- Fear of the unknown
- Loss of control
- Vulnerability

It is well documented that these stressors greatly affect us on physiological, psychological, and behavioral levels and that the environment has a tremendous effect on the healing process. The Robert Wood Johnson Foundation and the Center for Health Design convened national health care leaders in June 2004. The focus of the conference was on over 600 research studies that connect the quality of patient health and care with the way a hospital is designed. The report of the Foundation on "Designing the 21st-Century Hospital" reiterates many of the Feng Shui recommendations discussed in this book. The evidence is overwhelming that the hospital environment has substantial effects on patient health, safety, and care; on family participation in the patient's healing process; and on staff effectiveness, efficiency, and morale.

Entering a health care facility is a tremendous transition. To make this shift easier and the subsequent experience less stressful for both the patient and the family, your goal is to design facilities that resemble a more comfortable and familiar place—a home away from home. If this is a new facility, remember to begin with rectangular shapes, avoid slanted ceilings and angled walls, and follow the other recommendations in Chapters 2, 3, 4, and 5. Be conscious of the metaphors that designs may subconsciously project. Any image that is threatening or could connote illness or death in any way, such as a precarious-looking bridge over an atrium space, should be avoided at all cost.

FIGURES 8.7 and 8.8   *Doctor's Office Waiting Room*

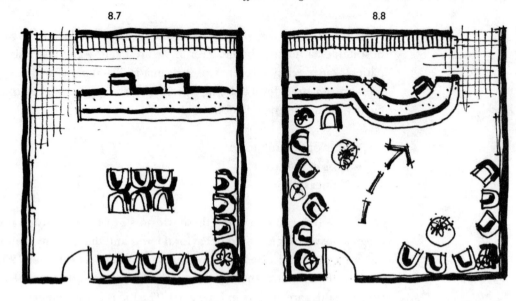

Doctor's Offices and Outpatient Clinics

Depending upon the doctor's specialty, some offices may benefit from an environment that will stimulate the patient, whereas others may be more suited to spaces that calm a person.

Patient Waiting Areas. Think "living room" when you design a patient reception and waiting area. Figure 8.7 is an example of a common plan that may increase a patient's stress level rather than reduce it. Figure 8.8 relocates some of the elements to create a more peaceful and healing environment.

Design a waiting area that is warm and friendly with a natural and easy flow of energy. Immediately seeing the corridor to the examining offices pulls our psychological energy too quickly into the "doctor's" space. On the other hand, centering the entry doors on the reception desk is too confrontational for the patient as well as the receptionist. By placing the receptionist off to the right with open floor space between the door and counter, the patient will move in a more natural curvilinear motion. Avoid having rows of patient records visible on the wall behind the reception desk, if possible. This view communicates that the patient is just one of many sick people.

The seating arrangement in Figure 8.7 places waiting patients either facing a stranger or sitting too close to other people in unnatural straight rows. The number of seats also indicates that many people are often waiting to be helped, another cause of stress. To avoid these conditions, Figure 8.8 has fewer seats, indicating that the wait will not be long. This arrangement allows people to sit in flexible groupings that are more natural and relaxing. The tables and lamps between the chairs create a feeling of separation from the stranger in an adjacent seat, and the added lighting on the human level adds warmth to the space. The open area in the center of the room, with tables and flowers, makes the space less personally invasive and contributes to the residential atmosphere.

In Figure 8.8, the seating arrangement is curved and suggests arms welcoming a patient. The light in the corner between the two chairs and real or silk plants in the corners enlivens the dead areas of the room.

Paint the waiting area a pale color other than white. Although white is traditionally associated with cleanliness, it is also cold and impersonal. Use light color values to make the room appear larger. Although green is a healing color, consider using warm creams and colors that are subtly reminiscent of sunlight to create an easier and more natural transition from the outdoors.

Carpet the floor to make the waiting area feel warmer, using dark brown or green colors to make the patients feel more grounded. Using reds could increase the stress energy of the patient. Keep the carpet simple and avoid patterns that would add a sense of busyness and chaos to both the room and the patients' subconscious mind.

If a restroom is accessible from the waiting room, make the signage very easy to see. Asking for directions will make a nervous patient even more uncomfortable.

Corridors. Because the corridor is the gateway between public and very private functions, keep it as open, well lit, and friendly as possible. Often many doors branch off the corridor. Avoid conflicting doors as well as centered and overlapping doors that are opposite one another. Locate doors so that they are unrelated to one another to increase the feeling of privacy. Use the same wall colors and flooring in the corridors as in the waiting room so that patients don't experience a sudden

FIGURES 8.9 and 8.10   *Exam Rooms*

8.9

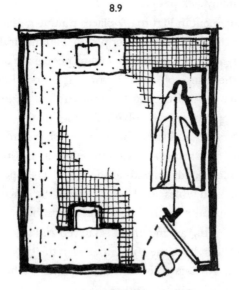

8.10

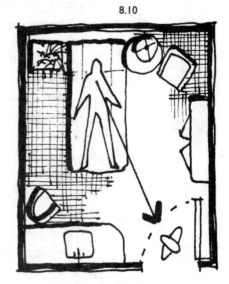

transition from the warmth of the waiting room to the treatment area. Add artwork that is horizontal in shape, contains very peaceful landscapes, and is calming in its predominantly cool colors. We recently saw in a doctor's office a large photograph of the New York City skyline with the World Trade Towers in the center—not an appropriate image.

Exam Rooms. This is where the tension mounts. The environment in this room will not only affect the patient but will also have an impact on the energy of the doctor, which will in turn further affect the patient's energy in a continuous cycle. A change in the environment from the waiting area and corridor may be appropriate, depending upon the nature of the practice. Painting the walls a pale green will expand a room that often feels claustrophobic and create a more healing feeling.

The room in Figure 8.9 is apt to maximize a patient's stress. The sharp corner just inside the door is too close and threatening, and the long wall of medical supply shelves sends the message that you will need major help. Whether one is waiting for the doctor or being examined, the only place to sit is on the examining table, which is behind the door in a vulnerable position. The sink, the sharp corner near the head of the examining table, and the empty space behind the table add to a patient's subconscious discomfort. Trapping the patient between the wall and the doctor causes additional patient stress.

In Figure 8.10, we have empowered the patient by placing him or her in the Commanding Position. Upon entering, the patient sees a comfortable chair, table, and lamp. The examining table is now in the middle of the room with the support and protection of the wall behind it and space on both sides, making it easier for the doctor to move around and certainly more comfortable for the patient. In addition, we have moved the bulk of the medical supplies out of the room and out of the patient's sight. The rounded edges on the furniture feel less threatening to both patient and doctor than do the sharp corners. This layout will work well for most medical specialties, but remember that the Primary Purpose might require a different configuration. For instance, in an OB/GYN room, a patient would not want to be in this particular Commanding Position. Turning the head of the examining table counterclockwise 90 degrees would make the patient feel less exposed and still give her some sense of being in command of the room.

If space is available, a plant on a countertop adds healing energy. In addition, horizontal artwork with a calm subject will create a peaceful atmosphere. Pictures of the skeleton and other body parts often can be negative images as we wait for the doctor, stare at all of those strange organs, and become convinced that our own body is failing. If needed, these diagrams can be pulled down as a chart for explanations during the exam. If patients are examined lying down and are looking up, "ceiling art" of natural sky scenes on acrylic lens can be installed in standard fluorescent fixtures and provide a stress-reducing focus.

Consultation Offices. After the exam is over, the patient often moves to the doctor's personal office. The traditional medical diplomas and certificates convey a sense of credibility and professionalism, but a wall covered with many certificates may communicate an excess of bravado or a feeling that the doctor is so busy that the patient is not of primary importance. This is the room for the medical books and charts that tell the patient that the doctor knows his or her job. Although a few pictures of the doctor's family can communicate that the physician is a regular person, the balance of the artwork should be consistent with the Primary Purpose of this healing environment and with the *Bagua*. A large photograph in the Path in Life area of the doctor sailing on a 65-foot yacht is probably not the best image for the office.

FIGURE 8.11 *Doctor's Office*

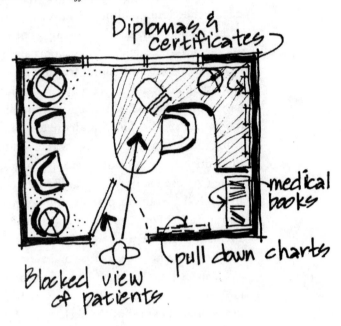

Although the doctor should be sitting in the Commanding Position in the office, avoid placing the chairs for the patient and a family member in a vulnerable position that is centered on, or in front of, the door so that every noise in the corridor or the opening of the door makes them feel vulnerable. Although not ideal, placing the patient chairs behind the door, as in Figure 8.11, is better. Round the corners on all of the furniture.

Hospitals

Most hospitals are extremely stressful for patients, their families, and the staff who work there. This stress can result in the psychological reactions of anger, anxiety, and depression; the physiological symptoms of elevated blood pressure, high levels of stress hormones, and lower immune function; and the behavioral patterns of aggression, resistance, lack of attention, and insomnia. Generally, hospitals have been designed to deliver technology effectively. We also need to focus on creating healing environments.

Every hospital has unique features that must be considered in its design, including geographical location, patient profile, and medical specialties. Regardless of differences, however, we need to make the hospital experience as physically and psychologically comfortable as possible. Whenever possible, introduce elements of nature throughout the hospital. Water features in the lobby; natural lighting; plants throughout the facility; landscaped courtyards with comfortable, small-group seating; and pictures of green and lush natural scenes are some ways to create a healing environment. Stay away from images of poor health and growth, such as leafless trees in a barren winter scene. Remember that the healing aspect of nature can also be introduced in every aspect of your design with round shapes, balanced colors and color values, the natural flows of energy, and the other tools that we discussed in Chapters 2 and 3.

Approaching the Hospital. The image of a hospital begins before the staff, patient, and family even reach the threshold. Clear, well-lit signage is critical to finding the emergency area, the main hospital entrance, the patient drop-off zone, and the parking lot. Remember that those signs must be as easy to read at 10:00 PM as at noon. Use the same color scheme for all of the signage throughout the entire hospital grounds to create a feeling of continuity and wholeness. Using the healing color of medium to dark green as the background and a contrasting value of gold for the lettering will create a feeling of balance.

Curving the driveway will continue a natural experience. A drive that curves in front of the entrance will feel more inviting than a drive that comes directly at the entrance or goes straight by.

The soft sound of soothing music in the parking lot begins to create a caring environment. Landscaping along the driveway, throughout an outdoor parking area, and around the main entrance will also have a calming and healing effect on everyone from patient to staff. Attractive and discrete, but visible, waste containers near the front door alleviate the anxiety of, "Where do I get rid of my coffee cup?"

A hospital entrance usually has a portico to shelter those who are waiting. Because the height of the portico ceiling is substantially lower than the sky "ceiling," make it as high as practical. Paint it a very light color and have the lighting evenly cover the entire semi-interior space, even during the daytime. The use of warm woods as trim in this area will continue the feeling of being in nature, the experience that we want to pervade the entire hospital.

Hospital Lobbies. Promoting a residential rather than an institutional atmosphere, the lobby area should incorporate the Feng Shui principles described in Section A: Hospitality. Include several immediately visible, comfortable seating arrangements, using upholstered chairs in muted, mixed colors and round tables with lamps. Bringing into the lobby some plants and the same music we heard outside the building will help ease the transition into the hospital. Continue to use warm woods as trim.

The floor of the lobby area creates an instant subconscious reaction. If patients step onto a carpet that feels softer than the outside pavement, the sensation will remind them of home. The darker values of earth tones add to the natural feeling of being stable and safe. If carpet is not possible, use either wood or a product that simulates a natural material to continue the impression of nature and stability and a feeling of warmth. Stone, slate, brick, and ceramic tiles appear harder and colder. If a modular material is used, the paving pattern should not be based on a complex graphic design but should direct people in the appropriate directions toward the registration desk or the elevators.

At the risk of overgeneralizing, using either yellows or greens as the predominate color scheme is usually safest in a hospital setting, with reds, blues, and purples as accents and balancing color elements. The green of Wood and the yellow of Earth are the more stabilizing of the Five Element colors, and the green is a healing color and the yellow a recuperating hue.

The artwork in the lobby and corridors is extremely important and should be positive and uplifting. Appropriate images would be sunrises, flower gardens, gently moving water, and happy groups of people and animals. Handmade quilts and other craftwork are often good pieces, because they communicate that someone cares. Always be aware of the psychological impact of the art. Every piece of art should be consistent with the Primary Purpose of creating a healing environment. I was recently in a hospital lobby where a large photograph of three airplanes in a dive formation was displayed prominently. I was tempted to turn the picture upside down so that the airplanes were soaring upwards.

Art will often say something about the style or direction of the hospital. One hospital that could not move forward into the 21st century had covered its walls with black-and-white photographs of its past buildings and people. The somber gray and sepia colors of old photographs can create a feeling of depression rather than of healing. Although our history is an important part of who we are today, it is more important for a hospital to look ahead to a healthy and prosperous future for itself and its patients. We recommended that the pictures either be arranged in a time line that culminated with some representation of plans for the future, or that the pictures be placed in a less prominent location.

Hospital Corridors. Good signage to help people find their way is extremely important in the corridors. Frequent, clear, and readable signage will reduce patient and family stress, reduce staff errors, and reduce the need for busy staff to take time to give directions. We recommend frequent directional signs, especially for long hallways. Because "You Are Here" maps are often difficult to understand, keep them extremely simple and place them frequently throughout the space. Directional artwork and paving patterns can also lead people in specific directions and reduce the amount of signage.

Because the family is still transitioning from the outside world as they walk to a patient's room and we want to make that process a gradual shift, continue the wall colors of the lobby and other public areas into the corridors. For the same reason, use the carpet or other flooring of the lobby and other public areas as far as possible, transitioning to medically required surfaces with similar colors and patterns to reduce the feeling of change.

Design corridors with occasional views off to the side or into landscaped atriums. Interspersed along the corridors, create intimate seating areas of three comfortable chairs with round tables and lamps to allow for family members to have private conversations. These "expansions" of the corridors will also break up the strong, unnatural flow of energy in a straight hallway.

Nurses' Stations and Offices. Make these areas as unobtrusive as possible but easily accessible. See Figure 8.12. The nurses' station placed in the middle of the confluence of several corridors is a constant visual reminder that everyone in the facility is sick and needs immediate attention. Removing the station from easy sight shifts this psychological impact away from illness and removes the nurses from the direct lines of energy rushing down the several straight corridors that are aimed at their fronts, backs, and sides. Put the most frequently needed supplies in the patients' rooms or within a few feet of the station so that staff doesn't need to expend extra energy away from the patient.

In locating and designing the offices and nurses' stations, follow the Feng Shui principles described in Chapter 7, Section C: Office Spaces. Particularly focus on the lighting in the nurses' areas, because inadequate lighting is responsible for a great number of human errors and will also lower staff energy and morale. Design stations to make the staff look accessible rather than barricaded. High architectural dividers or low transaction counters piled high with files say, "Don't bother me," to patients and families. By personalizing the stations and offices with different colors, materials, and details, the attitude of the nurses and other staff will be more peaceful despite a demanding, stressful job. The more pleasant their environment, the longer the nurses and staff will stay with the facility and the better the patient care and the hospital's reputation will be.

Private Patient Rooms. Private rooms are more conducive to healing and the reduction of nosocomial, or hospital acquired, infection

FIGURE 8.12 *Nurses' Stations*

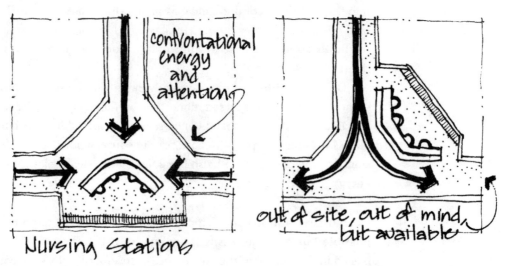

FIGURE 8.13 *Patient's Room*

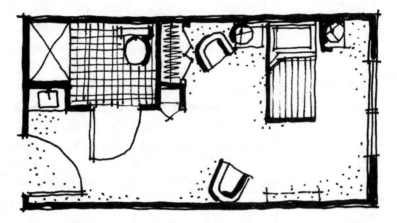

rates. Figure 8.13 depicts a hospital room that reminds patients more of home than an institution.

Ample space on both sides of the bed makes a patient feel less trapped. Lamps on both bedside tables add warmth to the room. They also eliminate the need for glaring overhead ceiling fixtures or a cold fluorescent tube over the headboard that seems fragile and out of reach. Warm-colored lighting combined with walls that are not stark white or gray will ease the patient's depression. To create a feeling of variety throughout the facility for both the patients and the staff, use different colors in each room: pale yellows, greens, blues, and purples. Avoid colors in the red and orange hues that may be too energetic for healing purposes.

Design the room so that the medical equipment and the guest chairs are on the same side of the patient's room as the door into the room, placing the patient in the Commanding Position. This placement will reduce the stress caused by having the energy of these activities on one side of the patient and the energy from the door and hallway on the other side. In addition, it will avoid having the patient looking at the reflection, glare, and chaos in the window that is backlighting the nurse, the doctor, or the guest.

Because stress increases with a loss of control, provide a shelf or surface for personal items that is easily visible from the bed without having to turn one's head. A picture hook across from the bed would give people the opportunity to hang a personal picture or a picture selected from the hospital's "art cart." A pin-up board for favorite pictures also allows the patient to personalize the room.

Separate the sink from the rest of the bathroom and place it near the entrance to the room. This location gives everyone—visitors, nurses, and doctors—the opportunity to wash their hands and reduce bacterial transmission without having to enter the resident's private bathroom. Specify extra wide bathroom doors to reduce patient falls by allowing the patient and an aide to move through together. By placing a locked cabinet in the room that contains items needed by the patient, the nurse can access supplies that are needed on a regular basis without having to go away, leaving the patient wondering when the nurse will ever return.

Install high-quality communication systems in each room that make it easy to reach a nurse. Lack of clear communication increases the patient's stress dramatically. If the patient room does not have a sound system, add a radio to the room. A radio, preferably with a headset, enables patients to escape to music of their choice and block out extraneous noises, such as hallway sounds and paging systems. These can be disturbing to a patient whose state of anxiety is already high.

Sound-absorbing ceiling tiles, draperies, and other materials will help reduce this distraction. In certain areas of the hospital, installing carpet tiles instead of hard surfaces could further reduce unwanted sounds.

Operating and Recovery Rooms. Light-colored flooring has been standard for operating rooms so that objects can be easily found. However, because a great deal of research and development has been done recently on hospital flooring, you will want to investigate recently discovered possibilities. Use the darkest values acceptable for these floors so that the staff and the patients will feel more grounded and stable.

Keep in mind that the subconscious is much more aware of energies in the environment than is the conscious mind, and remember that the patient who is supposedly under anesthetic is still reacting to the energies in the operating room. Although the patient may be sedated, paralyzed, and uncommunicative, the patient's subconscious is undoubtedly still active and affecting the healing process. The harshness of white walls, glaring lights, and the doctor's choice of music may not create a healing experience. The patient and the staff will benefit greatly if you can convince the hospital to use calmer, cool colors on the walls, a combination of overall even lighting and more focused light rather than bright spots, and nonverbal music with a slow rhythm. Lowering the stress level of the doctors and nurses may also reduce some iatrogenic injuries, those events resulting from a medical intervention. In recovery rooms, avoid contrasting ceiling tile and grid and patterned walls and floors, because they may increase the common conditions of headache and nausea.

Cafeterias. The cafeteria is often the only place where the staff and visitors can go for a break from tension. It should be a welcoming, relaxing environment. Designing it to resemble a restaurant with comfortable chairs and tables rather than a school cafeteria will help reduce the inevitable anxiety levels. Round tables with rounded edges will create a softer feeling. In general, avoid the appetite-suppressing color of blue. Also, the overly energetic colors of red and orange are okay for a fast food chain but not for a hospital.

Assisted-Living Facilities and Nursing Homes

Although assisted-living facilities and nursing homes have a different clientele, the approach to both types of facilities should be the same. They are "home" for those who live there. An assisted-living environment should not appear to be a transitional location, and a nursing home should not look like a place to die.

In designing these facilities, employ the basic principles of using as regular a shape as possible. Place the main entrance to the building facing the road. If the entrance is at the side of the structure, it implies psychologically that the building is hiding and people are ashamed to be living there. Center the main entrance on the front wall to convey a sense that the environment and the people within are balanced and still engaged in the world.

Lobby Areas. Treat the lobby areas of these facilities in the same way you would design the lobby of a hotel. Create an atmosphere that makes people feel as if their stay will be very pleasant. Review Section A: Hospitality, for ways to accomplish this environment. Be very conscious of the clientele of the facility so that nuances will appeal to those who live there as well as their families. Adding several small-group seating arrangements with comfortable chairs, occasional tables, and lamps will add to the feeling that this is a gracious living room. Use the Squint Test to make certain that the wall fabrics or flooring patterns are not creating a feeling of chaos.

A separate room off the lobby area that is designed like a private library or sunroom, depending upon its location, is a good way to give residents and their families and friends a quiet place to talk without having to enter a personal bedroom space. Placing this room off to the left of the main entrance will locate it in the appropriate Self-Knowledge area of the *Bagua*. This room should have a balance of warm and cool colors to accommodate the energies of everyone and should lean toward the medium values of mixed colors to create a feeling of close intimacy. As in most cases, a dark, green or earth-tone carpet will feel grounding, soften the atmosphere, and deaden the sound, making the room a more inviting space in which to have a personal conversation. Loosely woven carpets or wood floors with accent rugs are not practical for people who have difficulty walking.

Hallways. To reduce the institutional feeling, use different colors in each hallway. This technique makes each area special and helps residents feel less like one of many. Being able to say, "I'm in purple," introduces a personal element. Light colors will make the spaces seem more open. If particular rooms are always used for the same-sex patient, use light cool colors of green, blue, and purple for the female areas and light warm colors of creams and yellows for the male sections. Another very natural way to place colors is to order them in the same sequence as the color spectrum. As one proceeds around the building moving to the right, the colors of the rainbow reveal themselves in order.

Because these hallways need to be wide and clear of objects such as plants or tables, the best way to create the "meandering path" is with wall sconces that alternate on either side down the hall and with art that has depth and expands that particular part of the corridor. In most instances, a picture with a specific direction to the right or left may be confusing. Use horizontal images and select pictures, such as green and blooming spring and summer landscapes, to instill an atmosphere of calmness and nurturing. Avoid most images of solitary individuals, because they communicate a feeling of loneliness. Be very sensitive to the impact that an image and the energy of the artist will have on the viewer.

Insert small seating areas or rooms along the corridor that are similar in feeling to the "private library" off the lobby. These spaces give families a place to gather without being in either a bedroom or a very public space and add to a homelike environment.

Nurses' Stations and Administrative Offices. These spaces should follow the principles that we set forth above for hospitals. In addition, consider distributing the administrative offices throughout the facility, giving all residents the impression that they are part of normal society. People who are living far from the front door can easily feel outside the mainstream of life.

Private Rooms. Ideally, every resident should have a private room. Having one's own personal space increases the possibility of staying healthy and of healing by decreasing infection transfers, allowing more intimate time with family and friends, and providing personal control of space. The design and layout of these private rooms should be similar to those described for bedrooms in Chapter 6, Section A: Single Family Residences, and in Private Patient Rooms earlier in this chapter.

Avoid a sterile room with white walls, many metal finishes, and furniture with hard edges that create a cold, impersonal environment. Think "nature" and "residential." To the extent that carpet can be used, choose earth tones to create a feeling of being grounded. If carpet is impractical, use wood planking or a high-quality vinyl tile that simulates wood or a natural product.

Giving an individual the opportunity to choose the wall color begins to personalize the room. If this choice is impractical, use cream or pale yellow as the default paint color. Specify table lamps, standing lamps, and wall sconces rather than institutional ceiling fixtures to illuminate the room, because lamps and sconces bring the light closer to the human level and add warmth to the room.

Beds should always be in the Commanding Position, and the *Bagua* can be applied to the room to enrich the person's life. Remember the importance of a headboard. A solid, nonmetallic headboard will give the resident a much-needed feeling of support and stability. In a nursing home, separate the sink from the rest of the bathroom and place it near the entrance to the room in a manner similar to that in a private hospital room design to facilitate cleanliness and reduce infections.

It is always good for the resident to bring personal furniture and art into the room. If this is not practical, find other ways for people to personalize their space. Even providing a corkboard and clips or pins for the easy hanging of photographs of family and friends is a step in the right direction. We recommend giving the residents a simple booklet that describes some of the basic Feng Shui principles and explains how they can create a positive feeling about their space and improve their life. Placing the corkboard in the Family area of the *Bagua* is certainly a start. Giving the residents tools with which to personalize a space demonstrates a caring about them that will benefit their health.

Activity Areas. The activity areas of an assisted-living facility or nursing home should resemble those in a nice hotel. That does not necessarily mean they must be expensive. Provide generous entrances and spacious interior areas at a human scale to give everyone, including those with physical disabilities, the feeling that the spaces were specifically designed for their comfort. Consider the particular activity for which a space is intended and choose calming or stimulating colors accordingly. The spa and hairdressing salon should be a soft rose so that everyone looks healthy. The multipurpose activity room could use the recuperating atmosphere of yellow. And the dining areas would be more nourishing in burgundy colors, with the red stimulating the appetite and the blue in the burgundy causing the residents to eat more slowly. With every design decision, ask yourself, "Am I creating a home where I would want to live?"

C. RETAIL

The goals of a retailer are fairly straightforward:

- Bring the customer in the door.
- Have the customer buy the product.
- Provide a satisfying experience so the customer will return another day.

Retailing is all about creating an easy, comfortable, and positive shopping experience. By using the tools of Feng Shui, we can make that process a successful experience for the consumer and a profitable one for the owner.

In the Door

First, make it easy to find the store. The more visible and accessible the store, the more potential customers it will attract. Although the location of the site and the ease of parking or walking are clearly factors, we take those as givens and focus on the store itself. Signage and window displays are the two design elements that first attract potential customers.

The Signage. Signage is one of the most important features of retailing and is often a last-minute decision. If permitted, a distinctive sign that protrudes from the storefront is the most effective way to let people know well in advance that they are in the right place.

Use the company logo or colors to make it unique and graphics or window displays to make clear what type of product is being sold. The distinctive English tavern signs hanging over the sidewalk are a wonderful example of this marketing. If the company does not already have a logo or theme, Feng Shui principles can be used to create the desired energy for the image of the company. Focus on the market for the products. Are the shoppers primarily men or women? We can often tell the sex of the designer by the color choices that have been made, but the retail space design should be about the customers and what will pull them in. Although a generalization, remember that women tend to be drawn to the cool colors of green, blue, and purple and men to the warmer reds and golds. We recently analyzed a new wine store whose market was clearly masculine, but which had a pale green front with pale yellow-green lettering. The coolness of the front and the fact that the color values of the front and the sign were too similar to make the sign stand out do not bode well for easily attracting the target male customers. Regardless of the basic color direction you choose, balance the principal color with complementary colors.

The Window Display. Because many shoppers are impulse buyers, window displays are extremely important. The goal is not to display everything but to whet the appetite with a sampling that indicates the treasures waiting inside. Use the Squint Test to see if the number and grouping of objects has created a subconscious chaos that overwhelms potential customers, subliminally telling them to avoid the chaos and clutter inside. Design the windows to display a few strong items slightly below eye level and also to provide a view over these items of an attractive and organized store interior that will pull the customer in to buy.

The Door Swing. Because the goal is to make shopping easy for customers, have the doors swing in wherever possible so that people do not have to step back to enter. We realize this may take up more internal space, but it will make customers feel welcomed into the store. Outward swinging doors that are left open so they do not feel at all blocking may be as effective. If the doors can swing both ways, the process of entering easily as well as leaving with armloads of merchandise are both comfortable. If there are double doors, make certain that both doors are operable. Trying a locked door and then having to switch to the other one is not a good beginning. Automatic sliding doors are a good way to make the customer's path a smooth one in both directions.

The Buy

We have pulled the potential buyer into the store and now must make the interior inviting and comfortable. Although each store will have unique issues, following some general Feng Shui principles will make the experience feel more natural. Figure 8.14 is a small layout with several classic problems, and Figure 8.15 changes the flow of energy of the space in several subtle ways.

In Figure 8.14, customers enter directly into a harsh, flat display cabinet with open space on the left. The energy that immediately confronts the customer is unbalanced. The natural inclination is to move toward the customer the more open area on the left, because it is apt to be less of a dramatic change from the openness of the sidewalk outside the store. This directs the customer toward the cash register, the end of the shopping process. Customers may feel slightly awkward at this point, as if the experience should be over, and might turn around to go in the other direction and back toward the exit. Even if customers continue in the store, their entry progression has not been smooth. If they hurry by the cashier and proceed around the store in a clockwise direction, they

FIGURES 8.14 and 8.15 *Retail*

8.14

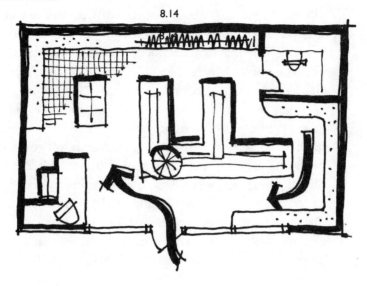

8.15

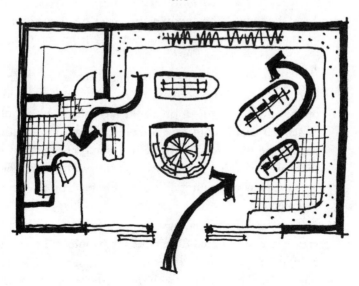

will arrive at the exit before returning to the checkout counter. Because the customers have moved past the register, they've seen the line at the register and subliminally know that the exit will come before the cash register. This experience is not conducive to buying.

The flow of energy in Figure 8.14 is tortured, with many sharp turns and a dead end in the middle of the store. The customer may feel a bit like a rat in a maze. The sharp corners on the furniture and display cabinets are also unfriendly. As customers proceed down the long corridor at the back of the store, they are aimed directly at the office door. This approach sends the negative subliminal message that this place is a business, not a fun shopping experience. This continuous flow of energy directed toward the office may also create health problems for its occupant, portending higher turnover in that position than would be expected.

We recently reviewed a store in which the two entry doors opened out and the door on the right was locked. Immediately to the left after entering were stairs to a lower level. Directly opposite the entrance was a short flight of stairs up to the main display floor. We watched what people did when they entered the store; of the 18 people that came into the store, 15 immediately went downstairs. When they returned, 12 of the 15 left the store and never made it to the main floor. Although the lower level was the less attractive floor, their energy had been pulled down the stairs. When people came back up, they more naturally turned to the right and went outside, escaping from the chaotic, negative energy below.

The potential customers could easily have been directed to the main floor by having both doors remain open. If only one door could be left open, an open right door would have directed people ahead and a closed left door would have discouraged easy access downstairs. A runner up the stairs to the main floor would also have directed people to the main retail floor, and a brightly colored or illuminated object in immediate view on the upper level would have pulled people's attention—and feet—up the stairs.

Because directional signs are rarely posted in a retail space, we must create easy subliminal directions for people. When customers enter as in Figure 8.15, they are greeted by a few beautiful or strongly designed objects on a display table with rounded corners, all welcoming features. Give the potential buyer the distance and time to adjust to the new environment and feel comfortable. Because roughly the same amount of open space exists on both sides of the center table, the natural inclination for a customer would be to move to the right and proceed around the store, ending up at the cash register at the end of the journey. If the front doors swing in and are left open, the right-hand door should be opened several inches farther back than the left, further directing the customer to the right.

The flooring of the store creates an immediate sensation. What effect and energy level does the store want to convey? Will the shopping experience be fast and efficient or more leisurely and luxurious? A carpeted area connotes more of a sense of leisure than a vinyl surface, and the thicker the carpet, the greater the feeling of luxury. In any situation, begin with the idea of a dark flooring surface to make people feel grounded. Avoid gray floors and walls that may lower the energy of the customer, making them feel tired and uninterested in shopping.

Generous aisles will present the opportunity to stand back at a comfortable distance to view the display shelves and still allow space for someone to pass behind. Crowded aisles and touching bodies are uncomfortable and divert attention from the merchandise.

When designing and arranging the display shelves, use the Squint Test to anticipate how they will look when full. Are the shelves so deep that they display layers of small objects, creating an overall image of clutter and chaos? If the merchandise is primarily smaller items, consider using narrower shelving units and additional aisles. Unfortunately, shelving is often used to stock items, not just display them, resulting in more chaos and creating a feeling of weight. Encourage your client to stock items in the backroom rather than on the retail floor. If customers only see one or two of each item, they may feel they should buy now before it is out of stock.

Avoid designing shelves more than seven feet high that place items out of easy reach or hold heavy-looking objects. Objects on higher shelves "shift" the feeling of weight in the environment from the ground to above us, making us feel uncomfortable. The corners of all display cabinets, shelving, and furniture should be rounded to make the space feel more natural.

By locating the office in Figure 8.15 in the Prosperity corner of the *Bagua*, we have placed it in a stronger position. We've also located the door to the office so that it is neither at the end of a long corridor nor directly in line with the cashier's position to avoid any feeling of confrontation. For maximum occupant productivity, the furniture in the office should be arranged in the Commanding Position in a manner consistent with Chapter 7, Section C: Office Spaces.

The lighting in the store should be warm and even throughout, with accent lighting to highlight specific products. Increase the lighting levels in the "dead" back corners, which often feel darker because they are away from the greater light, sound, and human energy at the front of the store. If the nature of the store's product would benefit from, and permits, the use of table lamps throughout the space, this lighting will add warmth to the human level and make the environment more inviting. If an item is being featured, place it in the center of a display area so that the objects on either side receive the overflow of light and the customer's attention. If the most important objects are all on one end of a display area, the objects on the other end could just as well be in the storeroom.

In selecting the wall color, consider the nature of the product and the desired psychological impact on the customer. Is it healing and calming or exciting and stimulating? In most cases, the walls are only a backdrop for the color and energy of the product and are relatively insignificant. This is one situation where white might be most appropriate. In a default situation, however, use a warm cream to imitate outdoor energy.

Return Again

Although the quality of the product is important, the quality of the shopping experience is critical. Which takes us back to the importance of the "in the door" and the "buy" issues. The ability to find parking, locate the store, enter easily, and circulate naturally as part of a smooth flow of energy will make the experience positive and bring the customer back.

D. PUBLIC RESTROOMS

We are focusing separately on restrooms because they are frequently, and unnecessarily, awkward. The Primary Purpose of a restroom is to give people a place to release toxins from their bodies and refresh themselves. This environment should be relaxing and free of stress. Our goal is to create a smooth flow of energy and enhance the space in a way that will calm people. A restroom should not be an after-thought in the planning process. The principal issues that we face in a restroom are generally location, the flow of energy, color, and decorative objects.

Location

In most public spaces, the restrooms are not easy to find, even hidden. We were recently in a new theater and had to search for the restrooms, passing the box office and its line of people and moving along a passageway that gradually narrowed into a long hallway with no indication of where the restrooms were located. No one likes to ask a stranger directions for a very personal purpose, and tension was created unnecessarily.

Keep the hallways wide and make it as easy as possible to find the restrooms. We are not suggesting that the facilities should be right inside the main entrance or in the elevator lobby, as we have occasionally found, because that raises first-impression issues! In a theater or similar public space, begin with discreet, but easily seen, signage near the main entrance or in the primary room. As one approaches the restrooms, good signage that can easily be seen at some distance is an effective way to reduce the tension one feels in what is often a hurried situation.

If you have the luxury of placing the restrooms side by side or across from one another, place the women's room on the left and the men's room on the right as people will approach them to conform to the natural juxtaposition of women and men that we discussed in Chapter 2, Section B: Balance.

Flow of Energy

A restroom should be an easy space to plan because we know how we move through the space. The normal traffic pattern in a restroom is to enter, proceed to the toilet or urinal, go to the sink, reach for the towels, dispose of the towels, and then exit. The problems occur when people cross paths. Bumping into another individual or having to stop to avoid hitting someone is uncomfortable in small spaces. In the following diagrams, we indicate the usual traffic patterns. Figure 8.16 shows an actual restroom where the normal path of movement results in repeated instances of making sharp turns to reach the next destination. In this layout, someone standing at the sink is also uncomfortably in line with the entrance.

In Figure 8.17, the flow of energy is smooth and reduces the number of times people's paths might cross. Having the flow of energy come in the door and move to the right, then continue in a counterclockwise direction, will feel the most natural and comfortable. The sinks are at a distance from the entrance and, with a mirror above the sinks, a person washing up will feel more in control of the space and less vulnerable.

We recognize that plumbing constraints may dictate the placement of the toilets, urinals, and sinks, but the towels and waste receptacles should always be conveniently located next to the sinks to reduce the crossing of paths.

FIGURES 8.16 and 8.17 *Restrooms*

8.16

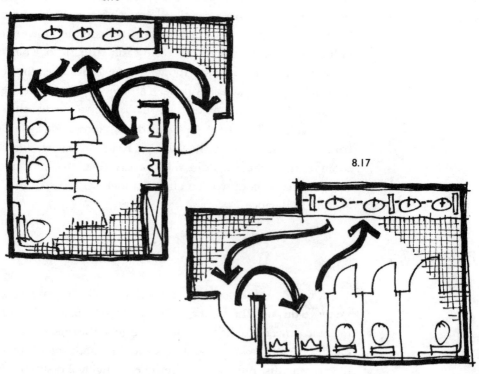

8.17

Because people often enter and exit the restroom at the same time and are frequently in a hurry, consider a slightly larger door than normal to avoid uncomfortable body contact or the interruption of movement. Avoid placing any active portion of the facilities behind the door, because this will increase the tension of those entering the space as well as those behind the door. If the space is large enough to have an outer vestibule area, the door to the vestibule can be a comfortable right-handed door and the restroom door can be eliminated. This transition area also puts private activity farther away from the public area.

Adding hooks in the toilets and near shelves in the sink area makes the experience easier by eliminating the uncertainty of, "Where will I hang my coat or put my purse?" Preferably not on the floor.

Mirrors

If the urinals in a men's restroom are placed so that the man's back is to the entrance to the restroom, placing a mirror in front of the urinal will make the man feel less vulnerable. Keep the mirrored wall at eye height. The purpose is to give a view of what is going on behind the user and nothing else. In several situations, we have seen mirrored walls that were so large they had just the opposite effect, making the occupant feel exposed and very vulnerable.

Color

Because white has a very clean look, it is a good color for the fixtures and any tile work in the restroom, although grout should be very dark so that the inevitable discoloration is not obvious. Having white throughout the entire space, however, pushes the room out of balance and creates a Metal harshness that increases the feeling of stress. Colored tile borders and wallpaper or paint on the upper portion of the walls can help balance the colors and elements in the space. Creams and roses as the predominant color will make everyone look more attractive. For accent colors, consider using sophisticated, mixed colors in the cool range for the women's room and mixed colors in the warm hues for the men's room. See Chapter 3, Section A: Colors for a more extensive discussion of color.

Art and Decorative Objects

Art is a very easy way to change a person's energy on entering a restroom. Pictures with humor are relaxing and reduce stress. The color in the art will also add energy to balance the neutral colors of the room. When placing art on a wall, be conscious of the direction in which the picture reads. We want to avoid walking into a space where the wall in front of us holds a picture that reads to the left when we are headed to the right.

A simple vase with real or silk flowers in the sink area will also add color energy and a feeling of warmth in the cold tile environment. The goal in public restrooms—as in every other type of project - is to create a space that is comfortable and relaxing.

9

THE TRANSCENDENTAL ASPECTS OF FENG SHUI

The most powerful and exciting Feng Shui work we do with clients and their environment reaches a deeper and more spiritual level than the ideas I've already discussed. This work can include shifting the energy of a physical space, as well as giving people the tools to shift their individual energy and move psychologically in a new direction. Very often, clients are a bit tentative when we move from the practical and mundane part of Feng Shui to the more transcendental methods. It is particularly rewarding when these clients begin to understand the impact of transcendental methods and the power of intention and start to experience desired changes in their life. I have discussed in great detail the impact that the flow and balance of energy, colors, shapes, materials, and the other physical aspects of our spaces have on us. Equally important are the unseen energies in our environment. In this chapter, "energy" takes on a new meaning. Remember as a child when you experienced something in the night and ran to your parents crying, "Mommy, Daddy, there's something in my room!" Well-meaning parents often assure their children that this presence is purely "imaginary" and there is nothing there. To the adult there wasn't. To the child there was. Many children do in fact experience something we do not understand. After being told by adults that there is "nothing there," children soon start distrusting their feelings and reactions and begin to shut them out. Eventually as adults, we often ignore the intangible energies around us. We have been trained not to trust those strange sensations we occasionally have when we "feel something in the room" that we cannot see. To counteract this conditioning, assure children or clients that their experiences are real and ask them to describe them to you. I advise my Feng Shui students that if they feel an energy or presence and are not up to dealing with it, they should merely say, "I cannot help you right now. I'll return when I know I have the strength to help." Say those words with love, not fear.

Even though we may have consciously blocked out the ability to perceive the unseen, we are still receiving those energies on a subconscious level. If we want to develop the ability to experience them, developing the right brain subconscious is critical. Because Feng Shui is about the impact that *all* energies have on us, the consultant must meditate in order to receive everything in the environment. Not always an easy task.

A. MEDITATION

As Anna Wise describes in *The High Performance Mind,* a person can develop the ability to be in the conscious mind and at the same time access the subconscious through meditation. Meditation is not prayer, as many people immediately think, but is a state of deep relaxation where the individual lets go of conscious thought. It is a way for you to go beneath the conscious surface, even to remember where you "lost" your keys!

There is no right or wrong way to meditate. You will eventually develop your own form. For those who have not meditated before, here is a way to begin.

- Sit very quietly with your eyes closed and both of your feet on the floor.
- Place your left hand (right brain receiving) on top of your right hand with your thumbs gently touching.
- Focus on your breathing, being aware of breathing in and breathing out.

- Let your body gradually relax.
- Feel the tension leave your body as you let go of your toes, then your feet, your legs and gradually work your way up your body to your shoulders, your neck, and your face.
- Once you have let go of the tension in your body, sit quietly for a few minutes, continuing to breathe deeply.
- You may then find yourself humming softly as you breathe out. Don't think about the pitch but just hum a single comfortable note. The more relaxed you become, the lower the note will be.
- Breathe in through your nose, if possible, and out through your mouth naturally and slowly, letting the sound envelop you as you breathe out.
- Envision that you are surrounded by a ball of pure light and feel the warmth, brightness, and clarity of the pure sound and light.
- As you slowly and deeply breathe in and out, your relaxed mouth and lips may have gradually parted and the hum may have become a very natural "ohm," the universal sound, or "mmm," a baby's first sound.
- The ball of pure light that surrounds you will now slowly enter your body through the "middle eye" in the center of your forehead.
- Let the light move slowly down through your entire body in a gentle circular motion, massaging every bone, muscle, and fiber of your body.
- As the ball of light moves back up your body, bring the light to any part of your body of which you are particularly aware. Be comfortable with whatever you feel, even if you are falling asleep.
- Continue to breathe slowly and hum as you exhale. If your mind wanders, think as you breathe in, "I am breathing in energy," and as you exhale, "I am breathing out." By keeping a pad nearby, you can write down a thought that comes to your consciousness and then more easily let it go and return to your breathing.
- As you move from the meditative state back into a state of consciousness, the energy that you have taken in will stay with you. If you meditate on a regular basis, you will find that you can go quickly into the meditative place and tap into your subconscious mind.

B. GOOD OR BAD ENERGIES?

What are these different types of energies that most of us can't see? On the most basic level, when we leave a room, house, or office, we leave some of our energy behind. For example, when I cleared the home of a woman who had been divorced for ten years, I could still feel the energy of her husband. I could identify his chair at the dinner table, where he'd sat to watch television, and where his desk had been located, even though his office had been turned into a meditation room. I have frequently found that when there is a history of Native Americans occupying an area, their energies are still present and can affect the life of the present occupants of the property. Their effect is not necessarily adverse as long as they are acknowledged and respected. This is the primary reason that we inquire about the past history of a space, a piece of furniture, or a work of art.

Are these "good" or "bad" energies? When we ask that question, we immediately move into a judgmental mode. Because being judgmental arises from our own personal value system it becomes difficult to help a client. We must remove our own personal feelings about what is good or bad because "One person's meat is another's poison." The real question is, "Can the energies in this space enhance the life of the occupants?" Many clients ask us to "clear the space." This involves various techniques to shift the energy of the environment to maximize it beneficially for the client and to help them "take possession of the space." This clearing can occur before a client moves into a space, after a renovation, or during occupancy, when something happens to create an uncomfortable atmosphere. Traditional clearing methods may involve ringing bells, burning dried orange peel or sage, or another technique that feels appropriate at that particular time and place. In very basic terms, when we clear a space or object, we use the following process, varying it as appropriate:

1. Meditate in the space.
2. Experience the energies in the environment.
3. Acknowledge and thank the energies for what they have brought to the life of the people who have lived and worked there over time.

4. Surround the energies with love, compassion, understanding, a ball of light, or other encompassing energy.

5. Invite the energies that can no longer enhance the life of the occupants to go forth into the light of the Universe and to be released from the space.

6. Ask those energies that can enhance the lives of the inhabitants to remain and nurture them.

Note that basically I have treated all energy alike and have not distinguished between "good" and "bad." If you have seen the movie *The Sixth Sense* and can ignore its more sensational aspects, some of this may sound familiar.

CHANGING PATTERNS OF BELIEF AND BEHAVIOR

This is one of the most powerful and rewarding aspects of Feng Shui. Feng Shui employs many techniques to change behavior patterns, always using the following underlying elements:

- Acknowledge where we are in our life.
- Decide the direction in which we want to move.
- Focus our intention clearly in the new direction.

Any physical object that may be a part of this process should be a very clear metaphor for the new direction and should not have any subliminal undertones. For instance, if a person uses a plant as an image for a flourishing relationship, then dead flowers or a cactus would clearly be inappropriate!

Many techniques involve rituals, the mere thought of which spooks some people. As strange as this may seem, remember that our daily lives are filled with rituals that we take for granted. A ritual involves the body, the mind, and the spirit. In other words, it involves the entire being. Shaking hands is a ritual. In shaking hands, a person physically reaches out and takes the other person's hand and says, "Good morning." The body and the mind are at work. The spiritual aspect of shaking hands is the intent of the person, usually reflected in the eyes, tone of voice, or body movement. It is this intention aspect of the ritual that communicates the individual's real inner feeling. The following technique is one that we often recommend to clients, because it is easily understood and accepted.

THE THREE SECRETS REINFORCEMENT

Throughout this book, I have referred to using a transcendental method or ritual when placing an object in a particular *Bagua* area to enhance that part of your life. The purpose of the Three Secrets Reinforcement is to implant an image in your subconscious mind of whom you want to become and to create a new belief about the direction in which you want to go. Once these new patterns of belief truly become part of you, then your behavior can go in the new direction. The word *secrets* is used in the sense of being *personal*.

Before using the following ritual of body, speech, and mind to empower adjustments with intention, calm yourself and clear your mind by meditating or sitting quietly and letting your body relax. Breathe deeply and let your mind focus on each in breath and out breath.

Because the following three steps are very personal, they must feel comfortable to you. The first two are from traditional Feng Shui but can be changed to any hand movement and verbalization you choose. One advantage of using these traditional recommendations, however, is that because they are not part of our experience, we do not have any conscious associations with them that could confuse our subconscious.

1. *The Body.* With your palm down and your arm comfortably extended in front of you, extend your little finger and pointer finger forward toward the object. Curl your third and fourth fingers under and hold them with your thumb. Flick these two middle fingers forward. Women should use the right hand, and men the left.

2. *The Mind.* Say aloud OM MA NI PAD ME HUM (pronounced ohm-mah-nee-pahd-mee-hum). These Sanskrit words contain a great deal of meaning but can simplistically be translated as, "So be it, so it is." A positive affirmation of one's intention.

3. *The Intention.* Visualize the specific result you wish to attain and the process that is needed to achieve it. This is the key. If you find

that the image shifts as you go through the process, let it happen. If the image becomes one that is contrary to the positive intention and direction with which you began, acknowledge that change and begin again and repeat until it is completely positive. Keep the word *not* out of the intention. Pardon the double negative, but the subconscious does not recognize the word *not*. If we say, "My partner and I are not going to argue any more," we have reinforced the word and impulse to "argue" in our subconscious.

Perform each of these three steps in succession, particularly taking your time with the visualization. Repeat the ritual nine times, beginning with the hand gesture, followed by the verbalization, and then by the visualization of your intention. After you do the process nine times, it truly will become part of your subconscious mind and can effectively shift the pattern of your behavior.

Remember that the power is not in the candle, picture, plant, or other object you are moving or installing but in your intention. Once you have gone through the ritual, the object will bring forth your intention whenever you see it, whether you consciously focus on it or subconsciously capture it out of the corner of your eye.

THE EXCHANGE OF ENERGY

If you begin to do Feng Shui consulting in addition to incorporating its guidelines into your designs, then you should know that a traditional part of a Feng Shui consultation is the red envelope that the client presents to the consultant containing the compensation. Because red is the most energetic color, the client is symbolically completing the flow of energy from the consultant to the client and back again by giving the consultant the red envelope. This expresses utmost respect and gratitude for the consultation.

Although the tradition is that the appropriate number of envelopes depends upon the magnitude of the problems and the solutions required, we approach this tradition as being one of respect. As a result, we consider the intention and feeling of the person who is giving the red envelope as paramount, not the number of envelopes. As the recipient, I follow a procedure that includes the Three Secrets Reinforcement and envision the energy flowing from the client to me and back again; a continuing cycle. This is an extremely important and moving ritual.

SUMMARY

The tools of Feng Shui are extremely powerful and can have an impact on people's life in many ways. It is exciting to see clients move in new directions and be freed from preconceived ideas, negative environments, and old patterns of behavior.

The principles discussed in this book are only the tip of the iceberg in the study of Feng Shui, but may help you appreciate some of the energies that impact people on a regular basis. Your role as architect or designer is to enhance your clients' environment and to create spaces that will further their goals. By following Feng Shui guidelines, being conscious of the effect that the various energies have on each space and the people who occupy it, and being aware of the nontraditional methods of changing the energy of a space, you can create an environment that "really works" physiologically and psychologically to improve the life of your clients and their families, children, friends, employees, customers, and clients. None of this is rocket science, but it does require an acute awareness of the small, medium, and large factors, seen and unseen, that play on both the conscious and subconscious minds of everyone who approaches and enters a space.

You have a tremendous opportunity to change people's lives in a very positive way to make the bottom line longer than the top and feel more grounded. Please use your power well and with care.

Note: When several dates are set forth below, the first date is the date of the first American edition, subsequent dates are the dates of subsequent editions, and the date in the ( ) is the copyright date if it is different from the publication date.

Abram, David. *The Spell of the Sensuous*. New York: Vintage Books, 1997 (1996).

Alexander, Christopher, et al. *A Pattern Language*. New York: Oxford University Press, 1977.

Cowen, James G. *Messengers of the Gods*. New York: Bell Tower, 1993.

Edwards, Betty. *Drawing on the Right Side of the Brain*. New York: Jeremy Tarcher/Putnam, 1999.

Govinda, Lama Anagarika. *Creative Meditation and Multidimensional Consciousness*. Wheaton, IL: Quest Books, The Theosophical Publishing House, 1990 (1976).

——. *Foundations of Tibetan Mysticism*. York Beach, Maine: Samuel Weiser, Inc., 1969.

Jou, Tsung Hwa. *The Tao of Tai-Chi Chuan: Way to Rejuvenation*. Warwick, NY: Tai Chi Foundation, 1981.

Lenz, Frederick. *Surfing the Himalayas: A Spiritual Adventure*. New York: St. Martin's Griffen, 1997 (1995).

——. *Snowboarding to Nirvana*. New York: St. Martin's Griffen, 1998 (1997).

Lima, Patrick. *The Harrowsmith Illustrated Book of Herbs*. Ontario, Canada: Camden House Publishing, 1986.

Lip, Evelyn. *Feng Shui for Business*. Union City, CA: Heian International, Inc., 1990, 1993 (1989).

Miles, Barry. *Paul McCartney, Many Years from Now.* New York: Henry Holt and Company, 1997.

Rinpoche, Guru. *The Tibetan Book of the Dead.* Translated with commentary by Francesca Fremantle and Chogyam Trungpa. Boston: Shambhala Publications, Inc., 1987 (1975).

Rossbach, Sarah. *Feng Shui: The Chinese Art of Placement.* New York: Arkana Books, Penguin Group, 1991 (1983).

———. *Interior Design with Feng Shui.* New York: Arkana Books, Penguin Group, 1991 (1987).

Rossbach, Sarah, and Lin Yun. *Living Color: Master Lin Yun's Guide to Feng Shui and the Art of Color.* New York: Kodansha America, Inc., 1994.

Sung, Edgar. *Classic Chinese Almanac.* San Francisco: MJE Publishing, published annually.

Webster, Richard. *Chinese Numerology.* St. Paul, MN: Llewellyn Publications, 1998.

Whitmont, Edmond C. *The Symbolic Quest.* Princeton, NJ: Princeton University Press, 1973.

Wise, Anna. *The High Performance Mind.* New York: Jeremy P. Tarcher/Putnam, 1997 (1995).

Wolverton, B. C. *How To Grow Fresh Air.* New York: Penguin Books, 1997 (1996).

Books on the *I Ching*

Leichtman, Robert R., M.D., and Carl Japikse. *Changing Lines.* Atlanta: Ariel Press, 1993.

Perrottet, Oliver. *The Visual* I Ching. Rutland, VT: Charles E.Tuttle Co., Inc., 1997.

Reifler, Sam. I Ching: *A New Interpretation for Modern Times.* New York: Bantam Books, 1974.

Ritsema, Rudolf, and Stephen Karcher. *I Ching.* Rockport, Maine: Element, Inc., 1994.

Wilhelm, Richard, and Cary F. Baynes, with an Introduction by C. G. Jung. *The* I Ching *or Book of Changes*. Princeton, NJ: Princeton University Press, 1977.

Wing, R.L. *The* I Ching *Workbook*. New York: Doubleday, 1979.

Books on Color

Albers, Josef. *Interaction of Color*. New Haven, CT: Yale University Press, 1975.

Amber, Reuben. *Color Therapy*. Santa Fe, NM: Aurora Press, 1983.

Backhaus, Werner G. K., Reinhold Kliegl, and John S. Werner. *Color Vision: Perspectives from Different Disciplines*. Berlin, NY: Walter de Gruyter & Co., 1998.

Birren, Faber. *Color and Human Response*. New York: Wiley, 1984.

——. *Color Psychology and Color Therapy*. New Hyde Park, NY: University Books, Inc, 1961.

De Grandis, Luigina. *Theory and Use of Color*. Translated by John Gilbert. New York: Harry N. Abrams, Inc., 1986 (1984).

Gimbel, Theo. *Healing With Color and Light*. New York: Fireside, Simon, & Schuster, Inc., 1994.

von Goethe, Johann Wolfgang. *Theory of Colours*. Cambridge, MA: Massachusetts Institute of Technology, 1970.

Kaufman, Donald, and Taffy Dahl. *Color*. New York: Clarkson Potter, 1992.

Kobayashi, Shigenobu. *A Book of Colors*. Tokyo and New York: Kodansha International, 1987.

Luscher, Dr. Max. *The Luscher Color Test*. Translated and edited by Ian A Scott. New York: Random House, Inc, 1969.

Mahnke, Frank H. *Color, Environment, and Human Response*. New York: John Wiley & Sons, Inc., 1996.

Recio, Belinda. *The Essence of Red*. Layton, UT: Gibbs Smith, 1996.

Rossbach, Sarah, and Lin Yun. *Living Color: Master Lin Yun's Guide to Feng Shui and the Art of Color*. New York: Kodansha America, Inc., 1994.

Stockton, James. *Designer's Guide to Color*. San Francisco: Chronicle Books, 1984.

——. *Designer's Guide to Color II*. San Francisco: Chronicle Books, 1984.

The Color Book. San Francisco: Chronicle Books, 1997.

Color and Its Use in Interior Design and Decoration. New York: New York School of Interior Design, 1983.

Books on Dowsing

Jurriaanse, D. *The Practical Pendulum Book*. York Beach, Maine: Samuel Weiser, Inc., l986 (1984).

Lonegren, Sig (compiled by). *The Dowsing Rod Kit*. Rutland, VT: Charles E. Tuttle Co., Inc., 1995.

Nielsen, Greg. *Beyond Pendulum Power*. Reno, NV: Conscious Books, 1988.

Ozaniec, Naomi. *Dowsing For Beginners*. London, England: Hodder & Stoughton, 1994.

Webster, Richard. *Dowsing For Beginners*. St. Paul, MN: Llewellyn Publications, 1996.

Books on Sound

Beaulieu, John. *Music and Sound in the Healing Arts*. Barryton, NY: Station Hill Press, Inc., 1987.

Campbell, Don. *The Mozart Effect*. New York: Avon Books, 1997.

Gimbel, Theo. *Form, Sound, Color, and Healing*. Saffron Walden, England: The C.W. Daniel Company Ltd., 1990 (1987).

Spaeth, Sigmund. *The Common Sense of Music*. New York: Liveright, Inc., 1924.

Tovey, Sir Donald. *The Forms of Music*. New York: Meridian Books, Inc., 1956.